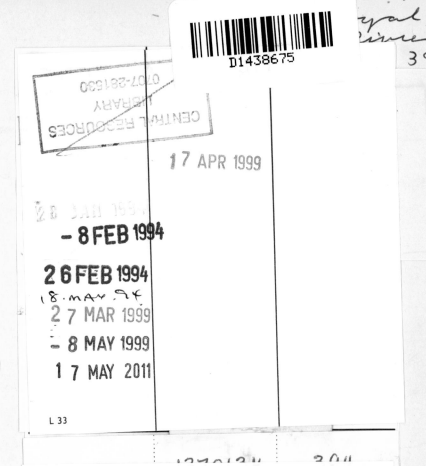
Please renew/return this item by the last date shown.

So that your telephone call is charged at local rate, please call the numbers as set out below:

	From Area codes 01923 or 0208:	From the rest of Herts:
Renewals:	01923 471373	01438 737373
Enquiries:	01923 471333	01438 737333
Minicom:	01923 471599	01438 737599

L32b

ROYAL RIVIERA

THE BEACH AT CANNES

CHARLES GRAVES

ROYAL RIVIERA

HEINEMANN

LONDON MELBOURNE TORONTO

William Heinemann Ltd

LONDON MELBOURNE TORONTO

CAPE TOWN AUCKLAND

THE HAGUE

*

Published in June 1957
Second Impression July 1957

PRINTED IN GREAT BRITAIN BY
EBENEZER BAYLIS AND SON, LTD.,
THE TRINITY PRESS, WORCESTER, AND LONDON

CONTENTS

LIST OF ILLUSTRATIONS

7

FANFARE FOR FOLLY

THE RIVIERA is the glamour strip of coastline of southern France extending 140 miles from Cassis, near Marseilles, to Menton on the Italian frontier. It has been successively occupied by the Ligurians, the Phoenicians, the Romans, the Saracens, the Spaniards, the Sardinians (in part), the Germans and Italians (in war time), the British, Greeks and Americans (in peace time).

Major townships are Monte Carlo, Cannes, Nice and Juan-les-Pins, with Cap d'Antibes, Cap Ferrat, Cap Martin, St. Tropez, Le Lavandou, La Napoule and Beaulieu as the smartest places in which the millionaires buy or build their lovely houses and swimming pools, have fun and play around.

Villa life – many villas are the size of palaces – has always been more fashionable on the Riviera than hotel life.

The first to become a real pleasure resort was Nice, but only for the winter season. It was later overtaken by Cannes which grew from a fishing village into the city elegant, almost over-night. It was Cannes which really inaugurated the plush summer season although the sad millionaire, Frank Jay Gould, had set the ball rolling at Juan-les-Pins a year or two previously. All the crowned heads of Europe for a century past have stayed privately at Cannes and gone over to Monte Carlo to gamble – always with the exception of that venerable Riviera *habituée*, Queen Victoria. To her, Monte Carlo was the hiss of death. Cannes, where she stayed first at the Villa Edelweiss, is elegance personified. The croupiers are elegant, the motor-cars are very elegant, the gigolos are the height of elegance. It is true that the mimosa and orange trees are not so elegant as they were before the blizzard in February 1956. It is true that we have seen an Englishwoman, who owns a mansion in Mayfair, chase her husband all round the high table in the casino because he was making eyes at a pretty lady gambling beside him. Nevertheless, though Cannes is one of the most cosmopolitan cities we know, this air of elegance envelops all visitors within a few hours of their arrival. The women yawn prettily, the men hit ladylike little drives off the tees of the three neighbouring golf courses.

But what is Cannes? Well, it is an elegant (dash the word!), an elegant city of 60,000 inhabitants with a narrow beach, a beautiful promenade known as the Croisette, with a summer casino at one end and a winter casino at the other. All along the Croisette are bars, miniature dressmakers and jewellers' shops interspersed with luxury hotels like the Carlton and the Majestic. On the beach are countless prostrate but sometimes not so shapely bodies, alfresco cocktails, nets for handball, god-like young physical training instructors as brown as coffee berries. Some girls actually get their bathing suits wet. Water skiing, speedboats and pedallos are watched lazily, while absurd little waves lick feebly at the aching silver beach. Occasional Algerians walk around offering carpets, beads and other North African knick-knacks. The sun blazes down relentlessly from the breathless pearl-blue sky. Here a woman's crowning glory is neither her hair nor her jewellery. It is her Tan. You can transform an ardent friend into a lifelong enemy seething with pure hate by the use of five simple words: 'Darling, you are burning badly.' It is like telling a highbrow author that he writes potboilers or accusing a Royal Academician of painting like a futurist.

It is the one unforgivable sin.

Beyond the winter casino there is a pretty harbour with

millionaires' gleaming white yachts cheek by jowl with grubby unpainted rusty tramp steamers lying there quite unabashed, though what tramps do in Cannes we cannot imagine. The big passenger liners – 271 calls a year – have to heave-to nearly a mile off shore.

In addition to the long narrow town with its bourgeois shops along the main street – the Rue d'Antibes – there are hundreds of elegant villas inhabited by the very rich, most of them in the hills behind: like the Villa Yakimour, the home of the Aga Khan, in the Californie section, and Les Glaieuls, the property of the former widow of Sir Mortimer Davis of Schenley Corporation, now Mrs. Eric Loder.

Cannes is towards the eastern end of the French Riviera. Its immediate neighbour is Golfe Juan, where Napoleon landed in 1815 on return from exile in the island of Elba.

Next comes Juan-les-Pins, which has quadrupled in size in the past fifteen years. It is followed by Eden Roc and Antibes. Antibes, where General Eisenhower relaxed for a week or two after the Rheims Surrender, has quite forgotten that for several months it was made the headquarters of American negro troops. In the old days it lived through stirring times – when the River Var was the frontier between France and Italy. The narrow streets and sixteenth-century ramparts are medieval. There are also indications of Antibes' Greek origin (its name was Antipolis). Near the Chapel of St. Roch are the remains of a temple of Venus, itself preceded by a temple of Aphrodite, built by the Greeks.

Antibes has always been associated with paganism, though in the last thirty years the cult has transferred itself in modern fashion to Cap d'Antibes, with its myrtle and rosemary, pine groves and wild lavender, and above all, the sea. The week before the outbreak of war, Eden Roc was stiff with stars. Marlene Dietrich was leaving within twenty minutes for Paris and Hollywood to make *Destry Rides Again*; George Raft walked down from the hotel to the bathing pool with Norma Shearer; tousle-haired Simone Simon in a flower-patterned bathing dress hurried past for a swim with hairy-legged Charles Boyer; while Edward G. Robinson was sitting at the bar looking more like himself than ever. Erich Maria Remarque just looked glum.

It was here, in 1939, that a Battle Royal took place. In the United States, a modern Battle Royal consists of a number of blindfolded negro boxers all pitched into the ring at the same time; on this occasion the boxers were white and not blindfolded. Ten French lightweights were engaged here to fight simultaneously in two relays, winner take all. To start, five of them were put in the diminutive ring with instructions to continue fighting until two had been knocked out or retired hurt. Then the second batch were put in, the three survivors being put back to fight in a free-for-all, with the other three left from the first quintet. Thus there were six in the ring at the final, which continued until only two survived.

To add a betting flavour to this hopelessly Roman event, ten sportsmen were invited to buy the chances of each boxer for 2,000 francs, the winning owner thus making 18,000. The boxers themselves were given varying sums of francs according to the length of time they stood up, the actual winner making 3,000 francs or so. It was an extraordinary scene – the 200 guests in beach costumes getting wildly excited at this astonishing breach of the Queensberry Rules under the very nose of the late Marquess.

An English Member of Parliament had bought the chance of the runner-up, known as Tigre, because of his trunks, and flapped the towel energetically, while his wife squirted soda-water over him. The Battle Royal began shortly before midnight, and within ten yards of the Mediterranean. Seeing six men simultaneously in the ring was rather like going to one's first bullfight – a kind of fascinated nausea was a typical reaction. Three men would all set on the same man at once, and then the other two would come up from behind and try to pick the three off. Yet none was seriously hurt, as might well have happened.

Cagnes, the last village before Nice, is a bohemian little place with an ancient castle and a pretty trout stream called the Loup.

Nice is the fourth largest city in France with a population of 300,000, its Battle of Flowers, casino, splendid hotels, excellent restaurants – altogether a very popular stop for motor-coaches. Once upon a time Rex Ingram had studios there. Once upon a time – but today Nice is Tourism personified. It has twice as many bedrooms as London itself. Nice is no longer the Miami of the Riviera; it approximates Blackpool. In its golden epoch a large hotel only required 400 clients who would stay, on an average, 120 nights each between November and May.

The Sanine family was typical. They took a complete floor at the Hotel Splendide for the whole winter. There were thirty-five or forty of them including Russian servants who slept in the corridors outside the bedrooms of their masters, not for economic reasons but simply to guard them against intruders. Every night the family would go to Monte Carlo to gamble. A complete buffet, including champagne and caviare, was prepared for them in a private room against their return at 2 a.m. to 3 a.m. Sometimes they did not bother to partake of it but they were still charged. The Hotel Splendide had previously been the private home of the King of Württemberg.

Today the hotels are open all the year round and, since the average stop is seven nights in the winter and two in the summer, twelve thousand clients are needed by each hotel every year to make ends meet. No hotelier has such a vast following, so he has to rely on motor-coach parties. It is as simple as that.

On the far side of Nice is Villefranche, once so popular with the British and American fleets. Cap Ferrat is followed by Beaulieu. Its chief disadvantage is its lack of bathing facilities. One corner of the village is known as La Petite Afrique, because of its tropical trees and flowers. Eze and Cap d'Ail separate it from Monte Carlo, beyond which there are only Roquebrune and Menton before the Italian frontier is reached.

Menton is a city of lemon trees surrounded by mountains. Many of the houses look tumbledown. Several of the palm trees still show the bullet holes used by Italian and German occupation troops for target practice. It has always had a reputation of being a sleepy, if not dowdy little resort. The casino, with its blue swimming pool and green palm trees, is the only large building which looks truly spick-and-span.

From Cannes to the west the road leads past La Bocca with the sea on the left and cactuses on the right, to Théoule, originally a Greek city called Theopolis, just as La Napoule was Neopolis. Like Miramar, they are pretty little villages on the shores of the Mediterranean.

At this point comes a very sharp turn in the road approaching Le Trayas, midway between St. Raphael and Cannes, with the Forest of the Estérels on either side.

The small coves, scarlet rocks and beach of Anthéor precede a deserted section of the coast with tiny forelands and still smaller bays of Agay with its unmistakable red rocks. Next come Boulouris and St. Raphael.

Considering that the Americans landed in force on the small sickle-shaped plage, it is astonishing how little damage was done to St. Raphael. It appears, however, that Intelligence work was so good that exact details of all the German blockhouses, with one exception, were known to the Navy and were immediately knocked out.

There had been three alerts on the night before the landing. During this period, American parachutists landed at St. Roseline. The barman of the Excelsior Bar described graphically how somebody banged on his door. 'I kept quiet like a rabbit,' he said, 'I thought they were Germans. Then a window was broken; then a door. I saw the helmets of the intruders. They were Americans.' The barman, having reassured them that there were no Germans in the neighbourhood, made tea for them and they slept the night on the floor. 'It was bang, bang, next morning,' the barman continued. 'As for the *débarquement*, it was frankly splendid, though a German Gestapo officer dressed as a *curé*, but with a *mitrailleuse*, jumped over a fence and escaped. I was to have been arrested myself, but the battle had begun and it was too late.'

At the back of St. Raphael is Valescure, reached by a pretty road shadowed by plane trees.

The eighteen-hole golf course open all the year round still belongs to Lord Ashcombe, although the bulk of the visiting golfers nowadays are Swedes, Belgians and Swiss. The brown-and-white, low-ceilinged club-house with its veranda, gay parasols and orange tiles bids everybody welcome. The course itself is not long, but the presence of three streams enabled the architect to have water hazards at eight different holes. So it is sporting golf.

Nearby is Fréjus, with its twelfth-century cathedral, the granite pillars of which were stolen from some Roman temple. Its chief interest is that Agricola, who conquered Britain, and whose daughter married Tacitus, was born there. Between the Wars Fréjus used to give performances of classical tragedies in the ancient amphitheatre towards the end of April. Fréjus is on the way to Val d'Esquières.

The road now curves away from the sea past another small hotel into the scrubby hinterland. The Americans landed at this point as well. There are still barbed wire and a number of shell holes. Fortunately, Val d'Esquières escaped all damage.

Next along the coast comes St. Maxime, which lies exactly opposite St. Tropez.

St. Maxime is a small gay town, the predominant colours of which are red, blue and ochre, but it is clearly getting too big for its boots, or perhaps one should say – for its sandals. Sunburnt cyclists, stripped to the waist, and piles of water-skis on the tops of motor-cars, are a common sight there in the summer, and its intention to become another Cannes is shown by the avenue of young palm trees planted shortly before the war.

The coast road now approaches St. Tropez. The first sign of it is Latitude Forty-Three – the huge white hotel which looks like a stranded yacht just above the former fishing village.

St. Tropez owed much of its sudden popularity before the war to the Duke of Windsor, who took a liking to it; and in summer it is crowded with semi-nude girls burnt almost black, their young men stripped to the waist, drinking through straws; while on the narrow roadway between the chairs and the edge of the harbour, small children chase hoops, dogs chase small children, and big cars with foreign number-plates crawl past avoiding both.

Cavalaire was best known for the healing hands of Father Nicholas. Admirals, lawyers, business men, their wives and sweethearts, as well as the local fisher-folk, went to his small white villa with its cherry trees, bougainvillaea, maize, pigeons, white kittens, blue beams, and white veranda. His pigeons used to coo while the clients waited under the strands of dried seaweed until their turn came. Sometimes he treated one hundred patients a day.

His own theory was that he was able to draw pain out of people into himself, which his own animal magnetism conquered in a moment. But it was only his theory. One could well believe that he was really an abnormal psychotherapist and osteopath combined. In other words, that he was good for pulled muscles, torn ligaments, and minor bone injuries.

Alas, Father Nicholas died in 1946.

But to return to Cavalaire. . . . The road now climbs nearly 700 feet above the sparkling blue Mediterranean. The Maures have crept close to the sea, rising sheer from the water's edge, and such is the denseness of the pine forests that they almost entirely obscure the villages of Le Canadel with its palm trees, wild olives and petunia, and Le Rayol with its Majorcan scenery and jolly garage, the temperamental owner of which has no time for smart Parisians, and being an inhabitant of the Midi feels he has to talk, and does so. Along the Corniche itself there are only two or three villas, a garage, and a little restaurant to signify the fact that Le Rayol and Le Canadel lie snugly in the pine forest below. True, one can catch a glimpse of pretty little bathing beaches and a few picturesque rocks, but you would never find either midget resort unless you knew that it was there.

Pramousquier has a rocky foreshore, tiny vineyards, and straggling cottages among the tamarisks. Cavalière lies on a charming little bay between Cap Nègre and Cap Layet. The road is now at sea level and one gets a fine view of the eucalyptus trees, saffron villas and small hotels.

Le Lavandou comes next. This honey-coloured little town is full of small stores selling straw hats, bottles of sun-tan lotion, parasols, smoked spectacles and Dubonnet. It is continually having competitions among the girl visitors for the best bust, the most beautiful bottom, the plumpest thighs, and the straightest knees. Prizes are anything from silk stockings to bottles of champagne, and sports include naked bathing by night, with searchlights playing on the sea.

A mile or two away is the Island of Levant, which is a nudist colony in the summer. It is rocky and small, the colony consisting of two or three hundred men, women and girls who spend their week-ends and summer holidays there. Officially, they are all supposed to wear the proverbial fig leaf, but most of them dispense with this compromise. It is really quite a community. But except for getting sunburnt and bathing, there is little to do.

Hyères is one of the oldest as well as the southernmost resort of the Riviera. People came to it before the railway had opened up the rest of the coast, and when highwaymen in the Maures and the Estérel mountains acted as a deterrent to further travel along the coast. And no wonder, with its palms, aloes, myrtle, orange groves and lemon groves. The orange tree, indeed, was originally introduced to France at Hyères – from Spain by way of China. Today, Hyères has fallen by the wayside.

Two miles on are Les Sablettes and Tamaris – delightful little places before the war.

Bandol comes next; its tiny promenade is stuffed with baby bars and restaurants.

The casino is rather large for so small a town, but *chemin de fer* is only played during the high season.

Les Lecques is the next resort along the coast. It was here that Caesar defeated Pompey's galleys. The road again curves inland from the very rocky coast through kilometres of wild olives before emerging on the Mediterranean again at La Ciotat. La Ciotat is half pleasure resort and half dockyard. To reach it from the east, you drive along the curving bay past the caramel-cream casino; past the little trees on the promenade; and past Les Flottes Bleus.

Once again the big road drives inland past topaz rocks and forests of pine trees until it descends steeply into Cassis, shady little town, surrounded by rugged limestone cliffs and draped in wisteria. It is dominated by the ruins of a fourteenth-century castle, last occupied by the English when Napoleon was first attracting attention at the Siege of Toulon.

The annual fête, which takes place in September, includes jousting from boats, but the reputation of Cassis depends largely on the excellence of the local beverage—export Cassis. At the far end of the harbour is the punk-pink, white-pillared Carlton Hotel – a favourite with the leading painters, like Salvador Dali. The latter is the creator of a brilliant bas-relief of a Louis XV admiral grinning at an English man-o'-war stuck on the rocks.

That is the end of the Riviera.

Of all the resorts, Monte Carlo is the one most continuously in the public eye. But it only exists by the patronage of a young man in his early thirties who reigns a mile away on the great Rock of Monaco, like his ancestors before him – an unbroken family dynasty going back seven centuries. Indeed, Prince Rainier III traces his descent officially from Otto Canella, born in A.D. 1070, whose great-great-great-grandson, Rainier I, finally set the Grimaldi seal on Monaco in 1297.

His power is absolute. Disloyal remarks about him or his princely family can result in expulsion not only from the Principality but also from the Departments of the Alpes Maritimes, the Var and the Alpes Basses. Prince Rainier carries the titles of Duc de Valentinois, Marquis des Baux, Comte de Carladès, Baron du Buis, Seigneur de Saint Remy, granted to his ancestors by the King of France in 1641. He is also Sire de Matignon, Comte de Torrigni, Baron de Saint Lô, Baron de Bambye, Baron de la Luthumière (as a result of the marriage of his ancestress Princess Louis Hippolyte to Count Jacques de Matignon in 1715); further, he is Duc de Mazarin, Duc de Mayenne, Prince de Château Porcien, Baron d'Altkirch, Marquis de Chilly, Baron de Massy and Marquis de Guiscard, as a result of the Duchess d'Aumont Mazarin marrying into his family late in the eighteenth century.

Through the female line Prince Rainier has Douglas-Hamilton blood in his veins which may have accounted for his being sent to school at Summerfields and Stowe. Later he spent three years in Switzerland and two and a half in Montpelier before studying political science in Paris. After the liberation he joined the French Army and served in Alsace where he was awarded the Croix de Guerre.

Prince Rainier is a devotee of underwater fishing, drives a number of fast motor-cars, the first four of which bear the number plates MC 1, MC 2, MC 3, MC 4, writes poetry, admires the Primitives, plays golf (handicap twelve) and tennis. He is well set up, dark with a clipped moustache, and has strong likes and dislikes. It is by no means unknown for him to refuse to accept directors of the casino whose names have been proposed to him for his official approval before election. Equally he is very fastidious on the subject of the various designs of the Monégasque postage stamps, particularly when they bear his effigy.

Monaco, owing to its extremely small size – eight square miles compared with the one hundred and ninety-one square miles of Andorra and the thirty-eight square miles of San Marino – is often the butt of humorists.

The royal household includes two privy councillors, ladies-in-waiting, a court chamberlain, an aide-de-camp, a chancellor of the Grand Order of Saint Charles, a secretary of state, a personal secretariat, a keeper of the archives, a court doctor, a court notary, a court architect and the palace registrar. The cabinet consists of a Minister of State who also acts as Foreign Minister, a Home Secretary, a Minister of Works, and a Chancellor of the Exchequer.

The consular service has representatives in almost every continental country as well as in Great Britain, the United States, Egypt and Morocco.

The National Council consists of eighteen members. But their powers are distinctly limited. They cannot change the cabinet, which is personally nominated by the Prince. They can, however, vote for or against the budget which was more than the equivalent of two million pounds in 1956. As the population of Monaco is less than 25,000, this works out at more than £80 a year for every man, woman and child. There is no income tax, but purchase tax becomes increasingly heavy. This provides the bulk of the revenue, aided by the profits from the sale of tobacco and postage stamps. In 1949 there was a national deficit of £150,000.

In contrast to what most people think, the contribution of the casino is nowadays only a small proportion of the total revenue. In 1956 £50,000 of the budget was earmarked for the Prince.

At present there is a waiting list of nearly 10,000 people anxious to become Monégasque citizens. It needs a five-year residence to qualify. On an average only twenty to twenty-five people are anually admitted to citizenship. Even they have to show that they have rendered some special service to the state.

CHAPTER I

DANGEROUS JOURNEY

THE VOGUE OF THE RIVIERA is founded on a myth and a song. The song was 'The Man Who Broke the Bank at Monte Carlo'; the myth was that the South of France was good for cases of consumption however advanced. It was nourished by three books written by two doctors and a doctor-patient: Tobias Smollett's *Travels in France and Italy* (1766), *The Ancient and Modern History of Nice* by Dr. J. B. Davies (1807), and Dr. Alexander Brown's *Wintering at Menton on the Riviera* (1872).

This trio of books made it clear that the winter sunshine was no cure-all for chest conditions, but in the process of so doing, contained so many references to the balmy air, pomegranates, orange groves, fig trees, lemon groves, mimosa and palm trees that invalids in all stages of ill health struggled out from the fogs and cold of England in late autumn and remained there either to die or return in April. (The fashionable physicians insisted on returning to their practices in London so that their poor wretches of patients had to follow suit.)

One of the most tragic cemeteries in the world is that of Holy Trinity Church at Nice. The Rev. H. F. Lyte who wrote 'Abide With Me', and was an early incumbent, was suitably buried here. Tombstone after tombstone is erected to the memory of girls and boys who died in their 'teens. None of them bathed in the sea and few, if any, braved the warnings of their doctors that after 15th May the Riviera was a death trap for foreigners, being riddled with malaria and every other known disease. In this connection it must be remembered that Cannes was 'discovered' by Lord Brougham as a result of a local outbreak of cholera which prevented him from crossing the Var (see page 43). But the suggestion that the local mosquitoes spread malaria was quite inaccurate and the tens of thousands who spend the height of every summer in the South of France today can only benefit from the vitamin D produced by the sunshine.

Smollett's account of his two years' stay at Nice on the advice of his doctors, eleven years before the American War of Independence, is most illuminating; it is the sole description of Nice in the eighteenth century, whether in French or in English.

To cross the English Channel, Smollett, already successful, hired a Folkestone cutter for six guineas, being transported by row-boat for the last mile or so over a rough sea. Both he and his wife were violently sick. The journey from Calais to Nice, with a servant on horseback, cost £120. The first British tourists in those days reckoned to take two and a half days to reach Paris, with another five days in the summer and six in the winter (which was the normal time to take the journey) to reach Lyons through Burgundy. This involved crossing the River Saône at Chalons by ferry; thereafter it was another three days to Avignon by boat on the Rhône. The vessel was a kind of eighteenth-century wherry on which the traveller and his carriage travelled, rather like the modern car ferries which cross the English Channel to the Continent. There was one large cabin, dark and dirty, into which the passengers, cattle and goods were huddled together.

After Avignon, the intrepid tourists had to cross the River Durance by boat or ford to reach Aix-en-Provence. The next stage – to Nice – could be done in three days, but as the roads were abominable and involved the crossing of the Estérel mountain range, at that time infested by bandits, many preferred to go by sea. The only vessels available were oar-propelled feluccas, large gondolas and skiffs unable to take the family coach.

The final stop before Nice was Cannes, where they crossed the Var from France into the Kingdom of Sardinia and so reached their destination after sixteen days of continuous travel since leaving London. (Today, of course, it can be done in under four hours by air or overnight by the Blue Train, the great aristocrat of French Railways.) Once arrived in Nice, visitors, mostly invalids, stayed in bed on a liquid diet for three days to recover from the food and the jolting they had received en route. Nevertheless, they felt it was well worth it; the sky was blue, the palm trees were green, the Sardinian Government was well disposed. There were no Customs nor Excise; nothing to stop them buying a house; a good police force, and a warm welcome from the inhabitants.

As to the hotels and inns at which they stopped during their pilgrimage, if one can use the word, there is many a story of unpleasantness and filthy lodgings. The names of a few good hotels are still on record, though practically none of them exists today. At Calais there was the Hotel Dessein. At Chalons, the Hotel de la Couronne was most luxurious, with silk counterpanes on the beds. In Paris, the best hotel was the D'Antragues in the Rue de Tournain, frequented by French aristocrats and foreign princes. Dinner cost not less than six livres per head. There were also the Auberge du Cheval Blanc – a departure point for the public coaches – and the Auberge of the Compas d'Or. Marseilles was noted for the Malta Hotel which was, however, very expensive by eighteenth-century standards.

Outside the big towns, single rooms were the exception to

the rule. Travellers had to sleep in dormitories like a public ward in a hospital, on beds in which, as at Amiens, Lord Walpole complained that he found 'enormous fleas and venerable bugs' – a reminder of what Locke wrote of the Inns of Picardy 'if Paris is the real paradise, as all the world is busy repeating, the inns on the main road are evidently the purgatory which leads to it.'

The ardours and endurances of the sixteen days' journey from London to Nice are admirably, if anxiously, demonstrated by the huge sale of a handbook entitled *A Manual of Conversation in Six Languages, English, German, French, Italian, Spanish and Russian*, printed in Leipzig. This neat little publication had an international sale. Carey and Lea were the agents in Philadelphia, U.S.A., with Black and Armstrong handling it in London. It was still a best seller half a century later, after having gone through seven editions with various improvements and augmentations. The first edition is famous for the phrase, 'Look, my postillion has been struck by lightning.' Consisting of sixty-four dialogues over 409 pages, it discussed such charming subjects as the cholera-morbus, fire, robbery, the purchase of arms, 'accidents that may happen on the road', and conversation pieces about crossing the water in the ferry boat or public conveyances, and useful phrases as employed between physicians, invalids and attendants, or wounded men and surgeons. Throughout, the manual suggests acute discomfort, slovenly postillions, greedy inn-keepers, dangerous roads, ignorant doctors, but also very considerable wealth on the part of the travellers.

Here are a few examples selected from those carefully underlined by the author's great-grand-uncle, John Graves, as being most useful to the travellers.

DIALOGUE 5
Of the cholera-morbus

You are going to N., Sir?

I am, Sir.

Are you not afraid of the cholera-morbus?

I need not fear it, Sir, because I have what may be called a wet nature.

Let us secure ourselves by a reasonable diet, and there will be no need of miracles to save us.

I do entirely agree with your opinion, Sir. I remember when I was once living at a place, where there was a contagion, I was advised by a physician, to eat and to drink more than usually, in order to keep myself free from infection; and this advice proved good, for I was always in good health, while many persons, which I knew, were infected and died.

DIALOGUE 6
Enquiries previous to entering upon a journey

Is the road good?

It is shocking.
It is very sandy.
It is full of mountains, forests and precipices.

Is the road broad?

No, rather narrow.

The road is full of deep ruts.

You must take care not to travel through the forests at night-fall or in the night-time.

Are there any lakes to cross over?
Is one obliged to cross them in ferries?
I shall go on horseback.

Is the carriage commodious and in good repair?

Is there room in it for a portmanteau?

I should like to send my harp and portmanteau by the stage-coach.

DIALOGUE 10
Conversation on board a ship

I think we shall have a storm. What is your opinion?

I am very sick.

Is there no means to keep one's self free from sea-sickness?

The best way is to stand and to go on board with one's knees loose and somewhat crooked.

How can the nausea be thereby prevented?

By the staggering of the knees caused by the reeling of the ship, the body is kept in equilibrium and repose, so that the stomach is not prevented from maintaining its regular motion.

I suffer extremely; I am sick; pray, hand me a basin.

I advise you to take a few of the ethereal, or Hofmann's drops, which are a sovereign remedy against sea-sickness.

I have the tooth-ache.

That happens frequently at sea. You must take care not to expose yourself to the morning and evening air. You must frequently chew sage-leaves. Wash your mouth with brandy mixed with camphire, in short take great care of your teeth.

DIALOGUE II

On crossing the water in a ferry-boat

Coachman, stop! I will alight before we go into the ferry-boat.

O, there is no danger, the horses are tame.

I tell you, I will alight and walk into the ferry-boat.

Now take off the horses. The horses ought not to be left attached to the carriage in a ferry-boat.

Why so?

Because nothing can be more dangerous.

Now that the horses are off, we may get into the carriage again; we shall be more comfortable there, than here.

DIALOGUE I3

Speaking to the postillions on the road

Hark ye, post-boy, drive at a good pace, when the road is good; but be careful in turning round and on bridges or in towns and villages; if you pay attention to this, you shall be well paid, otherwise you will only receive exactly what you are entitled to.

Stop, Driver!
Drive slower.
Leave the pavement and keep on the soft ground.

Have we lost our way, coachman?
Enquire of that peasant.

Driver, a man has got up behind; make him get down.
Don't go so near that precipice.

Keep as far from the edge of the precipice as you can.

The road is very steep here.
I desire you to fasten the drag chains to the wheels.

I think the wheels will be set on fire; look at them, and examine the carriage whether it has been damaged.

DIALOGUE 14

Of the accidents that may happen on the road

The head-pin is starting.
The leather-brace is torn.
The carriage is over-turned.
Lend me your hand.
Support me.
Take this luggage away.

Go to yonder cottage and call for assistance. Ask for nails, cords and a hammer; enquire whether we can have a wheel-wright.

Call to those country-people for help.

We are sticking in a hole. Lend us two of your horses, to draw us out of it.

I have lost a shoe in the carriage; look for it.

I was quite frightened.

So was I.

We must lift up the carriage. Is it quite shattered?

Reach me my small casket. In it are bandages of linen, very soft lint, Cologne-water, dried bladder, brandy, a vial of eau de Luce and a bottle with the juice of unripe grapes.

The coachman has fallen into a swoon.
Apply the smelling-bottle with eau de Luce to his nose.

One of the horses is just fallen down.

Is the driver hurt?

Yes, he is hurt.

That horse is dangerously hurt.
It is dead.

Disengage the coachman from under the horse.
He has broken his leg.
He has broken his arm.
He has a hole in his head.

He has fallen upon a flint, which has opened a vein, so that
the blood cannot be stopped.

Poor man, I sympathise greatly with your sufferings.

DIALOGUE 19

*On calling for food or refreshments
at an Inn*

This fruit is not ripe enough.

I like neither cinnamon, nutmeg nor cloves.

I will have no mushrooms in any of our dishes.

This must be tainted.
I won't have it.

This meat is so tough that I can't eat it; give us something
else.

Bring us coffee, but it must be hot and well-filtered.

Above all, let us have wine that is not adulterated.

Bring us boiling water and a teapot. Put some tea into it, put in two, three or four teaspoonsful.

Let it draw for some minutes. Now fill the teapot with boiling water. Pour out the tea.

DIALOGUE 24

Between a physician, a waiting-woman,
and a sick person, at an Inn

Good morning, sir.

Sir, your servant.

Pray, what is your complaint?

I have the gout. I have got a rheumatism, a cold, the gripe, the cholera-morbus. I have a fever and a nervous complaint. I have a diarrhoea, or a dysentery. I have a pain in my neck. I have a violent pain in my hip. I have an erysipelas, a ringworm. I have the colic. I have the obstructions, or pain in the liver. I have a pain in my breast. I have a violent headache and sore eyes. I think I shall get the measles or scarlet fever. I fear I have caught the small-pox.

Have you not been inoculated?

No, never.

Have you a pain in the loins?
Have you any appetite?
Is your stomach in order?
Is your digestion good?

Show me your tongue.

Do you sleep soundly?

31

No, I can't sleep at all.

Have you any qualms in your stomach?

I feel sometimes an inclination to vomit.

Have you had this complaint a long time?
How long, pray?

Do you think, sir, that bathing would be beneficial to me?

Yes, I think so.

But what shall I do for a bathing tub?

Have you a bitter taste in your mouth, when you are awake?
Are your legs swollen?

Are you thirsty?

Yes, I am frequently thirsty; I have the hiccough, the scurvy.

What regimen do you generally observe?
Do you go to bed early?
Do you take exercise?

Have you been subject to other disorders in your life-time?
What disorders have you had?
Are your nerves irritable?
Are your lungs weak?

Could I have a pail to bathe my feet in?

Yes, a bucket from the stable.

I want a larger one, in order to sit up to my knees in water.

We have none of that sort.

Smollett's house at Nice, with two small gardens well stocked

First issue of *The Cannes Gazette*.

'Victoria Charitable', water colour by J. Mossa. The Queen gives alms to peasant women at Cimiez in the 1890's. John Brown is on the right. *(From the Lawrence Venn collection)*

with oranges, lemons, peaches, figs and grapes, cost him £20 a year rent. He was offered furniture at a hiring price of two guineas a month, but he preferred to spend £60 on buying what he wanted; though he complained in his journals that he knew he would get less than half that price when he wanted to dispose of it. He found it difficult to secure a good cook, but was well satisfied with the beef, lamb and pork, ortolans, woodcock, partridges, *mostelle*, *loup* and *langouste*. Tavel wine cost sixpence a bottle; the price of malaga was fourpence a quart.

Smollett, however, took grave exception to the shopkeepers. He described them as poor, greedy and over-reaching. Many of them were bankrupts from Marseilles and Genoa who had fled from their creditors. As to the artisans, they were very lazy, very needy, very awkward and with no sense of improvisation. Against that, the police were well regulated and it was perfectly safe to walk anywhere in the city after midnight without anxiety, which was more than could have been said at that time for London. This was not surprising when one remembers that the penalties for crime ranged from hanging and lifelong slavery in the galleys to beatings and the strappado. The punishment by strappado consisted of hoisting up the criminal by his hands, which had been previously tied behind his back, on a pulley to a point thirty feet from the ground. The rope was then suddenly slackened, causing the unfortunate to fall within a yard or two of the ground; as a result of the shock, his shoulders were usually dislocated with incredible pain to him. Sometimes the dose was repeated, making him a cripple for life.

Cats, dogs and mules were pathetically underfed. The poverty of the inhabitants was largely due, said Smollett, to the number of religious festivals which had to be attended at regular intervals. Most of the window spaces were stuffed with paper instead of glass to keep out draughts. There were no regular libraries; not even a bookseller.

What really matters to the historian and to the ultimate vogue of the South of France, was Smollett's account of the weather. He sent to his patron and physician in London a special weather report which showed that there was less rain and wind at Nice than anywhere he knew, adding 'such is the serenity of the air, that you see nothing above your head for several months together but a charming blue expanse without cloud or speck . . . this air being dry, pure, heavy and elastic, must be agreeable to the constitution of those who labour under the disorders arising from weak nerves, relaxed obstruction, perspiration fibres, a viscidity of lymph and a languid circulation.' It is true that Smollett went on to say that the air was bad for scurvy, but he added that a friend of his who had apparently arrived at death's door suffering from loss of appetite, faintness, and a sharp pain in the chest, rapidly regained perfect health, eating heartily, sleeping well and able to climb to the tops of all the local mountains.

Smollett himself claimed that he was breathing far more freely after a few weeks at Nice than he had done for years and revealed the fact that he started the cult of sea bathing. This surprised all the local doctors who knew that he was consumptive and prophesied his immediate death. (It may be stated, in passing, that they charged the equivalent of sixpence a visit, so that medical knowledge was not likely to be much advanced.) When it became apparent that it was genuinely benefiting him, his example was followed by several other local worthies. Women, of course, could not imitate him 'unless they laid aside all regards to decorum. A lady should pay the expense of having a tent pitched on the beach where she could put on and off her bathing dress; she could not go into the sea without proper attendants.' Shades of Cannes today . . . And yet in another account of Nice, Smollett describes how, in the summer evenings, many of the so-called *noblesse* lay stretched in pairs upon logs of wood in the park, like so many seals on the rocks by moonlight; each dame with her gallant and each seigneur with his mistress. This phenomenon was attributed by Smollett to the complete absence of jealousy among the inhabitants of Nice. Husbands and the men who were cuckolding them lived together in the greatest friendliness, as did wives and their husbands' mistresses.

Other amusements available in those days were insignificant. A public *conversazione* was given every evening at Government House, where the local leaders of fashion played cards for a farthing. In carnival time there were two or three subscription dances a week. No private individual could give a ball without the Governor's consent or his equerry's perquisite of selling tickets for it at threepence each.

Perhaps the most fascinating aspect of Smollett's description of Nice concerns the temperature to which he refers again and again. The best-known doctor on the Riviera today claims that the theory of the alteration of the climate in the South of France is utterly fallacious. In his opinion, it is all a matter of clothes, hygiene and construction or re-construction of villas and hotels in modern times, intelligently designed to keep the interiors cooled. His only supporter, however, is the most successful architect in the South of France, Barry Dierks of Pennsylvania, who likes to be known as the Nash of the Riviera (see page 223). The fact remains that, according to Smollett, the heat was so violent from May to October during the two consecutive years he spent there, that it was impossible to go out at all after 6 a.m. until 6 p.m. Even in the winter, but especially in the spring, the sun was allegedly so hot that it was difficult to take any exercise without being thrown into a violent sweat, although the wind might be so cold that it gave people pleurisy. After all, he announced, there were only four doctors at Nice who could make a living out of medicine, a strong presumption in favour of the climate.

So much for the garrulous and embittered Smollett, except for his diatribe on the local *noblesse*. Nice, he said, abounded with marquises, counts and barons, mostly sons of shopkeepers who had paid for their titles. The father of one so-called count was still selling macaroni in the streets of Villefranche. The tariff, apparently, was £300 or £400 to be a count or marquis.

Directly as a result of Smollett's description of Nice, several members of the British aristocracy, headed by the ill-fated Duke of York, brother of George III, made their way to what is now the French Riviera. They included such personalities as the Duke of Gloucester, the Duke of Bedford, the Duchess of Cumberland, not forgetting Lord Bessborough, that famous dandy.

The roses, the olive groves, the blue sea, the carnations in the depths of what was winter in England, fascinated them. They lived in gaily decorated villas in the English quarter of Nice which they nicknamed Newborough. The rent was £20 a year for furnished apartments. A complete house, surrounded by a large garden, cost £130 a year. Soon, a large hotel was opened – the Hotel d'Angleterre – which became the focal point of their social activities. This was followed by the building of new roads and boulevards and long terraces facing the sea near the harbour. Next came the construction of a series of fine villas in the Croix de Marbre, near what is now the Promenade des Anglais.

CHAPTER 2

LORD BROUGHAM APPEARS

AT CANNES

In those days, it must be remembered, Nice belonged to the Kingdom of Sardinia, a close ally of Great Britain and hated enemy of France. The treaty between the two countries enabled the British fleet to use the splendid harbour of Ville-franche. The Kingdom of Sardinia exported silk, wine and oil to England; in return the British exported manufactured goods. Antibes, now a second-rate little provincial town, was then a major fortress, the last bastion between France and the Kingdom of Sardinia.

Everything was going splendidly for Nice. The number of British visitors was increasing by leaps and bounds and everywhere new villas and new roads were being built. Then came the French Revolution. On the day after the storming of the Bastille, the Duc de Tremoille put up at the Hotel York at Nice, followed by the Comte de Castellane, the Marquis de Grimand, the Marquis de Fare, and the Duc and Duchesse de Rohan. By January 1792, more than 1,200 French aristocrats who had escaped the guillotine crossed the frontier into Nice. Their impact was notably a mixture of talkativeness and ostentatious wealth, as exhibited by the throwing of silver through the windows of their villas to the beggars. These *émigrés* were accused of treating Nice not so much as an escape from France, but as a headquarters to enrol troops, to buy arms and to plot against the newly formed Republic.

In July 1792, war broke out between France and the Kingdom of Sardinia. Panic reigned in Nice. Half the inhabitants fled, leaving the dregs of the population to pillage at their will. French troops, singing the 'Marseillaise', entered the city, bivouacking in what is today the Place Victoria. Six months later, an official proclamation announced the absorption of what is now known as the French Riviera, by the French Republic under the title of the Department of Alpes Maritimes. The streets and boulevards were renamed Unité, Liberté, Egalité, Sans Culottes and the like. Properties and estates of the *émigrés* were sold at ludicrously low prices. One revolutionary leader bought the Episcopal Palace for £13,000. The huge estate of Lady Rivers was acquired for £3,000. In this general liquidation of society, everybody took advantage of the chaos. Church property was nationalised; the estates of the King of Sardinia were confiscated. The sceptre of the Prince of Monaco was sold for a song. During the Revolution, servile reproduction of what was taking place in Paris was painstakingly imitated in Nice. Wives of commissars grabbed gold in all directions. A crowd of camp-followers led a gay life in cafés, cabarets and restaurants. Theatres were always full, particularly the Maccarani, which quickly changed its name to the Theatre of the Mountain and presented a number of revolutionary plays like *M. Crac en Paris*.

Meantime, the strategic situation of Nice caused it to become the headquarters of the French Artillery, with seven barracks and innumerable troops to prevent the infiltration of the Sardinian army. Among the officers quartered there was Napoleon, then a young captain, who fell madly in love with Amelia Laurenti, daughter of a well-to-do merchant. Laurenti *père* decided that Napoleon's life was a bad financial risk and personally broke off the love affair. Indeed, his decision seemed wise when a few days later Napoleon was put under house arrest after the death of Robespierre, though quickly acquitted of any treasonable activities. When he returned four years later, Amelia had married another and was living in Grasse.

During this period, the English visitors to Nice were of course conspicuous by their absence; but they still remembered the mimosa and when the Treaty of Amiens was signed in 1802, they returned in droves, headed by the Duchess of Cumberland, sister-in-law of George III. Napoleon apparently approved of the visitation and it was at his personal instigation that a banquet, at which forty leading French citizens and a similar number of distinguished English visitors were present, was given by the local Prefect. Toasts were drunk to Napoleon, to 'the forgetting of political views which divided humanity', to the re-establishment of religion, to the British Commander-in-Chief, General Morgan. The respite was brief, the Treaty of Amiens was rudely broken and the British were unable to return until 1814, after Napoleon's defeat at the Battle of Leipzig, his abdication at Fontainebleau on the 4th April, 1814, and his exile in Elba.

Back came the tourists.

The journey from England was much easier than before, if only because of Napoleon's improvements to the main roads, designed purely for military reasons. It was now possible to reach the Riviera in less than a fortnight from London.

Apart from the Hundred Days of Napoleon's bid for power (from the moment he left Elba, landed at Golfe Juan, rode up what is now known as the Napoleonic Route via Grenoble, to be defeated at Waterloo) the British colony at Nice remained happily installed every winter on the Mediterranean coast until 1940. Such celebrities as the Marquis of Hastings, then Governor of Malta, the Marquis of Bute, Lady Olivia Sparrow, who built the first English Church at Nice, the Earl of Jersey, Lord Ashley, who spent his life trying to improve the pay and living conditions of the English working classes, appeared on the scene and behaved with the traditional British phlegm, just as if they were at Brighton; taking long constitutionals, reading their newspapers, riding on horseback, talking politics, drinking tea and entirely disregarding the local inhabitants.

In 1830, the English colony, encouraged by the Rev. Lewis Way, who spent his life crusading against anti-Semitism, took up a collection among its members to help the unemployed by enlarging the path used by invalids on the sea front to a width of two yards. Many of them had daughters who had been scared by uncouth beggars. Here was an opportunity to improve the local amenities, at the same time reducing risk of assault from the half-starved peasantry. It was a humble beginning and twenty years passed before the Promenade des Anglais was wide enough to permit horse carriages. Every morning, nevertheless, members of the English colony went for walks, many of them still in their dressing-gowns.

There were no trees on the promenade. (It was not until 1862 that the palms, mimosa and pepper trees were planted.) However, in the main boulevards there were numbers of splendid coaches to be seen, and on occasions a squadron of cuirassiers, in gleaming breastplates, trotted past – bodyguard of the Empress Alexandra of Russia, who had rented the Villa Robini and was the spearhead of the invasion of Russian royalty. Her acute neurasthenia had caused the court physicians in St. Petersburg to send her to Nice which she revisited later, renting the Villa Orestia on the Promenade des Anglais, sometimes occupied by the first Grand Duke Michael.

Another distinguished visitor at this time was the Emperor of Austria, who had taken advantage of the construction of the Corniche by Napoleon. Having heard Mario and Grisi, the famous opera singers, in *Robert the Devil*, he met them next day on the Promenade des Anglais. 'I suppose these are your little *grisettes*,' he said maliciously to Grisi, who was accompanied by her five daughters. 'Not at all, Sire,' was the reply, 'they are our little *marionettes*.'

Very soon Nice had become practically a suburb of London, with hundreds of fine villas, all of them boasting gardens of the most exotic character. French visitors preferred Hyères, which was still French. (Once again it is important to remember that the section of the French Riviera from Nice to Menton belonged to the Kingdom of Sardinia up to 1792 and then again from 1814 to 1860.) The famous composer, Berlioz, however, chose Nice. He had been driven almost mad by the suicide of the girl he wished to marry. His reaction to the orange groves and palm trees was immediate. He rented a house but was expelled by the police who thought he was a spy.

The English colony was not destined to remain the only foreign one. The Russians appeared in increasing numbers and, like the English, were fascinated by such local customs as the Feast of Reproaches at Cimiez – later to be the winter home of Queen Victoria – during which time young couples came to confess naughtiness committed during the excesses of the annual carnival of Mardi Gras. In those days, the carnival, already centuries old, was still a spontaneous demonstration of pagan feelings and salute to the sun; not organised or mechanised or publicised as it is today.

Famous writers like Georges Sand, Alexandre Dumas and Alphonse Karr also appeared on the scene and proceeded to write books and articles about the flowers and sunshine of Nice. Alexandre Dumas, in his travel book published in 1851, said that as far as the inhabitants of Nice were concerned, all visitors were from England. Every stranger irrespective of his haircut, beard, habits, age or sex was regarded as someone from London who had only heard tell of sunshine, knew

oranges and pineapples only by name and had no experience
of any ripe fruits, except cooked apples. One day while he was
staying at the Hotel York, a coach arrived. A few minutes
later, the hotel keeper entered his room.

Dumas said, 'Who are your new arrivals?'

Said the hotel keeper, 'They are certainly English, but I do
not know whether they are French or German.' Dumas added
that, needless to say, prices were very high because everybody
was called 'milord'.

Dumas' praise of Nice was by no means as important as the
efforts of Alphonse Karr, a typically lyrical passage of whom
was: 'Go to Nice, travel by electrical telegraph if you can. A
charming climate, delicious situation on an inlet aptly named
the Bay of the Angels, with the Italian sun overhead and only
half an hour from the fresh breezes of Switzerland . . . a veri-
table paradise . . . I have just given a luncheon out of doors in
this month of February for the Contessa Potocki and the
Princess Marcelina.'

Alphonse Karr's major contribution to the Riviera vogue
was, however, horticultural. The flowers of Nice had grown
haphazardly before his arrival. Karr made a scientific approach, importing plants and flowering bushes, particularly
roses, from France, Holland, Belgium and England. A year
later, he opened his own flower shop in the public gardens and
started a mail order business with places as far away as Paris,
Lyons and Marseilles. He guaranteed for twenty-five francs to
send a parcel measuring a foot and a half across, full of Parma
violets, carriage paid, to any destination. His friends thought
that it was a momentary caprice of this best-selling novelist.
They soon realised he was serious, especially when King Victor
Emmanuel of Italy, Prince Oscar of Sweden and the old King
of Bavaria came to see his roses and eat his strawberries.

Louis I of Bavaria was a regular boulevardier. The scandals

of his court at Munich, particularly his association with Lola Montez, had forced him to abdicate. At Nice he daily ogled the girls on the Promenade des Anglais, although his fat, ugly lined face was the reverse of the popular conception of anything royal. Close to his house was the villa of the Princess Souvaroff, one of whose guests, Mlle. Honorine, an actress from Paris, seems to have been the original character to drink champagne from a shoe. To celebrate an occasion, she said, when offered a glass of champagne, 'Do as I do,' took off her slipper, filled it with wine and drank it down. The rest of the guests followed suit.

Further along the coast, Cannes was beginning to attract an English colony. In the autumn of 1834, Lord Brougham, travelling in the South of France, had arrived at St. Laurent de Pont, at that time the frontier of France, on his way to Genoa.

He was there stopped by an officer of the Health Office who informed him that a *cordon sanitaire* had been established, on account of an outbreak of cholera. His passport being in the ordinary form, he was given the option of either undergoing a ten days' quarantine, or writing to Paris for a special permit to continue his journey. He chose the latter, and asked where he could be lodged during the five or six days it took to write to Paris and receive an answer. He was recommended to go to Antibes. On arriving there, finding the dirty cooking and inns of the garrison town by no means inviting, he inquired whether there was any other place short of Fréjus. The reply was, 'There is Grasse, a considerable town, with a good hotel, but some miles out of the road; on this road there is only the small fishing village of Cannes, where moderate accommodation may be found at the Hotel de la Poste'; so he decided upon Cannes, and drove to the Poste, kept by M. Pinchinat.

Having nothing to do during his detention, he occupied himself in walking about the neighbourhood of the village. At that time, Pinchinat's hotel was the only inhabited house to the south of Mont Chevalier. There was one other building near it, the office of the coastguard and custom-house officer, called La Cloche.

The village consisted of a row of houses beginning at the cross-street near the only confectioner, Blanc, and extending to what is now the Rue de Grasse; behind was the narrow street called the Grande Rue, the houses in the Suquée and a few scattered houses at the back of the cemetery.

To the south of La Cloche, the fishermen beached their boats, for there was neither pier nor harbour.

Lord Brougham was not so much struck with the beauty of Cannes and its neighbourhood as with the climate, and on being told that the winters were as mild as in Cairo, that frost was almost unknown, and that snow scarcely ever fell nearer than Grasse, he conceived the idea of buying a very small plot of land, on which he might build a house where he and his daughter (who had been an invalid, although not consumptive, from her infancy) might pass the winters, and escape the worse-than-winter, the cold springs of England. So he inquired whether there was a respectable notary in the place. He was sent to M. Violet, and with him took various walks in search of a building site.

The first he visited was on the route to Nice. It was a plot of ground extending from the main road to the Croisette. By a singular instinct, for which he never could account, he fancied the situation might not be warm enough, and proposed to M. Violet to try the other side of the village.

Unfortunately, there was nothing on that side to be sold, at least within a reasonable distance of Cannes. However, the attempt was made, and a narrow strip of land, less than fifty metres wide, but extending from the seashore to the top of the hill, was found. The price he paid for this, absurdly small as compared with the present value of land at Cannes, was, nevertheless, three times its market value then, no doubt because a Marseilles newspaper had announced that 'Lord Brougham, ex-Chancellor of England,' was detained at Cannes by reason of the sanitary regulations.

Lord Brougham then inquired for an architect and builder, and was recommended to M. L'Arras, Director of the *Ponts et Chaussées*, and to M. Guichard. Under M. L'Arras' direction, the house was begun in 1835 and finished in 1839.

Having thus acquired a permanent interest in the place, Lord Brougham soon afterwards asked the King of France whether a grant of money could be given for the purpose of making a harbour at Cannes. He satisfied Louis Philippe how advantageous this would be to the place and neighbourhood. All the produce, not only of Cannes, but the far more considerable exports from Grasse, were sent by carts and wagons to Marseilles. No merchant vessel, however small its tonnage, could load or discharge at Cannes. There was not even a jetty.

The form of the west side of the bay, ending in a reef of rocks at the south side of the Cloche, suggested to Lord Brougham that a harbour might be made at no enormous cost, and that, with a little more money, a pier might be extended, to afford ample shelter from all but the south-east winds. At his instigation, engineers were ordered to survey Cannes and report to the Government. The result was a vote of two millions of francs, to be laid out in the construction of harbour and pier.

The result has more than verified Lord Brougham's most sanguine calculation. Cannes, for many years past, has been the second port of export in the Mediterranean; Marseilles alone being before it. Today, on an average, five liners visit Caunes every week, among them the Export line, the Italian State line and luxury cruise ships.

Although the house built by M. L'Arras was not completed and habitable until 1839, Lord Brougham continued to pay a visit to Cannes most winters.

Lord Brougham never congratulated himself upon anything connected with his having settled at Cannes, so much as upon his choice of the locality where his house stands. If he had bought the ground first offered to him by M. Violet, he would have been on the limestone and clay, instead of being on the granite. In the one case, upon a retentive, in the other, upon an absorbent, soil. The difference in temperature, no less than in health, was remarkable, and he always entertained a profound conviction that for health, his side of Cannes was as superior to the east side as the climate of Cannes was superior to the climate of Westmorland.

What Alphonse Karr had achieved in publicising the flowers of Nice all over France, the Woolfield family did for Cannes' reputation all over England. Thomas Robinson Woolfield, a wealthy, religiously-minded Englishman, had travelled throughout Europe and the Middle East in search of a haven for his declining days and daughter. He selected Cannes, bought the Château St. George, at that time rented by Lady Nelson (the Duchess of Bronte) and later incorporated into the present Hotel Majestic. Not content with this, he built the Château du Riou, and sold it to Lord Londesborough before erecting the Villa Victoria on a cemetery of Napoleonic conscripts.

Thomas Robinson Woolfield was the first man to introduce the gooseberry, the Jamaican sweet potato and the acacia to the Riviera. He also grew the first eucalyptus tree. The seed was sent direct from the Royal Botanic Gardens in Sydney,

Australia. Sown in 1862, the trees had reached a height of sixteen feet in two years and were fifty-five feet tall nine years later, with a girth of four feet at their base. The leaves and small branches were used for distilling and sold to the local chemists. As a regular contributor to the *Journal of Horticulture*, Woolfield must have made the big English landowners green with envy by his accounts of the flowers and shrubs – such as his Chromatella roses, trained in pyramid form to the height of fifteen feet and with blooms measuring five to seven inches in diameter at Christmas. Long technical descriptions of other plants flowering out of doors in January must have induced many a rich Englishman to spend his winters at Cannes. Every year, new hotels sprang up for the English clientele and later for the German and Russian notabilities when the railway was completed in spite of strong opposition from Lord Londesborough, Richard Cobden and Lady Oxford, who all realised how it would spoil the amenities of their gardens through which, in many cases, it passed.

Socially, the Woolfields were very well placed. His Royal Highness Prince Leopold, the consumptive Duke of Albany and the youngest son of Queen Victoria, introduced croquet to Cannes in the gardens of the Villa Victoria. Incidentally, he went to Christ Church, the local church built by the Woolfields on the Sunday morning before his sudden death caused by a fall in the Cercle Nautique. The Crown Princess of Prussia, formerly the Princess Royal of England, later becoming the Empress Frederick of Germany, spent two months in Cannes with her sister, Princess Alice, accompanied by her two young sons. The elder, Prince Frederick William, was destined to become the Kaiser of the 1914–18 war. The younger was Prince Henry of Prussia. The local inhabitants, though amazed at the simplicity of their distinguished guests, complied with the royal request that they should not stare at them, follow them around or photograph them. Frequently, the Crown Princess and her sister borrowed the keys of Christ Church and spent wet afternoons there – Princess Alice playing the organ and the Crown Princess singing in her rich, pathetic voice, sometimes by the light of candles when they stayed longer than usual.

The Crown Prince, later the Emperor Frederick, also visited the Villa Victoria and Woolfield arranged that in future his croquet ground should be reserved exclusively for royalty every Tuesday. Large parties were mustered for this now despised game. They included Russian grand dukes from Nice, Prince and Princess Waldeck Pyrmont and the Duchess of Albany. A special party was given at the Villa Victoria for Prince Frederick William's eleventh birthday, Blind-man's-buff and musical chairs were played with enthusiasm. The future Kaiser showed everybody the gold watch and chain given him by his grandmother, Queen Victoria, but confessed that what he really liked best was the beautiful golden sovereign which his grandmother had also sent him. Prince Albert of Prussia, another regular visitor to Cannes, always made a special request that he should be notified when Hymn Number 349, 'The Son of God Goes Forth to War', was to be sung in the church. Six months later the Franco-Prussian war broke out. . . . Prince and Princess Christian were other visitors, as were the English Primate and three leading American clerics – Bishops MacIlvain, Dr. Kipp, the Bishop of California and Dr. Stephens, Bishop of Pennsylvania. They must have been some of the earliest American visitors to the Riviera which was still an unknown quantity even to the Vanderbilts.

Soon afterwards, the croquet ground was turned into a lawn tennis court, although the Cannes Lawn Tennis Club was not officially inaugurated until a generation later by the late Sir Sidney Waterlow. Such was the craze for lawn tennis that many players began at 8 a.m. Relays of enthusiasts occupied the court until nightfall.

On the death of Mr. Woolfield, the Villa Victoria was bought by Sir Charles Augustus Murray, who changed its name.

In the meantime, the original English gardener, John Taylor, to whom he had paid many tributes, blossomed out in a number of directions. It had frequently happened that Mr. Woolfield's guests asked him whether he knew of any villa in the neighbourhood for rent or sale. They were always told to ask Taylor. Realising quickly that there was money to be made out of recommendations, John Taylor left his employment and started an estate agency. The next step in his career was to found a bank to accommodate visitors who asked what they should do with their money while they were back in England. Another regular inquiry concerned the wines for the cellars of the villa owners, so John Taylor became a wine merchant, too. His great-granddaughter, Jacqueline, now runs the estate agency business. Over a period of years, the firm of John Taylor must have bought and sold, on behalf of clients, nearly 30,000 properties – villas, shops, hotels, factory sites, estates and garages. Of that, later.

The very same year that Lord Brougham discovered Cannes (although it was the Grand Duke Michael who made it truly fashionable and famous), Prosper Mérimée, that egregious character, visited the fishing village in his capacity of Inspector-General of Historic Monuments. He cannot have been much impressed because his next visit did not occur for another twenty-two years and, even then, the object of his sojourn was solely to avoid being presented to the Grand Duchess of Mecklenburg at Nice. He stayed two months and was delighted. In December he wrote that there was not a cloud in the sky and he had been eating wild strawberries in the woods. Prosper

C

was an asthmatic, even a hypochondriac, always swallowing pills. He now decided to spend every winter in Cannes, lying in bed until midday; writing official letters to the Academy and the British Museum in the afternoon, talking and smoking with his house guests – though ordered by his doctor to abstain from tobacco and to substitute dried eucalyptus leaves. In the early evening, he would go for a walk wearing yellow Chinese pantaloons and a panama hat, followed by two Englishwomen who were admirers of his genius. One of them carried the bow and arrow which an English doctor prescribed as good exercise for the neuritis in his shoulder. Sometimes he sat down on the future Croisette, still escorted by his two duennas.

Often he dined with Lord Brougham to meet his latest guests from England, noting their eccentricities with delight. Of Lady Cheney he wrote, 'She is passing the whole time doing silly things to entertain the idle.' Of the Marchioness Conyngham, the former mistress of George IV, he wrote, 'She lives in a baroque castle at Cannes with her son Lord Londesborough. She is eighty-four years old though no one would guess she is over sixty. She has the presence of a very great lady and I would very much like to make her talk. Her daughter-in-law is the most ravishing Englishwoman I have ever met. She has the appearance of a piece of porcelain; her skin is so delicate, transparent, diaphanous, that I feel that if I touched her she would break in pieces.' He describes Lord Brougham as seeming discontented with the whole world and complaining to high Heaven like Jeremiah. It seems, however, that when Lady Brougham died, his Lordship took her death very philosophically. Later Mérimée described Lord Brougham as having lost his reason, as being as deaf as a post, though carrying his eighty-eight years very cheerfully. 'He still hops around with the energy of a lean cat,' was his parting description.

CHAPTER 3

HIG LIF AT NICE

DURING ALL THIS TIME, Cannes and Nice still belonged to different kingdoms – France and Sardinia respectively. It was not until 1860 that Nice was ceded to France as the result of the Battles of Magenta and Solferino which produced the Treaty of Turin. One of the clauses in this treaty was that there should be a plebiscite as to the political future of the County of Nice. The figures were 25,743 for France and 160 for Sardinia. Some six months later, Napoleon III, accompanied by the Empress Eugénie and the Prince Imperial, paid an official visit to his new acquisition. Two days after a squadron of the Fourth Hussars had entered into a madly enthusiastic Nice, the Emperor and Empress arrived in their flagship *L'Aigle*, accompanied by four men-of-war. Ashore, they drove in an open carriage, preceded by mounted police and the French Life Guards in their gleaming cuirasses, to the Place Napoleon (now the Place Garibaldi) amid prodigious cheers. A series of presentations ensued, with a grand ball at the Théâtre Royal, which had been quickly renamed the Théâtre Impérial. Fireworks sputtered all over the sky; the Emperor kept on repeating to himself, 'It is far above anything I expected – is not it beautiful? . . . It is far above anything I expected – is not it beautiful?'

Long before Monte Carlo attracted the finest musicians and orchestras to its concerts, Nice was visited for months at a time by such celebrities as Offenbach and Paganini. Offenbach spent a winter at the Hotel des Etrangers, where he had a luxurious suite with a balcony. Passers-by who saw his hairy chest disclosed by his maroon dressing-gown, his astrakhan hat and sensational nose, decided that he looked more like an alchemist than a composer. Many people, indeed, failed to identify him; some thought he was a Pole, others that he was the husband of a Russian consumptive. Offenbach, at that time, was working on Varieties and the musical score of *Robinson Crusoe*.

Paganini, the miserly violinist, gave three concerts at Nice which produced what was then an incredible sum of money – the equivalent of £540 – although he was a very sick man. His laryngitis was so acute that he could only converse by forcing his nostrils together and emitting a kind of squeak through his mouth. To play his violin, he had to support his left arm on a tallboy. His meanness was notorious. A month before his death, he had refused to give a concert for the poor of the district, and as he died without the Last Sacrament being administered, the local clergy refused to have him buried in holy ground. His body was embalmed, grotesquely surmounted by a cotton night-cap with a very large blue ribbon and an enormous white cravat drooping from his skinny neck. The local bishop ultimately insisted on the corpse being expelled by the Government.

Marie Bashkirtseff, the Russian writer, was another celebrity who became a regular visitor at Nice for the sake of her health. As a young girl of fifteen, she would drive along the Promenade des Anglais, blue-eyed, blonde-haired, in a pony carriage. She had already started her famous journal but could not make up her mind whether to be a musician, a painter, a scientist or a writer. When the Duke of Hamilton appeared on the Riviera scene, complete with yacht and beautiful Italian mistress, the impact was immediate. Marie, though, was a consumptive and did not meet him until years later in Paris. Instead, she decided to make advances to Guy de Maupassant, then wintering at Cannes. She signed her first letter to him as 'Miss Hastings', giving a poste restante address, concealing her identity as long as possible to titillate his curiosity. It was a strange romance. Guy de Maupassant pretended to become surfeited with her amorous epistles. Nevertheless, he answered all of them. Eventually, Marie wrote, 'I can imagine exactly what you look like. You have a big stomach and a tight waistcoat with the bottom button undone.' She enclosed a caricature of him lying under a palm tree. Maupassant was furious. 'I have no wish to know you,' he wrote. 'I am convinced you are ugly.' However, he left Cannes and moved to Nice in order to identify his correspondent. This he did and, unannounced, entered the garden of her villa, 'No. 105' Promenade des Anglais, and engaged her in a long conversation. Marie was very ill at the time, but both she and Maupassant claimed afterwards to be most impressed by one another. The Rest is Silence.

Maupassant had a yacht, *Le Bel Ami*, in which he sought escape from the tourists and the hotels. In it he wrote at least two of his masterpieces – *Mont Oriel* and *Pierre et Jean*. He also explored the French coastline and was perhaps the first celebrity to discover St. Tropez, ultimately made fashionable by the Duke of Windsor, sixty years later, when Prince of Wales. Maeterlinck, who had first taken a villa at Grasse, came to stay at Nice. His enormous appetite, his passion for boxing and insectology, contrasted strangely with his delicate writing. Rodin personally sculpted the right-hand caryatid adorning the Villa Neptune on the Promenade des Anglais.

Victor Hugo came and wrote. Verdi was present when the first performance in France of *Aïda* was given at Nice. His Requiem was sung shortly afterwards at the Church of St.

Françoise de Paule. Rosa Bonheur first occupied the Villa Africaine, then the Villa Bornala. Square-headed, grey hair cut short, with her extraordinarily penetrating eyes, pleasant smile and clipped voice, she lived like a hermit with her faithful friend and fellow painter, Mlle. Nica. In the studio, a dog, a cat and a rabbit played around in complete amity. In pens, along the walls, were sheep and goats. Rosa Bonheur, dressed as a man, used to stride along the Promenade des Anglais in velvet pantaloons and an animal trainer's blue blouse, sporting the ribbon of the Legion of Honour.

In one typical fortnight of January 1861 the private parties began on the 5th with a musical soirée given by the Countess Orsini. On 6th January was a ball given by the Baroness Mercier. On 8th January there was a musical soirée attended by the King of Denmark and the Grand Duchess Marie at the villa of Baroness Vigier-Cruvelli. On 10th January, Prince Poniatowski gave a ball; on the following evening there was a masked dance given by Simon Malutine; on 13th January there was a reception at the home of Baroness Verschver. On 14th January a grand ball was held at the Préfecture. On 15th January the Marquise D'Espeuille gave a musical soirée at which Mlle. de Laigle sang. Next morning they said of her, 'What a pity she is a lady; her voice is worth five thousand pounds to any impresario.'

The villas where these parties were given were superbly decorated, magnificent in their proportions. Valrose, the château specially built for a Baltic baron, had an immense park with a hundred gardeners and a splendid theatre capable of seating an orchestra of sixty-six musicians. The Villa Arson, overlooking Nice, also had a huge park with shady avenues and a cypress grove looking like a gross of thin, green pencils pointing to the sky. Talleyrand, when inspecting it, said, 'If I had known how beautiful it was, I would never have allowed

Nice to be ceded to Sardinia.' Old Count Arson de St. Joseph, the proprietor, looked like a practitioner of black magic in his long red and black velvet robes, his hair dyed to match. His wife was quite a character, too. Once she sent to the local church a bouquet of flowers so enormous that it took eight men to carry it. The parties they gave were out of this world.

The nearby Villa Cessoles was a royal palace with an imposing orange grove. *Tableaux vivants* being fashionable at the time, the beautiful Countess of Cessoles and her two attractive daughters frequently took part in them. In the St. Philippe quarter of Nice, the wealthy Count Aprascine gave stupendous concerts: Seligman, Rubinstein, Blumenthal and Vieuxtemps made music for the guests. Costume balls were a favourite entertainment of Madame Audiffret, at her villa of the same name. Her Regency ball of 1862 was remembered for years. Next to her villa was the Château de Fabron, the home of the Prince of Saxe-Coburg-Gotha, an elderly relation of the late Queen Mary of England. He had five chefs whose sole job was to invent new dishes for their master or revive classic ones like *pâté* of swan.

At the other end of Nice were two spectacular estates, the first belonging to Baron Haussmann and the second to the otherwise undistinguished Colonel Smith. Colonel Smith's villa was quickly nicknamed the 'Englishman's folly'. As a former officer of the East India Company, he constructed a junior Taj Mahal, completely out of keeping with the Riviera scenery, but with a splendid view. Colonel Smith, according to local gossips, spent all his time drinking an incredible amount of Scotch whisky and soda, and finally sold the property to a Polish count who also stayed permanently indoors.

The architecture of Baron Haussmann's villa was quite simple with a still more perfect view which cost him the equivalent of £50,000 to guarantee, by purchasing the acres of arid rocks between him and the sea.

The wealth and the arrogance of these visiting celebrities was almost unimaginable. Study the case of the widow of the Grand Duke Constantine, Lord High Admiral of the Imperial Russian Navy, and herself a German princess. Deciding one day to visit Genoa, she instructed her major domo to organise transport. After despatching couriers hither and thither, he was able to inform her with satisfaction a few days later that a French steamer would soon be arriving from Marseilles, with a stop at Nice on the direct route to Genoa. It must be remembered that only the Upper Corniche existed in those days and Her *Altesse* was planning to take her grand piano, not to mention her other household goods, on the journey.

Said the Grand Duchess, 'You must be mad; I travel with the plebs? I, the widow of the Lord High Admiral of the Imperial Russian Navy, mingle with the common populace? I shall write to Napoleon III and demand a man-of-war! It is the least he can do for the widow of the Lord High Admiral of the Imperial Russian Navy.' Sure enough, she sent off a letter by special courier to Paris and Napoleon III dutifully ordered a frigate to go from Marseilles to Nice to transport her to Genoa. The frigate waited for some days at Nice while the contents of the villa were put on board. Finally it went off to Genoa. On arrival, the captain, saluting heavily, informed the distinguished passenger that a pinnace had been signalled to take her and her belongings ashore. 'A pinnace,' exploded the Grand Duchess, 'do you suppose I am going to risk myself and my grand piano upon some Genoese skiff? Certainly not, a pier must be built out to us here. I shall not leave this tub until it is completed.' Vainly the captain argued; the Grand Duchess was adamant. A fortnight elapsed before the pier was constructed, and clad in white from top to toe, the Grand

Duchess swept off the ship to be met by the Governor of Genoa. . . .

One must admit that the Grand Duchess's position had been strengthened by the meeting at Nice a few weeks previously of Napoleon III and Tsar Alexander II, who had come post haste to the bedside of his son, the Tsarevitch Nicholas. Nicholas, a consumptive youth, was being nursed in the Villa Bermond, a splendid property with fields of parma violets, groves of cypresses, fountains and (it is said) 200,000 orange trees; but he succumbed to his malady. His mother, the Empress, was with him when he died and accompanied his body on the Russian frigate *Alexander Nevsky* back to Kronstadt. The Villa Bermond was then demolished and the present Russian church erected on the spot in memory of the Tsarevitch.

The Russian grand dukes who stayed at Nice before Cannes was made fashionable by the Grand Duke Michael, lived in large villas. Russian princes and cavalry officers of high rank took furnished apartments. Immensely rich Russian merchants of no social standing also came to Nice in the hopes of being able to rub shoulders with their superiors in the casino and thus make them clients later on in St. Petersburg, or perhaps to introduce their pretty daughters to royalty at a masked ball. Such a man was Simon Malutine, who had made a colossal fortune in insurance. He gave unbelievable parties and used to throw money out of the window at hangers-on gathered in the street below.

Years later, a still more remarkable example of the importance of grand dukes and grand duchesses occurred. The old Grand Duke Michael, grandfather of Lady Milford Haven and great-grandfather, therefore, of the Marquess of Milford Haven, was told by his doctors that he must go to Cannes for his health. At this time he was very frail and ill, but looked

57   c*

rather like Father Christmas, with his long white beard. Unfortunately, he was unable to stand the shaking of the quick trains of those days. His journey was from St. Petersburg to the south of France, involving the Russian, German, Belgian and French railway systems. His doctors said that his private train of six coaches should not travel at more than twenty-four miles an hour. For a couple of days, therefore, the whole of the Continental schedules for railways were put out of joint, to suit the Grand Duke. The nearest equivalent to this was when the Prince of Wales, who was not allowed to fly back to George V's sick-bed, travelled from Italy to Calais in a special train which took precedence over all others. In this case, the precedence was speed, not slowness.

Those indeed were the great days of the Promenade des Anglais.

Englishwomen, accompanied by their husbands wearing tall hats with green bandannas, dashing Russian aristocrats, elegant Parisians, walked up and down in the gay sunlight. The carriages followed one another at short intervals, as on the Champs Elysées. Squadrons of English girls with long hair flowing behind them would trot or canter past; three or four British peers riding splendid horses, followed by their lackeys at a discreet distance, would stop and talk to their friends, rather like Rotten Row in Edwardian times. A Russian droshky, driven by a bearded major domo in the costume of a moujik, might contain two very pretty girls with ivory complexions and pretty blue eyes, accompanied on either side by a haughty officer of the Imperial Russian Guards, moustached like the Emperor Alexander, big-chested and aloof. Next might come the inevitable Parisienne *cocotte*, with her pony carriage and her groom, dressed in impeccable taste. Nonchalantly she would display her Prussian blue dress of Havana silk.

By six o'clock in the evening, all the fine people had retired to dress for dinner, and the Promenade des Anglais was occupied by the poorer classes on their way to the cafés after their day's work. Later in the evening the carriages would reappear at a slow jog-trot, full of befurred beauties and their escorts on the way to the casino.

Casinos, in Victorian times, bore no relation to those of today. The French Government had suppressed all games of chance for the previous thirty years. Gambling had also been forbidden in the Kingdom of Sardinia. The only places where it was allowed were in some of the minor German principalities like Baden and Homburg and, as from 1857, nearby Monaco.

CHAPTER 4

THE START OF MONTE CARLO

WHAT HAD HAPPENED WAS THIS. Charles III, Regent of Monaco, was faced with bankruptcy when his subjects in Menton and Roquebrune revolted against paying their stiff taxes on oil and fruit – his sole revenue. Monaco's only remaining asset was its climate.

Prince Charles and his mother, Princess Caroline, decided therefore to take advantage of the new fashion for sea-bathing and spas. The attractive climate and the ease of communications had already established Cannes, Hyères and Nice as watering places. Why not Monaco?

It was planned to form a company to build a sanatorium, a number of villas and a pump-room. The sum required was two million francs. Being unable to raise the capital, Princess Caroline sent Eynaud, her private secretary, to Baden-Baden, where the local Grand Duke had granted a concession for a casino to a Frenchman named Benazet. Eynaud's instructions were to find out the terms on which the concession was granted and how much money the Grand Duke made out of it. He quickly learned that the annual revenue accruing to the Grand Duke was nearly four hundred thousand francs, the equivalent of £16,000 a year. Not only that; he discovered that the Grand Duke benefited indirectly to an even greater extent from the thousands of visitors who came to the duchy and spent their money there. Eynaud advised his mistress that something on similar lines should be organised in Monaco, making it clear, however, that the first principle of running a casino successfully was to conceal its main object by disguising it as a spa. Nor was it long before various would-be concessionaires appeared on the scene, making extravagant offers of the palatial buildings they would erect and the money they would pay to the reigning family if they were given a monopoly for gambling.

The first concession of thirty years was granted to a couple of Frenchmen, Napoleon Langlois and Albert Aubert, for building and managing an establishment to be known as the Bains de Monaco, on the same lines as those in Homburg, Baden-Baden and elsewhere.

What really mattered was the clause which granted Langlois and Aubert the right to provide amenities of every kind, 'notably balls, concerts, fêtes, games such as whist, écarté, piquet, faro, boston and reversi, as well as roulette with either one or two zeros and *trente-et-quarante*,' all subject to the supervision of inspectors appointed by the prince. The official capital was to be £120,000 divided into six thousand shares. In point of fact, Aubert was penniless and Langlois had only succeeded in scraping together £8,000.

Their first step was to buy, at the equivalent of twopence a square metre, a large part of the rocky plateau, now Monte Carlo, on which they promised to build a fine casino, at some unspecified date. This done, they got to work on the only things which mattered to them, the start of gambling. All their fine promises of building hotels, villas and a pump-room were completely forgotten. In any event, they had not the money for such an enterprise.

In view of Princess Caroline's objection to having a gaming hell on the rock itself, they acquired the Villa Bellevue, the only private building in the Condamine. The actual surroundings were idyllic. The villa overlooked the harbour and behind it lay the gardens of the Rimmel Perfumery (in which was extracted the essence of oranges, eucalyptus, roses, jasmine and tuberoses) stretching uninterruptedly from the base of the rock to the Gorge des Gaumates. Behind the gardens there were groves of lemon trees and orange trees in what is now the Rue Florentine – headquarters of the Deuxième Bureau. Elsewhere eucalyptus trees and olives grew in picturesque profusion. The villa itself was sparsely furnished. Money was short. The maximum stake was £120, and the whole effect was cheapjack when, on 14th December, 1856, with garbage cans still cluttering the entrance to the villa, the roulette wheel was spun for the first time.

Most people imagined – as they still imagine – that a casino runs itself and invariably makes huge profits. But this is by no means automatic and the original concessionaires at Monaco were quickly made bankrupt. The reason in their case and that of their immediate successors was simple. The very inaccessibility which had enabled Monaco to remain an independent principality and permit gambling when it was forbidden in France, proved their undoing. The most luxurious casino in the world, serving free banquets and fine wines, has no hope of popularity if it is really difficult to reach. The only approaches to the somewhat sordid Villa Bellevue were by an elderly diligence with a maximum capacity of eleven passengers along the Upper Corniche (a picturesque but devious and dangerous route), or by sailing boat from Nice. The result is immortalised by an ancient print showing three croupiers in beards and morning coats, one of them looking gloomily through a telescope at a distant skiff battling through the mistral towards the harbour, in the hope that it contained at least a handful of gamblers. Worse still, there was not a decent hotel in the whole place and it needed a real addict to risk the double journey in the same day for a few hours' play in the drab gaming rooms which had no real supervision and where crooks congregated freely, some playing with counterfeit coins and others tampering with the roulette wheel. The Hotel de Russie, admittedly, had one or two uncomfortable attics, but the bulk of the visitors had to return home in the early evening before complete darkness set in and made their four-hour journey over the roots and boulders of the neglected roadway still more dangerous. No wonder that Langlois and Aubert were scared when, with only a handful of gamblers to patronize them, the casino lost as much as £2,800 in one day. They promptly reduced the reserves at the *trente-et-quarante* table to £400 and those at the roulette table to half that amount.

This had the immediate effect of discouraging most of the gamblers who liked to feel that they could win a relatively unlimited sum if they were in luck. As it was, between 15th March and 20th March, 1857, only one visitor entered the casino – and won two francs. On the 21st, a couple appeared on the scene and lost two hundred and eight francs. In a subsequent week, only two more gamblers chanced their luck and, though the casino was officially open for two sessions daily, play occurred only five times in eight days. In desperation, the concessionaires asked for and received permission to open a 'summer casino' in what are now the barracks in the square facing the palace. They thought, no doubt, that proximity to the residence of the Hereditary Prince would give a snob value to their undertaking, as indeed their gaudy brochure proved:

'A splendid mansion opposite the palace, belonging to His Serene Highness the Prince of Monaco, has been placed at the disposal of the company,' it began, following with a reference to the twenty-five hundred lemon trees, two thousand orange trees and the olive grove which surrounded the 'large and beautiful Villa Bellevue.'

All this was to no avail. The gamblers stayed away and the Langlois-Aubert partnership was glad to sell out on 17th November, 1857, to a certain Frossard de Lilbonne, the nominee of the Marquis d'Arnesano, who disposed of the white elephant on 31st December of the same year to a M. Daval.

Several of the croupiers left when it became apparent that Daval was just another semi-penniless adventurer. But at least Daval persuaded Prince Charles to arrive with the dessert at the gala dinner which inaugurated the new management. He was also responsible for laying the original foundations of a new casino on the site of the one existing today, in the presence of Prince Albert, the ten-year-old heir apparent. True, he failed to pay the local labourers who came out on strike, advanced angrily on the palace and were only dispersed when cannon were brought to bear on them. (Fifty were arrested and given prison sentences of up to two years, but were very quickly released because they cost too much to feed.)

The company of which such great things had been hoped was in the red to the tune of over £40,000, and Daval had to hurry to Paris in an attempt to raise more funds. All he succeeded in doing was to sell his concession at a cut rate to MM. Lefebvre, Jagot and Girois, the nominees of the wealthy Duc de Valmy. Daval himself died bankrupt some years later in a Marseilles hospital.

There was now a certain amount of working capital, but nothing like enough to carry out the original plans of a palatial casino surrounded by a garden city; and scarcely had the deal been completed when war broke out between the Austrians on the one side and the French and Sardinians on the other. Both casinos were closed during the two months of hostilities. However, Lefebvre used the time profitably by transferring the gaming tables to the Villa Gabarini at the eastern end of the

A contemporary drawing shows croupiers of the old Monégasque gaming tables watching for the arrival of players.

Countess Torby

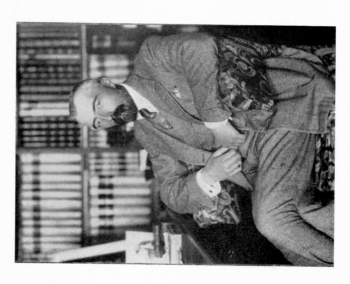

Grand Duke Michael

Rue Lorraine, known locally as the General's House because it had been the headquarters of the Sardinian garrison until they marched out against Austria, never to return. The new concessionaires organised a number of fêtes and concerts, the evening gaieties being embellished by the blaze of flaming torches on pedestals along the recently created boulevard, to cheer the gamblers on their way to Nice.

By now, an ancient tub called the *Palmaria* ran a semi-regular, completely unpunctual service from Nice to Monaco and back, taking two hours to go the fifteen miles. Moreover, the captain frequently delayed his departure if he thought there was any likelihood of more passengers being on their way to the harbour. Near the casino was the Café de Soleil which soon acquired a pathetic, if not sinister, reputation. The minimum stake in the casino was two francs. Broken gamblers who had only a few sous left, played in the café against each other to gain a complete two-franc piece and return to the tables. . . . Unfortunately for his partners, M. Lefebvre was a bad-tempered man who wanted everything run on factory lines, clearly impossible in so delicate an organisation as a casino where temperament is likely to manifest itself. Nor could he forget that his various predecessors had lost a great deal of money from their concession.

In October 1859 the new casino in the Rue Lorraine opened and during the next three months the gaming tables showed a regular profit of £50 a day. There were, of course, exceptions. One gambler was so *en veine* that the casino lost £2,000 in a single week. Lefebvre, like many ill-tempered men who had tried to be masterful, was a coward at heart and he now panicked badly, even to the extent of refusing to allow the *trente-et-quarante* table to continue when the reserve of £400 had been exhausted. This was doubly foolish because it prevented the bank from recouping its losses (after all, no run of luck is continuous) and produced the same kind of impression which had ruined Langlois and Aubert. Nevertheless, in March 1860, twenty-one weeks after the re-opening of the casino, the bank was still maintaining its profit of £50 a day.

Studying Monaco with the utmost vigilance from his temporary abode in Nice, was François Blanc. A great student of human nature, he knew there was a fortune to be made out of gambling on the Riviera during the winter months when the German casinos, including the one he operated in Homburg, were closed from October to April. He had already made a fortune out of roulette and *trente-et-quarante* at Homburg, and, better still, possessed a ready-made clientele – immensely rich clients – French princes and princesses, Russian grand dukes and German landgraves who would surely follow him to the Riviera if he guaranteed good hotels, good food, a smart casino and trouble-free gambling. Monaco's situation could not be bettered. True, it consisted of nothing but a little hill town with three churches, half a dozen parallel streets and a handful of alleyways, but it was swathed in orange groves, lemon groves, olive groves and fields of carnations and narcissi. As had been seen, it lacked one vital factor – accessibility. Another problem was whether the French Government would acknowledge the sovereignty of Prince Charles III of Monaco. After the Treaty of Turin in 1860, when the Sardinians relinquished all the territory from Nice to Menton, the situation changed rapidly. Prince Charles' negotiations with the French Government were conducted with unexpected success. What is more, the French Government promised a good carriageway to Monaco from Nice: what is now the Lower Corniche.

Monaco was now finally freed. It had been a Genoese protectorate, a Spanish protectorate, a French protectorate, and a Sardinian protectorate. There was no question of France placing an embargo on roulette or *trente-et-quarante*. Best of

all, railways were coming into vogue. There was already a
track from Paris to Lyons and plans to extend it to Cagnes,
maybe to Monaco.

Possibly it was Princess Caroline's agent, M. Eynaud, who
was responsible for the vital clause affecting the road connections between Nice and Monaco. Whoever it was, he laid
the foundations of the wealth later acquired by the Grimaldis.
The sea-going connections between Nice and Monaco were
also capable of rapid improvement. But instead of capitalising
the new situation and advertising in all available French newspapers that Monaco provided the only real casino in southern
Europe (which was perfectly true), Lefebvre drew in his horns
and made the inexcusable blunder of introducing a second
zero at roulette. Nothing could have been more – in modern
parlance – anti-box-office. He failed also to press the French
Government to carry out their promise of making a real
carriage-way along the Lower Corniche. In consequence,
Joseph, the solitary coachman who did the four-hour run from
Nice to Monaco along the upper road, still continued to run
his service most unpunctually. Nor did Lefebvre show any
signs of fulfilling his obligations under the concession to build
a garden city around the still undeveloped casino. So little did
the local population believe in his grandiose promises to turn
Les Spélugues into the paradise which is now Monte Carlo,
that offers of free land, on the condition that the recipient
would build a villa or a shop on it, produced no takers
at all.

Up to the moment, François Blanc had held only a watching brief. When Prince Charles' sovereignty was duly acknow-
ledged, he decided that the time was ripe, but still waited for
the Duc de Valmy, who held the gambling concession at
Monaco, to approach him. He felt sure that his agents in the
various German casinos would let him know the moment that

any other proposals, however provisional, were made. He must have smiled secretly to himself when, after tentative talk with an agent named Bigy, the approach to him was finally made in Paris by the Duc de Valmy and Eynaud, Queen Caroline's personal agent.

He pretended to be suffering from a boil on a certain part of his anatomy, which compelled him to stand up throughout the interview. He also pretended to be completely uninterested in the project, pointing out that his hands were wholly full with Homburg and that, in any event, there was little or no goodwill in the Monaco gambling concession, in view of the series of failures which had attended the efforts of the various concessionaires. All this was done to gain extra time; and when Prince Charles III invited him personally to Monaco, he asked for a few more days in which to think the matter over. In the meantime, he learnt that the balance sheet of the casino for the previous year had shown a profit of £3,000. This was little enough, but Blanc guessed that, properly handled, Monaco could be made a real gold mine by somebody who understood the business.

Having weighed it all up, he finally posted his proposals to Prince Charles from Paris. These included the financing of a company with a capital of £600,000 to acquire the assets of the existing company, to build a casino like the one at Homburg as well as hotels and villas like those at Nice, and, finally, to provide a proper working capital. He added that he would not consider the matter any further unless Prince Charles III could persuade the Duc de Valmy and Lefebvre to accept a reasonable price. Having dispatched the letter, he had a further conversation in Paris with Valmy and Lefebvre, who demanded £90,000 for the concession. 'Gentlemen, this is absurd,' said Blanc. 'If you continue to adopt this unreasonable attitude, I shall have nothing more to do with you. Go and find some other pigeon to pluck. I shall write to the prince tonight breaking off negotiations. Good day, gentlemen.'

He was as good as his word and wrote a second long letter to the prince that night. In it he pointed out that the price Valmy and Lefebvre were demanding was based not on the existing financial situation but on what might happen if he, Blanc, expended his capital and experience on the project. He further pointed out that Nice, Cannes and Hyères were attracting far more visitors for the winter season. He ended, 'I therefore request Your Serene Highness to intervene and reduce the demands of the present management to a sensible figure.' Prince Charles III was in a serious dilemma and Eynaud was given urgent instructions to carry out François Blanc's request. Lefebvre's intuition divined correctly that Blanc had, in fact, every intention of buying the concession, but was trying to acquire it at a knock-out price. He therefore persuaded the Duc de Valmy, who at the time was only too anxious to see some return for his original outlay, to stand his ground and refuse to lower the price. Blanc merely shrugged his shoulders and said the deal was off.

He was, at that time, fifty-seven years old, small, spectacled, with a ragged moustache, darting eyes, nervous gesticulations and, as described at the time, with his brain always in a 'ferment of ideas'. He talked with a strong provincial French accent, having been born near Avignon, the son of a clerk in the Inland Revenue.

Charles III was naturally anxious to see the deal go through and persuaded Jagot, as the chief debenture holder, to raise no difficulties. This offer was refused by the syndicate.

Further conversations took place in Paris with the Duc de Valmy, Lefebvre and Blanc, Eynaud holding a watching brief for Charles III. Blanc realised that he must pay his long-awaited visit to Monaco in person to conclude the deal.

Arriving by the morning steamer from Nice, he called immediately on the offices of the casino, where Jagot awaited him.

'You wish to sell your concession,' Blanc said abruptly, 'and I am disposed to buy it. My price is one million, seven hundred thousand francs (£68,000) in three bonds on the Bank of France. Think it over. I will return at three-thirty p.m., for I have to go back on the steamer leaving at four p.m., and I intend to have things settled one way or the other before I sail. *Au revoir.*'

There was no time to lose. Jagot hurried off to see M. de Payan, the secretary-general to the Government. He, in turn, had an audience with blind, bearded, drooping-moustached Prince Charles III, who gladly and immediately approved of the deal. Blanc returned and paid down the cash in the form of three bonds. Except for the four million francs compensation paid to Prince Charles III for the loss of Roquebrune and Menton, such a sum of money had never been seen in Monaco before. The bluff had worked.

Within twenty-four hours Blanc (who had not had the slightest intention of returning to Nice without acquiring the concession) drew up the articles of the new company. He founded the *Société des Bains de Mer et Cercle des Etrangers.* The capital of the company was £600,000 divided into thirty thousand shares of £20 each. Blanc received eighteen thousand shares. Of the remainder, four thousand were immediately taken up by Blanc's secretary and a nominee of his wife. After them, one of the earliest shareholders was Pope Leo XIII, at that time a cardinal. Further, Blanc was appointed general managing director for a period of ten years (the gambling concession was for fifty years). Against this, it was agreed that the sum due annually to Prince Charles III was to be greatly increased from the previous guarantee, never honoured, of £1,000 a year. It was also stipulated that his 'cut' was to rise proportionately with the profits of the casino. Blanc further promised to improve the road between Nice and Menton as the French Government had failed to carry out their obligations in this respect. His mere presence in the neighbourhood sent up the price of the land on Les Spélugues from twopence a square yard to ten shillings a foot. The future of Monaco was set fair.

Blanc's first action on taking control was to increase the reserve at the *trente-et-quarante* tables to £400 and to £200 at the roulette tables. His next step was to charter a Nice steamer capable of carrying three hundred people. In deference to the prince, he called it the *Charles III*. His third move was to acquire a fleet of hackney carriages drawn by first-class horses to bring the clients from Nice. He knew from past experience that transport was all-important to the success of any casino and did everything he could to press the *Paris–Lyons–Méditerranée* railway company to extend their track from Cagnes to Monaco.

The first of the English milords now appeared on the scene, notably, the Duke of Hamilton and Lord Strafford. Foreign visitors to Nice and Menton also made it part of their holiday to visit Monaco. The gaming rooms were full of distinguished people. Lord Brougham, one of the visitors during this epoch, wrote:

'In a single week I have discussed literature with the most renowned authors, gallantry with the Queens of the salons and theatres of Europe, politics with statesmen, art with the leading artists, and finance with M. Blanc.' Blanc, indeed, was regarded at the time as one of the great financiers and economists of the age. Against this, scurrilous French authors and pamphleteers wrote violent diatribes against Monaco. Thus: 'Near rustic cottages Satan has installed with all his vulgar seductions one of his most funereal industries. . . . In this corner

of Paradise amid giant olives, orange groves and fig trees,
blessed with air so pure that it is only agitated by the voice of
the winds and the streams or by the cry of birds – here the
genius of ill has established a gaming house. Youths who
throw away family fortunes, tradesmen with numbers of
children, daily meet with ruin and dishonour. Innocent bathers
are enticed into the labyrinth of evil, this cathedral of vice,
the casino of Monaco. The palace itself which dates back to
1538 is full of the sinister, mysterious dramas in which the
Guelphs and Ghibellines played their evil part.'

Nor did traducers of the casino confine their activities to the
public prints. Two blackmailers decided it would be a good
investment to take a lease of the hoardings at Nice railway
station and cover them with crude allegorical pictures of
widows being removed weeping after the suicide of their
bankrupt husbands in the casino, unprotected children being
removed to brutal orphanages because of the violent death of
their parents and, indeed, with any other fanciful defamation
which occurred to them or to the hack artists they employed.
In their particular case Blanc decided to pay no attention, after
a private inquiry into their financial background. Sure enough,
the two blackmailers were unable to pay the rent of the hoardings for more than a fortnight, and this particular nuisance
came to an end.

Success always breeds jealousy and malice. The community
of Nice had increased the virulence of its campaign against the
casino and seven hundred inhabitants sent a petition to Paris
demanding the suppression of gambling. It was the first of
several to be accorded the same answer – that Monaco was a
friendly, independent sovereign state and that the French
Government could not interfere with its internal workings,
however it might feel on the subject.

English writers also took up their pens against roulette.

True, Thackeray confined his attacks to the casino at Homburg in a now forgotten book, *The Kickleburys on the Rhine*,
as also did George Augustus Sala who spent some weeks per-
fecting an infallible system – operated cheaply enough at home
with beans taking the place of chips. The system broke down
at Homburg. John Addington Symonds, one of the earliest
English visitors at Monaco, arriving before the casino had
been completed on Les Spélugues, wrote:

'There is a large house of sin blazing with gas lamps by
night, flaming and shining by the shore, like pandemonium
or the habitation of some romantic witch. The air swoons
with the scent of lemon groves: tall palm trees wave their
branches in the garden, music of the softest most inebriating
passion swells from the palace, rich meats and wines are served
in a gorgeously furnished hall. . . . But the witch herself holds
her high court and never-ending festival of sin in the hall of
the green tables. . . . Splendid women with bold eyes and
golden hair and marble columns of Imperial throats are there
to laugh, to sing songs, to tempt. . . . Inside the gambling house
play goes forward like a business. Roulette and *rouge-et-noir*
tables are crowded. Little can be heard but the monotonous
voice of the croupiers, the rattle of gold under their wooden
shovels and the click of the ball spinning round for roulette. . . .
The croupiers are either fat, sensual cormorants or sallow, lean-
cheeked vultures, or suspicious foxes. Compare them with
Coutts' men. Note the difference. It is very discernible; these
men of the gaming bank show every trace of dissolute youth
in a vile calling of low sensuality and hardened avarice upon
their faces.'

At long last the railway reached Monaco – in October 1868.
The effect was immediate. Crowds of people poured out of
the trains and into the gaming rooms. Pickpockets abounded
and Countess Kissalev lost a pocket-book containing a trifle

over £1,000. The profits of the casino were tremendous and Prince Charles was able in the following year to abolish all direct taxation in the principality, while Blanc put up large sums of prize money for the horse races at Nice, in order to keep the inhabitants quiet. He also gave considerably to charity and even provided funds to pay for the gigantic masks for the annual Battle of Flowers. Very unkindly, the revellers used the money for making hideous effigies of Blanc and Prince Charles.

Blanc was now seriously threatened by the avalanche of his own success. The vast crowds of visitors were, in the aggregate, staking enormous sums. Six players who worked in a syndicate succeeded in winning £40,000. The success led to a whole series of similar syndicates. Most people will have forgotten the financial trusts formed in a number of continental countries, as well as in England, to employ professionals to win money at the tables. Their capital was anything from £1,200 to £20,000. Among these financial trusts were French, Armenian, Russian, Italian, Turkish and English organisations. The English society employed ex-bank clerks, thinking that, being good at figures, they would be most successful when staking on even money chances. The gamblers were paid a flat fee of £1 to twenty-five shillings per day, and every night there was a solemn post-mortem on the day's play.

The principle in itself would have been sound if it had not been for the imposition of maximum stakes at both roulette and *trente-et-quarante*. It is always the gamblers with small funds who, in the long run, provide the bulk of the profits for the casino. They do not have enough capital to fight a bad losing run at the start. But even these syndicates soon ran out of cash. As Dostoievsky said, 'the roulette wheel has no memory and no conscience.' And the croupiers continued to pull in the gold coins with the ruthless efficiency of a suction pipe.

A few weeks later the Franco-Prussian War broke out. France capitulated swiftly and Prussia imposed a seemingly vast indemnity on her victim. Blanc thereupon instructed his bank to place £80,000 of his own personal fortune at the disposal of the French Government. Nor was this a great strain on his resources. The casino at Homburg had made immense profits. Once again it was the old story of what is lost on the roundabouts is won on the swings, and there were still two more lucrative years ahead of Homburg before the ban on gambling came into effect.

The post-war depression in France was of short duration and more than one hundred and forty thousand people visited Monte Carlo in 1871. Blanc imported André, the famous landscape gardener, to lay out 'The Cheese' and the Boulingrins, enlarged the casino and started the infamous *Tir aux Pigeons*, giving a first prize of £400, by far the largest ever granted for this form of sport. The pigeon shooting took place on one of the terraces immediately below the casino. The first winner was an American who caused the greatest excitement in Monaco by spending £20 on a cable to his friends in New York to announce his victory. Very quickly, crack shots from all over the world entered the annual event, which continued with only the interruption of the First World War until the thirties, and was later revived.

By now there were eighty furnished apartments, four doctors, nineteen hotels, twenty-four villas, eighteen cab-drivers and one midwife. Within ten years the furnished apartments had increased to four hundred and thirty-three, the doctors to thirty-one, the hotels to thirty-five, the villas to one hundred and sixteen, the cabs to ninety-one, and the midwives to five.

CHAPTER 5

BARON RENFREW AND

QUEEN VICTORIA

In 1872 Dr. Alexander Brown, a well-known physician who had practised in India, wrote a best-seller, *Wintering at Menton on the Riviera*. The worthy doctor had the sense to travel as far as Nice by sea, thus avoiding the laborious overland journey, and then proceeded by carriage along the Upper Corniche. It is noticeable from his account that the various villages such as Eze and La Turbie were still given their Italian names of Eza and La Turbia, twelve years after the French annexation.

Dr. Brown, like Smollett, provided weather statistics – in his case over a period of ten previous years – showing per annum an average of 214 days of unclouded sunshine, forty-five when cloudiness was occasional, twenty-four rainy days and eighty-two of alternating bright sunshine and 'genial' showers. Medical practice in those days seems to have been strongly in favour of stuffy rooms for chest complaints. 'Sleeping with windows open, a process of ventilation amounting to exposure and fraught with the greatest danger is,' he wrote, 'simply absurd and requires much more moderation in prescription than is generally observed in the system now in vogue at Menton.' Elsewhere he comments: '. . . for fellow-islanders, to whom at any season sunshine is a novelty, are liable to forget it is still winter, and severe enough within a day's journey. Faithful to prescribed rule or capricious fashion, they live in a manner as utterly opposed to physical and sanitary needs as is possible to conceive; both sexes, at all ages, affecting an eccentricity of style and costume as ridiculous as inconvenient. On a sharp, clear December morning it is amusing to meet our fellow-countryman among the hills astride a donkey, beneath a huge white umbrella and harnessed with botanic cases. Besides the goggles and odd clothes, he wears a formidable hat and puggaree, for which he cannot even plead the sufficient French excuse of having been in India. Near him is the little Mentonaise damsel carrying his block, stock, stick and other impedimenta. To the uninitiated his delusion is that of doing the Pyramids and feeling very hot. This love of sunshade and fear of sunshine, so amazing, does not prevent him committing a thousand extremes in other respects. In the case of the ladies, boots of the period, as elegantly slight as those of the gentlemen are fashionably heavy, with dresses to match, slight and flimsy as for summer air without wind, which have no existence there; frequent out-of-door fêteing, picnic and gipsying, the best English weather would scarcely justify; and, added to all this, the *à la mode* church-going excess, with all its formality and display, though none to please but themselves, and serious risks are run. Still, it is respectable, and the only passport to the set. Children also suffer from the same cause, conventionalism being all the more irksome that they have no choice in the matter. With every facility for enjoyment the juvenile ought to expand. Sunny rambling by hill and dale, the donkeys, and the pebbly shore, with all its charms, are there; but style and cherishing of the bazaar toy haunts them at every turn. They are only in some degree more artificial than their elders, and suffer even more from what is unsuitable in dress. You meet them on excursions daily at the sunniest hours, half clad, with an atmosphere at something like freezing point, when the addition of a cloud upon the sky would drive them to the rug or near the fire. The prevailing mania becomes positively painful when good health or recovery from serious illness is the object.'

However wrong Dr. Brown may be considered by modern standards, he was at least the first to recommend patients to stay in the South of France until midsummer. He also deplored the lack of sanatoriums with permanent medical and nursing staffs away from the bustle of the ordinary hotel.

A brief description of what is now the Menton casino – one of the most charming on the Riviera – shows that it was, in those days, a kind of club-house, rejoicing in the title of Cercle Philharmonique, elegant and by no means so pretentious as the one at Nice. The interior consisted of a large ballroom for dances, concerts, receptions and other entertainments, sitting-room for women, a reading-room, a billiards-room and – quite an innovation – a smoking-room, but no gambling-rooms of course.

Robert Louis Stevenson, one of the first Englishmen to discover the joys of Monterey, California – in October 1879 – was another distinguished writer who went to the Riviera in search of his health. He first stayed at the Grand Hotel, Nice, and wrote the *Child's Garden*. Thence he moved to La Solitude, Hyères. It was here that he composed one of his most delightful letters. 'My dearest people,' he wrote to his parents, 'I have had a great piece of news. There has been offered for *Treasure Island* – how much do you suppose? I believe it would be an excellent jest to keep the answer until my next letter; for two cents I would do so. Shall I? No, well, a £100 all alive-o! A hundred jingling, tingling, golden, minted quid. Is it not wonderful? *Silverado* is done, too. I have today paid my rent for the half year.' In a subsequent letter to Edmund Gosse he talks of his roses, marigolds and olives. While at Hyères he also wrote *The Black Arrow*, but the climate was not helpful to him. He became dangerously ill again, with haemorrhage of the lungs, and hovered between life and death for several months (although he was only thirty-four), before returning to England by very slow stages. At least he was luckier than J. R. Green, the author of *A Short History of the English People*, who was buried at Nice, while still in his forties.

Edward VII as Prince of Wales paid his first visit to the South of France in 1872, where he stayed at the Hotel Gray d'Albion at Cannes. The owner, Mr. Gray, was proud of being an Englishman, but little else is known of him. Edward VII was, on this occasion, accompanied by his wife, later Queen Alexandra, but preceded by a certain M. Fehr, of Swiss origin. Intelligent, incisive, he was detailed to see that his Royal master was not overcharged. Edward VII's entourage consisted of a physician and two equerries. General Sir Stanley Clarke was the senior equerry. The physician was later on supplanted by Sir James Reid, Queen Victoria's doctor. He had, in addition, two valets, a butler and a first footman. The senior valet was an Austrian, the junior was an Englishman. It was the English valet's job to make the Prince's bed every day, always remembering not to change it on Fridays. Edward VII, who travelled incognito as Baron Renfrew, was superstitious.

The butler and first footman were respectively German and English. Hopfner, the butler, was a fine figure of a man. Willard, the footman, had a special job of keeping an eye on Caesar, the royal fox-terrier, who followed his master everywhere and slept at night on a sofa on the right of the royal bed. Caesar had to be washed, combed and brushed with the greatest care every morning. He appeared at all receptions and was admired and caressed by everyone in the royal circle. Round his neck was a collar labelled 'I am Caesar. I belong to the Prince of Wales.'

Edward VII went everywhere. He visited assiduously all the sovereigns visiting the South of France, such as Queen Isabella of Spain, Queen Natalie of Servia, the Archduke Charles of Austria, the King and Queen of Württemberg and the Duchess of Saxe-Coburg-Gotha. He paid a call on the Prince of Monaco and in later years never failed to call on the Empress Eugénie when she was in residence at Cap Martin. The Empress Eugénie frequently asked him to luncheon. He always accepted.

In the meantime, the Duke and Duchess of Edinburgh and the Archduke Victor of Austria-Hungary, after visiting the Isle of St. Margarite, were welcomed on their return by the Prince, who was staying at the Union Club in the grounds of the Grand Hotel, on his way to pay a visit to the Princess of Saxe-Coburg-Gotha. The Prince did not always stay at the same hotel. On his next visit he stayed at the Hotel Provence, where Caesar Ritz was enjoying his first management of an hotel. (It is now a block of flats.) Another year he patronised the Hotel Estorel. Yet another year he stayed at the Hotel de Pavillon at the far end of the Croisette. Later he brought his yacht *Britannia* and took part very successfully in a number of the regattas, but never slept on board. He preferred the Hotel Mont Fleuri at this stage. His arrivals and departures, however, were never allowed to appear in local newspapers, nor of course his flirtations with such beauties as Alice Keppel, whom he first met at the Villa Kasbeck.

Ritz's arrival in London at the Savoy Hotel was the direct result of his successful management of the Hotel Provence. Richard d'Oyley Carte, the impresario of the Gilbert and Sullivan operas, came to Cannes while still planning the famous hotel in the Strand. His original thought was to employ Romano. Lily Langtry heard of this. She said, 'It is all very well to get Romano, but he specialises in a male clientele. No doubt they will buy large numbers of cigars and drink innumerable bottles of champagne, but Romano is a man's man. Why don't you get hold of Ritz? He will bring the ladies.'

Richard d'Oyley Carte accepted her advice and advised Romano to buy the empty building in the Strand, opposite what is now the Savoy Hotel. This Romano did with great benefit to himself, hiring Luigi (later the famous club proprietor of the Embassy in Bond Street, London) as his restaurant manager of Romano's.

Much less did the public know that the Prince of Wales had any idea of baccarat, which he played at the Cercle de la Méditerranée at Nice and at the Cercle Nautique at Cannes. It was the Cercle Nautique, alas! pulled down to make way for the present Cannes Film Festival hall on the Croisette, which saw most of him. Charles Forrester, who has unquestionably shaken more cocktails (incidentally for more celebrities) than any man alive, recalls him well. Although whisky and soda was still very proletarian in those days (most gentlemen preferred brandy and soda), it was Edward VII's favourite tipple, and specifically John Dewar's Black Ball, though Victoria Vat succeeded it shortly in popularity.

The Cercle Nautique was approached by two winding staircases from the Croisette. The entrance fee was a hundred guineas. The annual subscription was twenty-five guineas. Multiply that by four to reach present-day monetary standards and it will be realised that it was an expensive club to join, considering that it was only open for about four months in the year. Not that anybody was eligible. On the contrary. A prospective member needed to be of excellent family, practically princely or royal.

Besides the seventeen bedrooms there was a big bar and smoking-room and a long gallery with a stage at one end for private theatricals, dances, bridge and *chemin de fer*. In those days there was no casino, and *chemin de fer* was still forbidden by law.

Charles Forrester recalls that powdered footmen in knee

breeches served caviare and smoked salmon from 11 a.m. until luncheon time. As barman he always had six bottles of vodka in an ice-tub ready for the grand dukes. They helped themselves to it in claret glasses. On one occasion Lord Portarlington called across the room to Forrester. 'Charlie,' he said, 'bring me my drink.' Forrester unthinkingly took it over to his Lordship. Next day he was informed that Captain Sheldon, the secretary, wished to see him. Captain Sheldon said, 'I have a serious complaint about you. It seems that you had the effrontery to serve Lord Portarlington without wearing white gloves.' Forrester apologised profusely, explaining that the footman had not been immediately available. Captain Sheldon said, 'You must always keep gloves in your pockets for emergencies like these.' Forrester recalls that on one occasion there were no fewer than seven grand dukes in the Cercle Nautique at one and the same time. They were the Grand Duke Michael ('Mich-Mich'), the Grand Duke Cyril, the Grand Dukes George, Andrew, Serge, Dimitri and Nicholas.

On another occasion he was in the bar when the Duke of Cambridge sent for him. 'Charlie,' he said, 'Her Majesty requires a glass of port.' Looking out of the window, Forrester espied Queen Victoria in her donkey cart, the English tiger, Jacko the donkey, two ladies-in-waiting and two men-servants in Highland dress. He brought the glass of port. Queen Victoria drank it. As usual she was clad in black. Strange as it may seem, the inhabitants of Nice and Cimiez who saw most of Queen Victoria, were inclined to the belief that she sometimes drank more than she should.

Forrester was the first person to introduce the Bronx cocktail to the South of France. Originally, it was known as an H.P.W., named after Harry Payne-Whitney, for whom it was invented at the Piping Rock Club. Then, as now, it consisted of the juice of an orange, Italian vermouth and gin. Forrester, now in his eighties, but still doing his annual stint as barman at Evian-les-Bains, spent his first season on the Riviera in 1898. When the Boer War broke out he joined the 8th Hussars and saw service in South Africa.

An Englishman, he decided that he wanted to see still more of the world and, armed with letters of introduction to Oscar, the famous manager of the Waldorf-Astoria, made his way to New York. One day, walking down Peacock Alley he encountered Prince Lichtenstein whom he knew from the Hotel de Paris at Monte Carlo. The Prince was looking for a rich wife. Forrester was looking for a job. Said the Prince, 'I have an idea. Let us have luncheon at the Café Martin.' Forrester accepted gratefully. Barnum and Bailey were giving their annual New York presentation at Madison Square Garden. As they walked along, Forrester noticed their poster advertising the Biggest Man on Earth, as a major attraction. Forrester knew him. His name was Hugo and he was born at St. Pol near Nice. Disengaging himself after luncheon from his princely host, he went to the Freaks department of the circus and asked for Hugo. Hugo suggested that he should join the circus, which was leaving in two weeks' time, and introduced him to the personnel manager. When asked how he could justify a job with the circus, Forrester replied that he had been in the Cavalry and could speak French and German. He was given the job of showing people round the Freaks. They were all, it seems, delightful people with the exception of the dwarfs, who were always fighting one another. The Siamese twins were particularly charming. Forrester, realising that it was a wonderful education for him to meet Americans in all walks of life, preferably the higher grades, stayed with the circus for three months, and had a splendid time. Whenever they came to a different town, he would accompany Hugo after the performance was over, to a nearby saloon The proprietors were insistent on providing drinks free. In Philadelphia George Karer, the current owner of the Waldorf and also of the Philadelphia Club, invited him to work as supernumerary bartender. Thus Forrester met the Wanamakers, Jason Walters, the Biddles and Drexels. This is no digression. Forrester became quite unintentionally an honorary Public Relations Officer for the South of France and was responsible for many rich Americans making their first trip to Monte Carlo and Cannes. On his return to the Riviera in 1905, cocktails were still competing in popularity with egg drinks, like a 'Tom and Jerry' an egg-nog served with boiling water instead of hot milk. Dry martinis were already on the map; but champagne cocktails consisted only of orange juice, champagne and grenadine. There was no sugar, brandy nor angostura bitters in them. Manhattans, always rye whisky and vermouth, had not yet reached the South of France.

Forrester's first job was at the Café de Paris at Monte Carlo with occasional visits to the Cercle Nautique in Cannes. As a result of this, he was invited by the famous Ruhl to open the bar at the Carlton Hotel. Next to it, in those days, was the Hotel La Plage where the secretaries of the grand dukes were housed. Until then, only professional beauties had the nerve to go into a bar.

The first place where ladies of rank ever frequented a mixed bar was much later at the Carlton Hotel, Cannes. It was the Grand Duke Michael's idea that the three rooms alongside the bar should be turned into a club. Mrs. William Leeds, later Princess Christopher of Greece, was persuaded without difficulty to give a tea party to launch it. She was in those days the most beautiful widow in Europe. Thereafter, one room was set aside for men, another for women, the third being a common meeting place for both sexes. Bridge was played, and when cocktail time came Forrester dispensed the drinks, and incidentally taught the future Lady Milford Haven and her sister, the future Lady Zia Wernher, how to use a shaker.

It was in those rooms, later on, that Marconi talked of his earliest radio plans with his backers and Lloyd George had private conversations during the famous treaty of Cannes in 1922, which so many people have forgotten.

CHAPTER 6

DUKES AND DAMES

IN 1879 the Empress of Russia arrived with her sons Paul and Serge at the Villa des Dunes. The Russian flag was hoisted at once and the French fleet at nearby Golfe Juan fired a salvo of 101 guns. The Grand Dukes Alexis and Vladimir arrived later, followed by the Tsarevitch, the future Alexander II. His wife, the Grand Duchess and the Empress' brothers, Prince Alexander of Hesse, the Duke and Duchess of Edinburgh paid a return visit a few days later, the Duchess of Edinburgh being the daughter of the Empress of Russia. The Archduke Renier of Austria and the King and Queen of Württemberg added further lustre to the scene. Shortly afterwards the Marquis de Nores, son of the Duke of Vallombrosa, married Miss de Hoffmann of New York. Wedding guests included the Comte de Paris. In the following year, Mr. Gladstone, Prime Minister of England, stayed at the Château Scott belonging to Lord Wolverton, doubtless on instructions of Queen Victoria, to find out about the movements and amours of her son and heir who appeared a week later at the Hotel Pavillon. A ball in his honour was given at the Cercle Nautique. That was the month when the Duke of Albany died as a result of a fall at the club.

The grand dukes regarded themselves as a race apart. In all, ten or a dozen of them frequented Cannes in the winter season. The senior quartette consisted of the sons of Tsar Alexander III – Michael, Boris, Andrew and Cyril; the last three were real glamour boys. Grand Duke Cyril was in the Imperial

Russian Navy. He was a survivor when his flagship blew up at Port Arthur and was fantastically good-looking. In the Russian Revolution of 1917 he was commanding the Guards Marines. Before the Tsar abdicated, he unwisely paid tribute to the Kerensky Government. Many White Russians feel that if he had not done so the situation might have been salvaged. The Grand Duke Boris was in the Guards Hussars. Grand Duke Andrew, who was in the Imperial Artillery, became addicted to ballet and particularly to Mathilde Mala, who loved Monte Carlo, and jewellery. He built the Villa Alam for her. Among the other grand dukes of the next generation to visit Cannes were the Grand Duke Michael, grandson of the Tsar, the Grand Duke Nicholas, the Grand Duke George, the Grand Duke Serge and some of their cousins, such as the Grand Duke Dimitri and the Grand Duke Vladimir.

Of the four brothers, Nicholas was much the brightest. He was a first-class historian, a great wit and a far greater gambler. He would never sit down to gamble because he was allergic to seeing his money raked away. His method of playing was to back some number which took his fancy with every possible combination on half a dozen tables simultaneously. To do this he had to dash around in all directions. He then turned away to learn from the *chef de partie* what had happened. On one occasion just before leaving to catch the train to Paris he plastered zero and its neighbouring numbers, 1, 2 and 3. He then turned to a perfect stranger beside him.

'I must rush off now,' he said. 'Please look after my money. If it wins, double up.'

He was gone in a flash. Zero turned up twice followed by 2, with the result that the maximum had been reached. The *chef de partie* turned to the stranger (Captain, later General, Polovtsoff, the President of the International Sporting Club).

'What shall we do?'

At that moment the Grand Duchess Anastasie passed by.

'Shall I give her the money?' he asked.

'No. Don't. Send it to the Crédit Lyonnais in Paris.' This was done, the only time that money ever went direct from the tables of Monte Carlo to Paris.

The Grand Duchess Anastasie was a more colourful gambler even than her brothers. Her semi-oriental green eyes went quite opaque as she concentrated on her next *mise*. Slim, dark, exquisite, she was completely indifferent to anything but her own desires. She married the Grand Duke of Mecklenburg-Schwerin who had a splendid villa at Cannes. Their retinue included a Master of the Court, his sister and an A.D.C. This was Graf Voss, tall, dark, boorish, good-looking. The garden of Villa Wenden ended abruptly in a parapet festooned with roses. One day the Grand Duke, who was a sick man, jumped over it to his death.

The Grand Duchess had many adventures. One of them was with a member of her staff. Disguising her pregnancy as long as possible, she wore loose dresses and claimed that she had a tumour. She announced later that she had caught chicken-pox and had to go into quarantine. Her child is now a successful wine salesman in London.

One of the Grand Duchess's theories was that croupiers could roll the ball into a particular section of the wheel, if they wanted to do so. Her favourite section was the *tier de sedan*.

She finally died of what was said to be an overdose of sleeping tablets. In the meantime she had bought the Villa Fantasia at Eze.

The Grand Duke Dimitri, who married an American heiress, had strange blue eyes and walked in a cat-like way. He was the son of the Grand Duke Paul. It was in his house that attempts were made to shoot, stab and poison Rasputin, the strange, ignorant Russian priest who had such a diabolical effect on the wife of the Tsar. Some fabulous vitality enabled Rasputin to survive three attempts on his life. He was finally discovered under the ice of the frozen River Neva.

Protocol among the Imperial Russian set at Cannes was very carefully maintained. If a carriage contained a grand duke or a grand duchess, the coachman had to wear his cockaded hat sideways and, incidentally, use white reins. If any relation of a grand duke was in mourning his fellow-guests at a private dinner party also had to wear black.

The Grand Duke George, who married the sister of the King of Greece, lived in very fine style. He brought not only butlers, valets and chefs and coachmen, but also four generals, two doctors, a master of his household and four aides-de-camp. He occupied the Villa Valletta on the edge of the sea, the one in which Lloyd George spent his visit during the negotiations for the Treaty of Cannes.

The Grand Duke Michael was invited on one occasion to inspect the British Fleet at Villefranche. He accepted and after inquiries had been made on his behalf, presented the midshipmen with boxes of sweets. After all, they were only fourteen or fifteen years old. Soon afterwards, the French fleet arrived. He decided to follow the same procedure which had been such a success on the previous occasion. After inspecting the flagship he asked to see the *enseignes*. To his horror he was confronted with a file of bearded men. By this time his equerry had already arrived with boxes of candy. Quickly he waved the equerry and the boxes away, and at the French Admiral's suggestion announced that he would give each *enseigne* a packet of tobacco instead.

The Grand Duke was not always so formal. Baroness Stoeckl recalls an occasion at the Café de Paris at Monte Carlo, when having ordered a superb chocolate *soufflé* as a climax for his luncheon guests, he put a napkin over it, placed it on a chair and then sat on it, squirting the creamy *soufflé* in all directions. Not very witty, in spite of the Grand Ducal laughter.

One of his neighbours was the Archduchess Stephanie, widow of the Meyerling suicide, the Archduke Rudolf. She had consoled herself by marrying Count Lonyay and lived in the same royal state as if she were at Schonbrunne.

On one occasion her guests who had been invited to dine found a large notice on a tree near the front door of the villa announcing 'Carriages 9.15 p.m.' They could scarcely believe their eyes; nevertheless at 9.10 p.m. the Archduchess threw a deep curtsey at them and went upstairs. The discomfited guests retired to the Cercle Nautique.

The Grand Duke Michael made many contributions to the social life of Cannes, his greatest undoubtedly being the golf club at Mandalieu. It quickly became a rendezvous for the rich English and aristocratic Russians. In the centre of the restaurant was a horseshoe table at which the Grand Duke Michael sat. Nobody was allowed to start from the first tee until he appeared on the scene. Every year he gave spectacular prizes for the spring golf meeting. Tea sets of inlaid red enamel, made by Fabergé, were routine rewards for the golfer with the best score. Mandalieu remains one of the most attractive golf courses on the Riviera and was responsible in 1922 for the resignation of Briand, the French Premier.

It was at Mandalieu that Bonar Law and Rufus Isaacs, later Lord Reading, played a game of golf with Lloyd George just before the Marconi scandal and neither of them said a word to him about it.

Two years after the short-lived Cannes Cricket Club had been founded, the *Cannes Gazette* made its first appearance. The editor was Mr. Lumbert, an English tailor whose villa was later converted into the famous Sunny Bank Hospital. An illustration of the Croisette on page one of the first issue shows that it contained only three villas, seven palm trees and one bathing cabin. There were references to the Cercle Nautique, and the local theatre which was showing *Les Surprises du Divorce*.

The names of all the thirty doctors were also printed with their addresses. Five were English, one was Scots – Miss Agnes MacLaren – one was German, two others were Belgian and Swiss. There were no American physicians. Thirty-six hotels and fourteen *pensions* took care of those visitors who did not have villas. English villa owners numbered 140 including the Duchess of Montrose and the Duke of Newcastle. To keep their staffs in a religious frame of mind Bible classes were given every week for English maids, but not for their mistresses. There was only one estate agent, John Taylor. Today there are 800 between Menton and St. Tropez.

In the meantime Cannes became a little kingdom of its own, populated by almost all the Russian Imperial family and German royalty. The Grand Duke Michael not only built the Russian church at Cannes but laid the foundation stone for the casino and also the Carlton Hotel. It is strange that no statue has been erected to his memory. During the Russo-Japanese war, he provided a convalescent hospital for Russian officers. On Sundays a luncheon was provided for them, over which the Grand Duke presided. After each Sunday, plates and silver were openly removed by the army officers as souvenirs of their visit. As for the English visitors to Cannes, if any of the young men misbehaved themselves in the slightest way, they were informed by some senior aristocratic Englishman that they were to pack their bags and leave on the train that evening. And they did.

Where Lord Brougham left off, the Grand Duke Michael carried on. Under his patronage the city elegant housed not only the most fashionable, but also the gayest, craziest, most amorous, not to say promiscuous society in Europe. With the exception of Francis Brantingham, the local correspondent of the *Paris Herald Tribune*, there were no newspapermen to draw attention to the intrigues, naughtinesses and excesses of the distinguished winter visitors. Francis Brantingham, moreover, had the good sense to smile at scandals and never report the nightly gaieties of the Russian, French, English, Spanish and German nobility, except in the politest way. He was received in most villas. When parties took place to which he was not invited he would call at the Villa Balibouze belonging to the Baron de Stoeckl, equerry to the Grand Duke Michael, and son of the man who sold Alaska to the U.S. for seven million dollars. The Baroness thoroughly enjoyed herself by supplying him with the details of the jewels, celebrated names and other titbits for publication. Naturally, she never disclosed the amours, practical jokes and other integral ingredients of a typical party given in a Cannes villa.

Perhaps the best proof that high society at Cannes was so incredibly promiscuous was the complete absence of *demi-mondaines*. They were only to be found at Monte Carlo. On Tuesday and Thursday there were dances at the Cercle Nautique. It was the quaint custom to make them 'Dutch' affairs. Dinner cost fifteen francs, the equivalent of three pounds, exclusive of wines. There were twenty tables of varying sizes. The object of the exercise was to sit at one of those most favoured by royalty or grand dukes.

In the absence of Edward VII, the Grand Duke Michael was the uncrowned king of Cannes. He was the third son of Grand Duke Michael Nicholaieff and therefore grandson of Tsar Nicholas I. He had been madly in love with the Countess Ignatieff in St. Petersburg, but because a Grand Duke was not allowed to marry a commoner, he was forbidden to marry her by the Tsar, who advised him to go on the Grand Tour. According to the Grand Duke's daughter, Lady Zia Wernher, he met his future wife in the flower market at Cannes, having been introduced to her by that celebrated character Quentin Dick. The more probable story is that of the Baroness Stoeckl. She claims that the Grand Duke met his future bride at Biarritz. She was then the Countess Sophie Merenberg, but was later given the rank of Countess Torby by her uncle the Grand Duke of Luxembourg. Wherever they met, they married at San Remo in the face of the Tsar's furious disapproval. The Grand Duke was forbidden to return to Russia, even for a brief visit. He promptly bought a property in Cannes, making it his headquarters during the winter months.

The Villa Kasbeck, now a block of flats, is in the Californie section, up on the hill behind the Croisette. It was a vast place needing a staff of five footmen, a butler, a valet, a maid, a governess, a nursery-maid and half a dozen chefs. The villa had no great character, either in architecture or décor, except that the reception rooms were full of gilt *jardinières* with flowers and ferns round the walls. The table decorations were, however, unique. The Grand Duke set the fashion of having spring flowers looped from candlesticks on the table which were then linked to the candelabra above.

The Grand Duke, who wore a small, pointed beard, dyed until the Russo-Japanese war (when it suddenly turned white), was very elegant, always in love with someone – though nothing really came of it – and a very charming man. His Christian name was the same as that of the first of the Romanoff Czars (1596–1645). Not surprisingly, the Soviet control of Russia gave him later on good reason to feel that his every movement was being watched by the Communists, who always ascribed the worst motives to the most innocent acts of any Grand Duke. No wonder that he became highly suspicious of strangers. Incidentally, his private diaries, now in the possession of Lady Zia Wernher, have never been published.

His apanage, withdrawn on his marriage, was later re-constituted. In any event, his father, the Grand Duke Michael, owned among other things most of Tiflis and in particular a mineral water spring which was in those days as popular on the Continent as Evian water is today. Money had never meant much to 'Mich-Mich', but when his father died he became immensely rich.

Gambling being still forbidden in France, it became the accepted tradition to go to the Principality three times a week. From Cannes the journey took one and a half hours. The usual procedure, therefore, was to send a valet and lady's maid to the Hotel de Paris with the gowns and dress clothes necessary for gala occasions. The distinguished visitors themselves followed on the afternoon train, then spent perhaps two hours dressing themselves before dining at the Hotel de Paris as a prelude to going to the casino. As often as not, the men would be so obsessed by gambling that they would miss the last train home and stay the night without their wives and probably with some *cocotte*. The wives and their husbands if they noticed the time (no casino has ever had a clock), would catch the midnight train back to Cannes, or, if they missed it, would hire a carriage to take them as far as Nice and embark on the local train returning them to Cannes at 2 a.m.

Before Grand Duke Michael inaugurated the golf course, there was nothing to do except flirt, play occasional bridge or have tea at Rumpelmayers next door to the Cercle Nautique. Only a few people played lawn tennis. Midday was the earliest time for anybody to be seen on the Croisette. Surprisingly enough there was no *maison de rendez-vous*. If a wife cared to *tromper* her husband or the husband wanted to *tromper* his wife, they went to the villa in question at a time when they knew that only the servants would see them. Just as Smollett observed about the lack of jealousy among the Niçois a century before, husbands and wives were very complaisant. Divorce in those days was almost unknown. Most wives had their lovers and vice versa. Both parties led their own lives so long as there was no public scandal.

The leaders of French society were the Marquise de Gallifet, the Princesse de Sagan, and the Comtesse de Pourtales. Their nicknames were 'Cochonette', 'Cocodette' and 'Coquette'. Each name speaks for itself. They were in the entourage of the Empress Eugénie. Quite apart from being introduced to the Empress herself it was a great compliment to be allowed to curtsey to the Princesse de Sagan. The Princess was plump, blond, elegant. Beautifully dressed, the daughter of a French banker, the Marquise de Gallifet was tall, dark, slight and rather sarcastic. Like the Comtesse de Pourtales, the most beautiful of the three, she enjoyed life to the brim.

It was not, however, so much beauty that attracted the men in those days. Mrs. Clayton, the tall, thin, fair, very French, but not particularly pretty wife of the A.D.C. to the Duke of Connaught, was very much in demand.

Mrs. Keppel, a dark woman with a generous figure, was quite lovely, very brilliant, full of charm and never malicious. It was around Edward VII, the Grand Duke Michael and this quintette that Cannes society revolved giddily between Christmas and April 1st. When anybody was so unfashionable as to stay a few days longer, he had the embarrassment of hearing the carpets in the closed villas being beaten by the servants who had been left behind to clear up.

Princess Daisy of Pless, one of the most beautiful women of her generation, fortunately kept voluminous diaries of her visits to the South of France. As the sister-in-law of the Duke of Westminster and a member of the inner coterie of Edward VII, she was able to shed a great deal of light on the more intimate side of the grand ducal scene in her day. After her first introduction to the Riviera, by taking a villa at Grasse, she became a regular guest at the Villa Kasbeck, the home of the Grand Duke Michael. Her observations in 1904 and 1905 are of particular interest, these being the years of the Russo-Japanese war. The grand ducal set at that time included the Grand Duchess Anastasie, the Grand Duke George and his wife, the daughter of the King of Greece and her son, the Grand Duke of Mecklenburg-Schwerin and his young wife, daughter of the Duchess of Cumberland, and her second daughter, Cecile, who married the German Crown Prince.

She noted in her diary of her stay at the villa that on one occasion the dinner was awful – badly served and everything overcooked. After dinner some played bridge and others played poker. The Grand Duke George quarrelled with his sister all the time, shouting at her dreadfully. It seems that finally the Grand Duchess, red in the face, said, 'This is not really my brother, I should never have introduced you.' Princess Daisy could not help telling the Grand Duke Michael that she much preferred him to his brother George; but confided to her diary that Grand Duke Michael was nothing particular though, compared with his brother, an incomparably nicer man. Princess Daisy took a dim view of the failure of the grand dukes to maintain the prestige of Russia during the unfortunate war with the Japanese. She went on to say that if they had been men of character, strong will and perception, the fiasco of the Russo-Japanese war would have served as a warning and would have awakened them to the dangerous position of Russia, not only abroad but at home.

It was not until some time later that Princess Daisy dined at Monte Carlo for the first time. Her host on this occasion was

Nada, Lady Milford Haven

Lady Zia Wernher

Villa Kazbeck, Cannes, built for the Grand Duke Michael. (*Joe Hollander*)

Mr. Drexel; her fellow-guests the Duchess of Devonshire, very cheerful and very rouged, Mr. and Mrs. Derek Keppel and Lord Charles Montagu. Princess Daisy and Mr. Drexel went to the opera after dinner and heard the young Russian singer, Feodor Chaliapin. Afterwards, Mrs. Clayton (formerly Jeanne de Fougère) took her backstage to ask Chaliapin to sing at her home in Cannes. Chaliapin at that time was only twenty-six, but his acting astounded everybody. Mrs. Keppel who, according to Virginia Cowles, first met Edward VII at Sandown Races, was actually introduced to him for the first time at the Villa Kasbeck, which was named, incidentally, after the highest mountain in the Caucasus of which the Grand Duke Michael had been titular governor.

We have two favourite stories about dukes during this epoch. The first concerns an English duke's valet. When asked how his Grace was feeling, the valet replied:

'His Grace is in very good spirits. He actually helped me button up his braces this morning.'

The second story concerns a very pompous Scottish duke who thought it smart to travel under an assumed name. One evening he was telling his brother-in-law, Charlie Forbes, all about it.

He said: 'Yes, I travelled across the Channel incognito and nobody knew who I was. It was the same in Paris. I was incognito and nobody knew who I was. Even at Cannes I was incognito and nobody knew who I was.'

Charlie Forbes, bored to distraction, said: 'And who *were* you?'

Dukes, whether Russian, English, French, Spanish or Hungarian, always brought a retinue of servants with them when they came to Cannes, even if they stayed at a hotel or at the Cercle Nautique. The Duke of Devonshire, for example, used to bring seven servants including a chef. Whenever a private banquet was given at the Cercle, therefore, there was no need to import local waiters. English butlers and footmen served the guests. Later on the Grand Duke Michael quarrelled with the Duc de Vallombrosa and set up a rival club at the Malmaison, formerly the Villa Dubosc in the grounds of the Grand Hotel. This belonged to a Mrs. Howlands. The membership was purely masculine and the primary attraction was bridge in the afternoon. While a member of the Cercle Nautique, the Grand Duke let his bills run right through to the end of the season before Captain Sheldon, the secretary, received a cheque.

It was in the Cercle Nautique that the fashion for *pousse-café* and after-dinner cocktails was introduced. A *pousse-café* is a series of liqueurs poured into a glass one by one in order of gravity, the lightest on top, with the result that there is a series of different coloured drinks in layers. After-dinner cocktails had always the same basic ingredients of cherry heering and brandy and Cointreau, with the addition of cochineal. They could be tinted any colour to suit the gowns of the women who ordered them. The idea seems ripe for revival today.

Oscar Wilde, a frequent visitor to Cannes after his release from prison, was naturally barred from the Cercle Nautique. Instead he frequented the Grand Hotel, running up a considerable bill, in return for educating the kind-hearted Charles Forrester who not only served him champagne, but also gave him chicken sandwiches when he could not afford them. It was incidentally Forrester's idea that Ruhl, who owned the Grand and was a substantial shareholder in the Carlton Hotel, should build the tennis courts and form the Carlton Tennis Club, with the Duke of Westminster as president.

Blanc was now reaching the end of his life. His asthma was growing worse and although he went every year to the little Swiss spa of Loesche-les-Bains, he grew more nervous and pallid every day. Threats of personal violence, which had always been frequent, now began to agitate him. He became more and more embarrassed when waylaid by gamblers who had lost everything and pleaded for their wives and children. At least, however, he had the vast satisfaction of marrying off his elder daughter Louise to Prince Constantine Radziwill, though he did not do it without a great deal of previous investigation.

Within a year he was dead.

The funeral service, which took place in the same Church of St. Roch, was almost as impressive as his daughter's wedding. The whole façade was covered in black crape like one of his roulette tables.

Blanc left £3,600,000 of which £40,000 was willed to the Church. Whatever might be said about him he ran his casino on scrupulously honest lines and was always able to justify his strange vocation by claiming that gambling is a universal passion, will always flourish and therefore, as M. de Sartines had announced a century before, it was far better to bring it out into the open and run it with scrupulous care, instead of driving it underground into private clubs where the roulette wheel could be rigged and the cards marked.

Camille Blanc was now appointed managing director and proved in many ways that he was as great as, if not greater than, his father – at any rate in elaborating the existing success of Monte Carlo. He was a small, stout little man with a grey flowing moustache, light blue eyes set like a Red Indian's, very great charm and an admiration for beautiful women, notably Mlle. Chinon.

CHAPTER 7

EDITORS AND EMPRESSES

VERY SOON Camille Blanc persuaded Massenet and Saint-Saëns to write operas specially for Monte Carlo, where they had their world *premières*. *Don Quichotte, Ivan le Terrible, Thérèse, Le Jongleur de Notre-Dame*, were all seen first at Monte Carlo, which soon became the rival to Paris, Berlin, London and New York. Puccini, Bellini, Leoncavallo, Gounod, Bizet, Offenbach and Berlioz all came under his sway. In one season all three *Fausts* by Gounod, Berlioz and Boito were performed. In those days a performance of opera was regarded as exceptional and yet in Monte Carlo operatic performances were being given twice a week. The orchestra was international and far better paid than any other in the world. In addition, each member of the orchestra was promised a comfortable pension when he retired. At one moment, sixty-three of the orchestra had won first prizes at the principal *conservatoires* of France, Italy and Belgium.

Madame Patti was paid £400 for a single performance. Jean de Reszke received £240, Sarah Bernhardt was frequently seen on the stage in the latest French plays, many of them also having their world *première* at Monte Carlo. Camille Blanc knew well enough that these world-famous artistes were not really expensive, however much he paid them. All were born gamblers and, like Chaliapin later on, lost most of their fees in the casino. Bernhardt was particularly unfortunate at the tables.

In 1887 the Hotel de Paris had among its guests, during the

brief three months' winter season, the Emperor and Empress of Austria, the Dowager Empress of Russia, the Queen of Portugal, the King of Sweden, and the King of Servia.

Other reigning monarchs in search of sun and seclusion gravitated to the wooded headlands of Cap Martin and Cap Ferrat. Leopold II, King of the Belgians, after a number of visits to Nice and Monte Carlo, decided one day to secure a property at Cap Ferrat which he could transform at his leisure. Xavier Paoli, chief of the French Security Police in those days, and therefore entrusted with the arduous duty of having to protect visiting royalty from attempts at assassination – somewhat popular during that epoch – tells the story. During a drive, King Leopold noticed the Villa Passable, surrounded by high walls and apparently abandoned. 'Whom does it belong to?' he suddenly asked. Paoli said, 'To an Englishman, Sire – to an Englishman who never comes here, Sire.' Leopold said, 'We have got time to inspect it before the train takes me back to Nice. Let someone look for the gardener.' The gardener could not be found, but the main gate was open. King Leopold did not hesitate. He pushed through it and entered, followed by Baron Snoy, Paoli and Olivier, another police officer. He walked rapidly down the paths between the trees, exclaiming ecstatically about the beauty of the flowers. When he decided to leave, Paoli discovered that someone, during their visit, had closed the main gate. There was no key and it was impossible to open it. The party shouted; nobody answered. The train was due to leave quite soon. King Leopold was impatient. Olivier had a bright idea. He ran to a shed not far away and returned with a ladder. 'Sire,' he exclaimed, 'there is nothing else for it. If Your Majesty agrees, we can lean it up against the wall.' King Leopold agreed to the suggestion and Baron Snoy climbed up first, followed by Paoli. King Leopold took his place behind with Olivier to bring up the rear. They clambered up to the top of the wall. Baron Snoy and Paoli hoisted the King up and Olivier followed suit. At that moment, the ladder quivered and fell to the ground. All four men were now isolated, their legs hanging down and with no means of descending on the other side. 'We look like burglars,' said King Leopold, laughing uncertainly. 'The only thing to do is to jump down.' True, it was not much of a drop and Snoy, Olivier and Paoli landed easily on their feet. King Leopold, who had a bad leg and was by no means mobile, refused to jump. Olivier, the resourceful detective, solved the problem. He suggested that he and his companion should provide a kind of human ladder. As a result, King Leopold allowed himself to slide over the shoulders of Baron Snoy who passed him on to Olivier's back while Paoli grabbed his long legs and enabled him to reach the ground safely.

A few weeks later, Leopold bought the villa and thoroughly enjoyed pulling it down, rebuilding it, redesigning the gardens and planting more flower beds every year. He was most meticulous in other matters but in this case he spent a comparative fortune. He renamed it Les Cèdres.

It did not take long for people in close contact with him to learn his habits; for example, every morning he would have three or four gallons of salt water poured over him as a morning bath. He insisted on game being served at every meal and he hated creases so much that he insisted on a hot iron being used, not only on his handkerchiefs, but also on the newspapers before he would read them. When he addressed the servants, he always spoke of himself in the third person. Instead of saying, 'You will wait for me,' he said to his coachman, 'You will wait for him.' This stupefied people who did not know the mannerism and made them wonder what on earth he was talking about, or who the third man was.

Nevertheless Leopold was in some ways a simple soul,

ready to gossip with the locals but always grabbing the bill when it was presented to him and scrutinising it very harshly. He was always afraid of being overcharged and ran the villa with the strictest economy.

When he was sixty-five, he made the acquaintance of Mlle. Blanche-Caroline Delacroix, a girl of eighteen, on whom he later bestowed the title of Baroness de Vaughan.[1] She was blonde and gay and made a strong impression on the King who started by flirting with her and then married her in secret – according to some people, at San Remo. At first they took every kind of precaution to conceal their liaison. Though they travelled on the same train, they never spoke a word in public, pretending not to know each other. However, they descended at the same railway station, stayed in the same hotels with adjoining suites, sat in the same restaurants, but always at different tables. Later on, when the association was more or less official, they relaxed rules and the King gave her a charming villa which connected with his official residence outside Brussels at the Château de Laeken.

At Cap Ferrat, he built a charming little house for her on the estate. According to Paoli, he used to walk across to her every evening, armed with a lantern. On arrival, he spent two hours playing cards with her, and at 11 p.m. returned to his own villa, while the French detectives hid in the shrubberies and maintained security measures without his seeing them. He always liked to be watched carefully provided the detectives were not obviously placed to guard him. Needless to say, the locals learnt all about his foibles, but after their experience with so many extraordinary people, nothing surprised them.

Cap Ferrat was studded with beautiful homes, one of the most important of which belonged to the sister of Baron Edward

1. Purely to irritate Cardinal Vaughan, who disapproved of his amours.

de Rothschild. She was a Madame Ephrussi. Today it is open
to the public in its capacity of the local museum. To build it
and design the gardens took ten years and the work of fifteen
architects. The style is more Spanish than Italian or Provençale.
It is a real treasure house with a dozen salons and boudoirs and
bedrooms, furnished in the most luxurious way with Gothic
tapestries and splendid iron-work. The carpets date from the
seventeenth and eighteenth centuries; some Aubusson and
some Gobelins. There is an extraordinary collection of Sèvres.
A Japanese boudoir is full of Chinese lacquer screens. Frago-
nard, Watteau, Monet and Renoir are all represented on the
walls. The park which surrounds the villa has majestic walks
through cypress groves.

Not far away was the more modest villa of James Gordon
Bennett, the famous proprietor of the *Paris Herald Tribune*.
Bennett, the man who sent Stanley to find Livingstone, was a
strange character with a passion for owls and replicas of owls.

When he founded the *Paris Herald* in 1857, he was already
an international celebrity, head of the *New York Herald*, to
which he had succeeded on the death of his father. Many
stories of his wild parties and eccentricities were told. He
moved in a whirl of royalty and took the view that the public,
particularly the American public, were snobs who liked to see
their names in print. The very first item in the Social columns
in the first issue of the *Paris Herald* began: 'Mr. William K.
Vanderbilt will return from London on Wednesday.' This
was followed by the announcement that Mr. and Mrs. James
Blain were on their way to the Riviera at an early date.

Bennett's policy of printing the names of celebrities and
would-be celebrities when they arrived in France, and particularly on the Riviera, made Americans socially self-conscious.
The high season at Monte Carlo, Cannes and Nice was literally
heralded by Francis Brantingham, sent to collect names of

visitors at the various hotels and galas. It is said that 200 copies were sent every day to St. Petersburg. One of his first acquisitions was a villa at Beaulieu. He also had a yacht, the *Mamouna*, which he replaced with the *Lysistrata*, said to have cost him 625,000 dollars.

The former Consuelo Vanderbilt, later Duchess of Marlborough, and still later Madame Balsan, recalls that he invariably ran to the window to watch the train-de-luxe rushing through the bottom of his garden; but Bennett was a real eccentric. On one occasion, he invited a number of handsome American women to dine on board his yacht. In the middle of dinner, Bennett retired to his cabin, and the yacht moved out to sea. Adèle, Countess of Essex, noticed the coast of France was disappearing and dashed off to question the first mate. (One of James Bennett's eccentricities was to dispense with the services of a captain. Another was to pay the deck hands, first mate, second mate and chief engineer exactly the same wage – £480 per annum.) The first mate replied that he had been given instructions to proceed to Egypt and nothing could be done about it. The guests spent an agitated night, the sea was rough and they were in evening dress.

Next morning, Bennett changed his mind, and the yacht returned to Beaulieu, where the angry guests went ashore in broad daylight still, of course, wearing evening dress.

Bennett never hesitated to insult anyone he felt worthy of insulting. Another of his eccentricities was to publish the same Letter to the Editor every day for nearly nineteen years, exactly as it had appeared the first time. It read:

'To the Editor of the Herald.

I am anxious to find out a way to figure the temperature from centigrade to fahrenheit and vice versa. In other words, I want to know, whenever I see the temperature designated

on a Centigrade thermometer, what it would be on a
Fahrenheit thermometer.

An Old Philadelphia Lady,
Paris.'

Bennett's affection for the sea was quite genuine. Before he
had become the United States' most famous expatriate on the
Continent, he had twice been Commodore of the New York
Yacht Squadron.

He claimed that after fifteen years, the *Paris Herald* had cost
him two million dollars, but had been well worth it. Certainly
the French tourist office never had a better publicist, though it
is strange that it was not until 1920 that the American Express
found it worth while to start a branch in Nice, to be followed
by others in Cannes and Monte Carlo. One of his most famous
staff men was Sparrow Robertson, a tiny little man, who
quickly became the most famous sports writer in Europe.
Sparrow referred to everyone as his 'dear old pal', and although
he confined his activities mainly to Paris, he frequently found
a reason to visit the South of France.

James Gordon Bennett and Lord Northcliffe were the first
newspaper men to realise the importance of aviation. Bennett
not only instructed his newspaper to write about flying, but
himself did a series of round trips by air between Monte Carlo,
Nice, Beaulieu and Menton. Bennett was also responsible for
establishing two of the most famous restaurants on the Riviera.
The first was the Reserve at Beaulieu, the second was Ciro's,
in Monte Carlo. Ciro, an Egyptian pastrycook, born in Italy,
had been Bennett's favourite waiter at the Café Riche, where
he liked to lunch out of doors. One day he found that all the
tables had been moved inside to keep the terrace free for
people who wanted drinks in the sunshine. This so infuriated
him that he bought the restaurant, handed Ciro the bill of

sale, and said, 'Now you own this place. Get those tables back, and go cook my chop.' Ciro made his fortune, and before Bennett died, sold out to an English syndicate which included the late Earl of Rosslyn, and which opened branches in London, Paris and Deauville.

Bennett's approval of a restaurant, whether in Paris or the South of France – such as the Café de Paris – at once guaranteed its success, at least among Americans. He saw to it that the *Paris Herald* gave the most flowery descriptions of the cuisine and wine cellar. Nor was bad weather on the Riviera ever mentioned.

One of the *commis des rangs* at the Café de Paris was none other than Henri Charpentier, later to become one of the most famous *restaurateurs* in the United States, best known perhaps for his management of the restaurant at the Rockefeller Centre in New York. Henri was only fourteen when Edward VII, then Prince of Wales, arrived at the Café de Paris for luncheon. One day it was Henri's lot to wait upon the Prince and his party.

'Good morning, Your Highness,' said Henri.

'Bon jour, Henri,' said the Prince. 'What are we going to have for luncheon today?'

'Sir, today it will be a sweet never before served to anyone. I have contrived out of something – ' According to Henri he was planning to make an ordinary French pancake with curaçao, kirschwasser and maraschino to be poured on just before serving. Quite by accident, as he worked in front of a chafing dish, the liqueurs caught alight. He thought he was ruined. The Prince and his friends were waiting. Nevertheless, he tasted it and suddenly realized that the accident of the flame was exactly what was required to give that extra flavour. Again inspired, he added two more measures of the three liqueurs. The pan was alight with blue and orange flames. As the colours died, he looked up to see the Prince of Wales, dressed all in grey that day, with a cravat of light blue, a carnation in his buttonhole. The royal chin was up, and the royal nostrils were inhaling. The Prince ate the pancakes with a fork, used a spoon to capture the remaining syrup; then asked Henri the name of what he'd eaten with so much relish. Henri said, 'Mon Prince, it is Crêpe Princesse.' The Prince, although recognising that the gender was inevitable, protested, with mock rage, that there was a lady present. 'Will you,' said the Prince, 'change Crêpe Princesse to Crêpe Suzette?' Who Suzette was will never be revealed. She has become immortal anonymously.

Still earlier, at the age of nine, Henri, who came from the neighbourhood of Nice, was a diminutive page-boy at the Hotel Cap Martin, where his half-brother was chef. Dressed as a page in a suit of blue with a wide collar of white linen and a blue cap with a gold button on top, he soon found himself running errands for the Duchess of Rutland, the Prince of Wales, and Leopold, King of the Belgians. King Leopold always held his grey melon-shaped hat and his cane in one hand. One day, a band of dark blue velvet was sewn to the right sleeve of Henri's coat between the wrist and forearm, with an edging of gold lace, and the two-headed eagle emblem of Austria-Hungary. The Empress Elizabeth had come to stay. The significance of the decoration was that Henri had been appointed special page-boy to Her Majesty. Whenever she arrived or departed, a red carpet was unrolled and Henri's job was to stand stiffly with his arm extended so that she could use him as a living balustrade. It was Henri who carried the telegrams, packages and letters to her apartment where he handed them to a major domo.

The Grand Hotel, owned by Ulrick, a dignified Englishman, had a superb view all the way from Monaco to Bordighera. Four tall fireplaces were in the lobby. The walls were cream. The marble stairs were beautifully covered. Tapestries, thick carpets and rugs softened the conversation in the vestibule where the files of the great newspapers from London, Paris, Madrid, New York, Berlin and Buenos Aires were daily replenished.

The Empress occupied the whole of the ground floor of the right wing of the hotel. Her furniture was very simple, mostly Sheraton. Her bed was gold-plated with a mosquito net above. Unknown to everyone except her intimates, the Empress was a gymnast. Above the top of her bed was a swing on which she did a private trapeze act for her own amusement and to keep her figure. Incredible, but true.

Every Sunday, the billiard room was reserved for her, as her personal chapel. The Empress, who was very pious, had asked about the nearest church on the day of her arrival. She was told that there was nothing nearer than the one at Roquebrune. Church ritual demanded that all the furniture should be consecrated before the room could be used as a chapel. But this could only be done by the Bishop. The problem was solved in a curious way. There was an ancient law which enacted that the chief dignitaries of the Holy Order of the Knights of Malta could consecrate anything on which they had placed their cloak. It was then remembered that General Berzowicz, the Empress's Chamberlain, was entitled to this privilege. He duly obliged by dropping his cloak and the Abbé Rosso, a magnificent-looking priest from Roquebrune, held the service every Sunday with Henri Charpentier acting as altar boy, putting wine in the chalice, moving the Book, uttering the responses, and stealing glances at the Empress, as she sat in a big chair in front of a velvet stool on which she stooped to pray.

Every day the Empress, accompanied by her Greek secretary, went for long walks. Complaining that her dress interfered with her stride, she used to change her skirt in mid-walk for something lighter. The transformation was done very simply. She would disappear behind a bush or a tree, while her companion looked discreetly the other way. The Empress then handed him the heavy skirt which she had replaced with a lighter one, and the walk continued. The young Greek's job, besides making conversation to Her Imperial Majesty, was to read passages from a book whenever they stopped for a breather. This occurred fairly frequently, because although the Empress was an indefatigable walker, she was fond of climbing up any goat track which came into view, and there were many of them.

On one occasion she told Xavier Paoli, the security officer, to take her to the casino, which she had never visited before. 'I really must know what a gaming room looks like before I die,' she explained, as they drove off with a lady-in-waiting to Monte Carlo. On arrival, the Empress slid her way into a crowd of people round a roulette table, and stood there watching ecstatically. 'Let's see if I am lucky,' she said. 'I think thirty-three will win,' and placed a silver coin on the number. She lost twice. On the third occasion 33 obliged. The croupier passed her 175 francs. Gaily, the Empress said to her two companions, 'Let us leave at once. I have never had so much money in my life before.'

On her other visits to Monte Carlo she always paid a call at Rumpelmayer's, where she could be sure of her favourite delicatessen. She used to sit down at a small table near the counter, joke with the waitresses and cashier – nobody having the slightest idea that she was the Empress of Austria-Hungary. Like Queen Victoria, who occasionally called on her at Cap Martin, she loved visiting the farms of peasants, very frequently nursing their babies on her knee, asking for a glass of wine and then paying royally. But then, she was a member of the Bavarian royal family which has always been the most friendly in Europe towards its subjects. What also differentiated her was her strange premonition that she was going to be drowned, or that her death would have something to do with water. It sounded more like a shipwreck and not the assassination by a lunatic which ended her life on that lake steamer in Switzerland.

While she was at Cap Martin, the Emperor Franz Joseph, her husband, came and spent a fortnight regularly with her. Nothing could have been more charming than their regular meeting at the railway station at Menton, where the Empress awaited his arrival from Vienna. The Emperor would always jump down from the railway coach, hurry to her, bareheaded, kiss her on both cheeks, smile broadly, take her arm and lead her off to the waiting carriage.

The Empress Eugénie, the Spanish girl who became the wife of Napoleon III, also visited the Hotel Cap Martin, where she took an apartment on the first floor. Henri Charpentier first encountered her, when she was seventy, wearing a *peignoir* of lavender silk, grey lace and white, and a spicy perfume of carnations. Like the Empress Elizabeth, she was a gymnast. Both went for long walks, both were fond of swimming and hid their pearls in the same hiding place in the same rock when they went for a bathe. Both Empresses were very abstemious, dieting themselves largely with fruit juices. The Empress Eugénie, however, had a dress for every day of the week. At Cap Martin they were chiefly cottons and muslins.

According to Prosper Mérimée, the Empress Eugénie had been advised by him to buy an estate at Cannes before her husband was dethroned. She had not taken his advice. It was not until the Third Empire had crumbled that she thought of acquiring a permanent home at Cap Martin. After two or three visits to the Hotel she bought some land from the widow of the Duke of Aosta and built a villa, which she called by the Greek name of Kyrnos. It was a large white building facing Monaco with a splendid terrace and a delightful garden. Her original intention was to turn it into a salon for poets and authors, but somehow this idea fell through. However, she entertained a great deal, particularly all her former friends who had remained faithful to her in spite of her husband's abdication. Among them was a Dr. Egen Schmidt, who was supposed to look very much like Napoleon III. As long as the Prince Impérial was alive, the Empress refused to meet him. After the Prince's death, she asked him to come and see her. The doctor acceded to her wishes. The Empress looked at him for some time and then murmured, 'How much you resemble him.'

During her stay at Cap Martin, she frequently walked to Monte Carlo, taking pleasure in studying the latest fashions as worn by the *haute monde*. When any of them wore a dress which in any way resembled the Empire style, she would say gaily, 'But that is *my* fashion.'

Later on, during the 1914–18 war, she offered to provide an ambulance at her own cost. By some stupidity, her offer was refused by the authorities. So she gave her yacht to the British Admiralty.

At her death the Villa Kyrnos went back to the Duchess of Aosta, who left it to a Captain Fischer. When Captain Fischer died it was inherited by his widow, Madame Bovie, the opera singer. In 1956 Sir Winston Churchill was offered it by its present owner – but at a price which he decided was too high.

Queen Victoria, preceded by Edward VII and other members of the British royal family, made the French Riviera famous throughout the British Empire. After the death of the Prince

Consort, she paid several visits to the Continent, first to Switzerland where her trip to the top of the Rigi brought incalculable benefits to Geneva and the surrounding Swiss towns. In the spring of 1882, Queen Victoria spent two months at La Mortola, the internationally celebrated home of the Banbury family a few kilometres from the French frontier. She arrived by way of Menton and returned by the same route. In 1891 she spent five weeks at the Grand Hotel in Grasse. From 1895 onwards, she took up residence for five consecutive years at Cimiez, arriving punctually in the middle of March and leaving at the end of April. Her first choice was the Grand Hotel; later she stayed at the biscuit-coloured Regina Excelsior Hotel, known as the Pavilion – now a home for old people of both sexes.

At the Grand Hotel, her apartments cost the Privy Purse £2,000 for six weeks. At the Regina Excelsior Hotel she was charged £4,000 for two months.

The reason for her preferring hotels to a villa was that she always brought a prodigious pile of luggage, not only her clothes and table linen, china, glass and cutlery, but also much of her furniture from Balmoral, even down to her narrow little acanthus-wood bed. Her retinue was numerous and always consisted of exactly the same people. The man in whom she had the most confidence, Sir Henry Ponsonby, acted as keeper of her Privy Purse and private secretary. When he died, she replaced him with Sir Fleetwood Edwards and Sir Arthur Bigge. Her private physician was always Sir James Reid.

Among her ladies-in-waiting were Lady Churchill, Lady Southampton, Lady Antrim, Lady Lytton – and Miss Harriet Phillips, who never left her. In addition to these palace dignitaries, there were six chambermaids, a head chef, several kitchen hands, John Brown, her famous kilted manservant, a coachman, an outrider, and a dozen grooms, because the Queen always brought her own coaches and horses with her. Besides all these, there were her Indian servants. These mysterious, imposing and aloof men wore large turbans and were clothed in gorgeous Kashmir silk uniforms. They surrounded their Queen with silent, attentive protection and enjoyed various privileges, including the practice of all their Hindu rites.

The Queen lived a punctual life. She rose at nine o'clock in the morning, and dressed, breakfasted and read and wrote letters with the aid of two secretaries. Correspondence was brought every day by special courier from England. At eleven o'clock she removed her white tulle bonnet which she wore in the house, put on a garden-party hat and a silk cloak, then, leaning on her walking stick, walked slowly to the flight of steps where her little carriage, drawn by the famous grey donkey Jacko, awaited her. Jacko played an important part in the life of the court. He was the Queen's favourite and always drew her donkey carriage in the gardens of her various residences. The Queen had bought him at Aix-les-Bains from a peasant who was driving him along the Lake of Bourget. Taking pity on his skinny appearance, for she loved animals, she acquired him on the spot. Jacko soon showed exemplary docility and obedience. He retired some years before the death of the Queen, eating his last carrot at Windsor.

In the afternoon, Queen Victoria went for long drives in her landau, sometimes not returning before nightfall. She was particularly fond of going to local fêtes which recalled the old customs of the country, like the Feast of the Reproaches.

Every year she brought a trunk full of presents for railway porters, hotel staff, minor officials and other people with whom she came in contact. At the end of her visit, she would give away over a hundred watches, watch chains, tie pins, rings, bracelets, pocket books, photographs, ink pots and the like. From the Inspector of Police, down to the plain clothes man, each gendarme received a little memento. No mistakes were ever made. Although the Queen visited the Riviera several years in succession she never once gave the same present to the same person. For example, the station-master at Nice might be given a cigar case one year and a watch the next and a tie pin the year after. But never another cigar case or tie pin.

On one occasion she reviewed the local troops at Nice. There sat the little old lady under her black umbrella facing the bright blue sea, while 10,000 troops in red, white and blue uniforms marched past her. At the end of the procession came the *Chasseurs Alpins*, their band playing a lively tune which drew tremendous applause from the crowd.

'What is that march?' asked the Queen.

'It's the *Marche Lorraine*,' she was told.

'Ah yes, I quite understand,' she said, and looked very pointedly at her informant as she recalled the fact that Alsace-Lorraine had been taken from France by Germany some twenty years before.

Many stories are told of her removing her patronage from Menton to Cimiez. The real truth is that a royal commission of physicians was detailed to inspect the various resorts in the South of France with a view to finding the most salubrious spot for Her Majesty. After profound inquiries and innumerable statistics the commission decided that Cimiez was the place for her. One scandalous explanation of her forsaking Menton was that a high-ranking lady-in-waiting had fallen madly in love with a horse-tram-conductor and frequently spent the whole day going to and from Cannes on his tram. Finally, so the story goes, she died in childbirth and was buried privately in the cemetery at Menton with the inscription on her tombstone, 'Here lies the body of Lady . . . who died in disgrace.'

But nobody has ever found the grave.

As matriarch of European crowned heads – there cannot have been a single royal family on the Continent except the Habsburgs which was not intimately connected by marriage with one of her sons, daughters, nephews, nieces or grand-children – Queen Victoria's choice of the South of France in which to spend her declining winters set the seal of official approval on it for all royalty, quite apart from her immediate family, such as the Duke of Connaught, the Duke of Cambridge, the Princes and Princesses of Hesse, Gotha, Mecklenburg, Battenberg and Schleswig-Holstein.

It is notable that Edward VII, when he came to the throne, never once returned to the scene of his princely escapades on the Riviera. Travelling under the incognito of Duke of Lancaster, he chose Biarritz.

In 1887, the year that Gordon Bennett started the *Paris Herald Tribune*, Queen Victoria spent a holiday at the Villa Edelweiss at Cannes. While there she inflicted the famous snub on Prince Charles III of Monaco by driving over to Menton by way of Monaco. Prince Charles, learning of her impending visit, had given hurried instructions to the officer commanding his carabiniers to practise various ceremonial drills. The casino authorities sent a gigantic bouquet of flowers to the villa. Queen Victoria completely disdained the bouquet, returning it two days later to the casino, still in its original casket. Then she drove up to the Rock of Monaco but deliberately abstained from paying a state call on the Prince. It was the complete squelch, and Prince Charles never recovered from it.

Shortly after her departure from Cannes the celebrated earthquake took place early in the morning of Ash Wednesday. Dr. Ginner, the famous physician of Cannes, recalls it vividly. 'I was 11 years old at the time. At 6 a.m.,' he says, 'there was a violent tremor with a noise like thunder. It lasted a minute, to be followed by another. The third and final one took place at 8.30 a.m. Nobody was killed in Cannes, but several died in Nice, where the houses collapsed and no fewer than 300 were killed in the Church of Diana Marina at San Remo. The Prince of Wales was staying at the Hotel Estorel at Cannes and had intended to leave that afternoon. He stayed five days longer to allay any panic among the populace.' In Monte Carlo the superstitious thought that the earthquake was an act of God, as with Sodom and Gomorrah. Numbers of visitors were returning home after a fancy dress ball. The Place du Casino was crowded with terrified people. A French baroness, who announced hysterically during the tremors that if she were spared, she would devote the whole of her life to religious works, would never set foot in Monte Carlo again, and would give all her winnings to charity, was back at the Hotel de Paris within a week. When asked by a friend, who had not seen her since the earthquake, whether she had carried out her promises, she shrugged her shoulders and said, 'After all, it was such a tiny earthquake that I thought it would be quite enough to give half a dozen candles to the Virgin.'

Sir Arthur Sullivan once said that the most wonderful sight during the earthquake was that of a well-known lady, who had lost her wig, trying to climb up the monkey-puzzle tree in the Boulingrins.

CHAPTER 8

THE MAN WHO BROKE THE BANK

IN THE SAME YEAR the attempts to suppress the gambling monopoly of Monte Carlo were frustrated for all time by the official French Government pronouncement that 'the Principality of Monaco is absolutely independent and its independence is recognised'.

Now arrived Charles Deville Wells, the original of the famous song 'The Man Who Broke the Bank at Monte Carlo.' He was a common little man who claimed to have found an infallible system and there is no doubt that he turned his original capital of £400 into £40,000 in the course of three days. But this was the result primarily of luck, secondly, courage and, thirdly, his adaptation of the Martingale system.

He doubled up to the maximum and then left the money on three times running, if he won. Then he withdrew the £1,920 thus won and started again with a stake of £100. If, however, the roulette wheel was running against him, he kept his stakes down.

In three days he broke the bank several times. In other words, he won at least £3,500 on various occasions, which thus denuded the reserves at his particular roulette table and more gold coins had to be brought in boxes from the head office. While this was happening, the roulette table was covered with a huge black crape sheet, a brilliant publicity scheme originated by Benazet at Wiesbaden and copied by Blanc, first at Homburg and then at Monte Carlo. (Today the losing table is no longer put in mourning and, if there is any sign of the reserve being denuded, new boxes of plaques appear smartly. The casino has always £100,000 worth of plaques on the premises and a cash reserve of half a million pounds' worth of francs in the nearest bank a quarter of a mile away.)

Having played solidly for eleven hours a day for three days, Wells decided to give himself a break. On his way out, however, he threw some money on the *trente-et-quarante* table where his phenomenal luck continued, and within half an hour had won over £6,000, putting this table, too, into mourning. Everybody showed the greatest interest in this somewhat unpleasant little man, not only the casino authorities but also the inevitable hangers-on, always to be found in close proximity to a lucky gambler in Monte Carlo.

The month of July in those days was, of course, quite unfashionable. There was no summer season. Sun-bathing was unknown and the scarcity of visitors made Wells's winnings all the more spectacular. Camille Blanc smoothed his flowing moustache quite calmly. 'They always come back,' he said. Sure enough, Wells returned in November, just at the start of the main winter season, but had another astonishing run of luck, winning £10,000 in a very short time. Once again he left after three days and, cleverly enough, bought £2,500 worth of shares in the casino, feeling quite sure that other gamblers were not as smart as he was.

Back again in January at the height of the season, this time in a palatial yacht suitably dubbed the *Palais Royal*, he was accompanied by his mistress, Jean Burns, a former artist's model from Chelsea. This time he lost heavily. But instead of using his own money to recoup his losses, he sent a telegram to Miss Catherine Phillimore (sister of the famous judge) who promptly wired him funds.

Wells was a confidence trickster with thirty aliases, and the reason for his yacht was his story that he had invented a new type of fuel-saving device for coal-burning ships, which it was necessary to test under active conditions. His telegrams, never sent from Monte Carlo, always claimed that the apparatus had temporarily broken down and that he needed the extra money to get it working again. He described himself as an inventor and civil engineer, though the only invention ever traced to him was a musical skipping rope which sold quite well and might easily become a craze again.

Some of his rich victims, hearing of his success in Monte Carlo, began to grow suspicious. But when they asked him what on earth he was doing down there, he replied that he had an infallible system in which they were participants. This kept them quiet for some time. A year later, when his yacht was in the harbour at Havre, he was arrested by French police officers while trying to sell the coal out of the bunkers to a local merchant. The arrest followed an extradition order issued by the British Government and, less than a month later, he appeared at Bow Street on a charge of obtaining £29,800 by false pretences. At the Old Bailey he was sentenced to eight years' hard labour.

Jean Burns remained faithful to him. Now completely penniless, she became, in succession, a cook, a kennel maid, a governess and a lady's maid, ultimately becoming proprietress of the Terminus Tea Gardens at Uxbridge, which she promptly gave up to rejoin Wells when he came out of prison and went to Paris. At his trial, Wells's defence had been that he had lost all his money by taking out too many patents for inventions which had not come up to expectations.

What he had really done was to invest his Monte Carlo winnings and the money he had obtained by false pretences. So, though adjudged bankrupt while still in prison, with liabilities of £35,000, he was potentially a rich man.

On his release he soon got to work in Paris with a long-firm fraud based on lending money at one per cent per day. This time he used one of his many French aliases, and within a short space of time had sixty thousand clients from whom he obtained £80,000. Of this, on the usual long-firm principle, he had repaid £35,000 when he was once again arrested on a yacht, this time at Falmouth, and given another five years' imprisonment.

In 1919 it was discovered by the authorities that he was in a destitute state in Paris. He was therefore officially allowed 2,500 francs a year to keep on living, so that the French Government could obtain as much as possible from his annuities for the benefit of his victims. He ultimately died at the age of eighty-five. Needless to say, he had never been able to return to Monte Carlo, because a prison sentence at once debars anyone from the casino.

Another famous plunger was Jubilee Juggins (alias Ernest Benson) but he was a less successful one. He had taken £5,000 with him to Monte Carlo, lost it all, and had to borrow a five-pound note to come home. Another five-pound note figures pleasantly in the annals of the casino. An English gambler who wrote home for financial assistance received a five-pound note through the post, changed it at Ciro's in Monte Carlo, and won £10,000 before Ciro himself discovered that the five-pound note was a bogus one used by the late Augustus Harris at Drury Lane as a stunt for one of his spectacular productions.

In the meantime, the tune of 'The Man Who Broke the Bank at Monte Carlo', popularised by Charles Coborn, became a national favourite. It was hummed, whistled, sung and – the supreme compliment – played on the barrel organs of London. It swept two continents, doing Monte Carlo infinite good.

For the next twenty years, before the motor-car became

popular, the Riviera boomed and boomed. Crowned heads, grand dukes, the cream of the English aristocracy, millionaires from all over the world, and the most beautiful and expensive women frequented the gaming rooms in full evening dress, listening to the music of the world's finest singers, composers, violinists, pianists and 'cellists, and applauding the star artistes. If gossip columns had existed in those days they would have been devoted exclusively to the winter season from December to March.

The South of France was still a long way from the capitals of Europe, particularly St. Petersburg, in spite of the speeded-up train services from Paris and Rome. This meant that it was scarcely worth while for the wealthy to come for less than a month. There was no question in those days of motoring overnight from Paris, stopping three or four days and continuing the journey to Italy, particularly as casinos were still taboo everywhere else in Europe.

There were two routes from St. Petersburg to Cannes. The first involved taking the Nord Express at 6 p.m. from the Russian capital, arriving in Berlin at 8 p.m. the following evening. At 3 p.m. on the day after that, Paris was reached. The tired travellers reached Cannes at noon next day. The alternative route was to leave St. Petersburg at 6 p.m., say on the Tuesday, reaching Warsaw at 4 p.m. on Wednesday and Vienna at 7 a.m. on Thursday. The train steamed into Cannes by way of Venice at 3 p.m. on the Friday. Nobody went by motor-car before 1914 from Russia. A grand duke's staff was a minimum of ten people. It consisted of three personal servants, two aides-de-camp and one aide-de-camp general, one physician, one chef, four kitchen hands and the court's chamberlain.

The journey from England was much simpler. It was possible to reach the Riviera in thirty-three hours. However, the continuous jolting and lack of meals on the ordinary *Rapide* caused most travellers to break their journey at Paris, Lyons and Marseilles. The extra cost of a night's stop in an hotel in each of these three cities amounted to less than the price of a ticket on the *train de luxe*. Return fares on the *Rapide* were £13 2s. 6d., seventeen shillings less than the single fare on the *train de luxe* which left London at 3.15 p.m. and reached Cannes at 1.16 p.m. A sleeping berth car cost another £14. The top hotels charged sixteen shillings a day for bed and breakfast.

For people who drove along the Corniche from Cannes to Monte Carlo instead of taking the train, the main method of transport was a *berlin de voyage*, a kind of landau, with two high box seats, the back one equipped with a hood so that in case of rain nobody except the coachman could get wet. The coachman wore a glazed, sugar-loaf hat which looked as if it could smile at a trip-hammer, surmounted by a cockade like a red and blue cabbage, together with high boots, buckskin gloves, a red waistcoat, a tight, bright blue jacket covered with gold lace and exactly sixty gilt buttons. The landau was drawn by four horses, each with a fox's brush dangling at its ear to keep off the flies and a harness which jingled at every stride.

The first book written specifically for U.S. visitors was published in 1891, entitled *Monte Carlo and How to Do It*. It must have induced a number of Americans to try their luck on the Riviera. 'In the free and easy republic of nations which constitutes Monte Carlo,' wrote W. P. Goldberg and G. Chapman Pierce, 'it is not unpleasant to find oneself rubbing elbows with an English Cabinet Minister, to stand by and stake on the luck of a Russian prince, or to follow the fortunes of a great Berlin banker who thinks nothing of winning £12,000 in an afternoon, to be able to let one's friends know what the Prince of Wales wore in the way of tweeds and the exact cut of the corsage of the notorious Marquise. . . .'

Meantime, Prince Albert of Monaco had disassociated himself as far as possible from Monte Carlo. He had joined the French Navy in the Franco-German war, after which he bought a yacht at Torquay, calling her the *Hirondelle*. In her he sailed all over the world, indulging his passion for oceanography. Altogether he made twenty-four world trips, discovering one or two previously unknown types of octopus and ordering the construction of entirely new cables for deep sea work. When he came to the throne, he revived an ancient Grimaldi custom by inviting the head of every Monégasque family to his Court of Honour in the palace and asking them whether they were satisfied to have him as their prince. For a time he resided in the Principality, indulging his other passion, anthropology, and making a number of interesting discoveries of troglodyte caves in the neighbourhood. Later he returned to his first love – oceanography – and arranged for the first series of international marine conferences to be held at Monaco. His autobiography is well worth reading.

CHAPTER 9

SYSTEMS AND SUPERSTITIONS

BY THE TURN OF THE CENTURY, Europe had been at peace for an unusual number of years and the Boer War was too remote to affect the situation at Monte Carlo. England was rich; so were the United States. France had quickly recovered from the Prussian War indemnity and, with relatively low income tax, and no death duties, there were many wealthy people who had little or nothing to do except gamble. There were no night clubs, little dancing, golf or tennis, and no contract bridge.

The technique of gambling, particularly at roulette and *trente-et-quarante*, therefore became as popular a subject as gin rummy or canasta in the 1950's. Article after article appeared in the newspapers and magazines on the subject of system. Culbertson and Jacoby, if they had been alive, would have made a fortune by writing books about them. The whole situation between the casino and the gambler was discussed extensively. It was solemnly pointed out that the gambler had all the advantages of being able to play when he liked, stop when he liked, double up his stakes to the maximum, reduce them when he felt sure that his luck was out or had passed its zenith. The disadvantages of the gamblers were listed in an equally elementary way – the question of nerves, desire to win too much, mental fatigue, the effect of having lunched or dined too well beforehand, the bad advice from friends standing near by, the women who borrow from the gambler, the women whom the gambler wants to impress by his plunging. Oddly enough, no reference was made to the greatest disadvantage of all – 'No. 37', as the old stagers call the slot into which the chips are placed when given as a *pourboire* to the croupiers after a lucky win.

From the earliest days the casino had laid down a law that no individual croupier could be given a tip by a gambler and that the money had to be pooled for the benefit of the whole staff of croupiers. Hence the phrase, '*Merci, Monsieur, pour la personelle.*' This etiquette of giving a percentage of a big winning stake or even a small winning stake to the croupiers was soon exploited by the management. Most people imagine that the tips they give go direct to the croupiers. This is by no means the case. Until 1948, when the croupiers staged a sit-down strike, the management took fifty per cent of the tips. Even now the croupiers only get seventy per cent.

The advantages to the casino were also set down in somewhat portentous fashion. These, obviously enough, were zero at roulette and its equivalent at *trente-et-quarante*, the *refait*. At baccarat, the mathematical advantage in favour of the bank is 0·8 on the turnover if the banker plays well; if he plays badly his benefit is reduced to 0·6. The reason why there is any advantage is because the rules of the game compel a punter to draw on a four and forbid him to draw on a six. The banker is not restricted in any way. He can draw on a six or stand on a four or even on a three or two if he thinks it wise.

At *trente-et-quarante* the odds in favour of the bank are 1·45, and on individual numbers at roulette 3·26.

Having nothing better to do, various leading mathematicians compiled learned tomes on the laws of chance as related to gambling. Professor Earl Pearson wrote a series of articles in the *Fortnightly Review*, afterwards reprinted in book form. He made a scientific study of roulette on the spot and soon found

himself baffled by the divergence between the theoretical deviation of red and black over several thousand throws, and the
actual deviation which he recorded. The professor came to only
one conclusion which any gambler could have told him from
Dostoevsky onwards: the succession of red and black sets the
law of chance at defiance in the most persistent and remarkable
manner.

Now Sir Hiram Maxim appeared on the scene and devoted
the same careful study to roulette as he had to the manufacture
of his famous gun. He realised that most people find gambling
to be exciting and exhilarating and, although it may be expensive, they are quite willing to pay their money and have their
fun. Landowners in England spent thousands of pounds a year
in breeding partridges simply to shoot them – a sport with
absolutely no chance of gain. Roulette and *trente-et-quarante*, he
realised, were to many people just as exciting as shooting and
there was always the chance, however remote, of not only paying for one's holiday but even of taking away large sums in
cash. Of course it always was, and always will be, absurd to go
to Monte Carlo with the deliberate intention of making a
fortune. And in the late 'nineties and early 1900's there were
thousands of people with large incomes who went to Monte
Carlo every year, playing steadily for months at a time and
losing philosophically. When asked why they played per-
sistently year after year at systems which did not have the
slightest chance of beating the table, the reply was always the
same: 'I never bet more than I can afford to lose.'

By now the casino was making a steady annual profit of a
million pounds a year. This meant, said an official handbook
on the Principality, that the average gambling relations between the players and the bank were as sixty is to sixty-one. In
other words that the gamblers took sixty-one million pounds
to Monte Carlo every year, staked it, won back sixty million

pounds – and left one million pounds behind them on the tables.

After a very short study of the scene, Sir Hiram came to the conclusion that what really happened, if the latter figure of one million pounds was correct, was that the gamblers took about £1,100,000 with them to Monaco, of which the bank won ninety per cent. Taking the matter a step further and arguing from the plane of pure mathematics, Sir Hiram flatly denied that, because red had appeared, let us say, eight times in succession, it was increasingly certain that black was due to appear; indeed, that even if black had turned up twenty-one times running, it was just as likely to appear on the twenty-second occasion. He claimed in fact that each particular throw was governed by the physical conditions existing at that particular instant.

There have always been people who think that they can break the bank with some sort of system. One man arrived at the casino with a gigantic ledger and asked permission to spread it out in front of him at the roulette table. The authorities, who have no fear of systems and, indeed, show the greatest interest in them, told him regretfully that the ledger was so large that it would make it impossible for the usual number of gamblers to stake their wagers at the same table. This was indeed self-evident. They compromised, however, by giving him a special table to himself at the bar nearest to one of the roulette tables. The head of the syndicate thereupon spread out his ledger and, while keeping one accomplice at the roulette table to call out the numbers (as a result of which he made furious calculations), instructed the second accomplice to hurry over with chips to put on the number or numbers which he decided were most likely to win. This continued all summer without any loss to the casino.

Lord Beaverbrook in the pergola of his villa.

Sir Winston
Churchill's
painting of
Lord
Beaverbrook's
Villa
Cappocina.

Another system-man asked permission to bring a small adding machine with him to the tables. This took up so little room that he was granted immediate permission. But unfortunately his calculations were so complicated that he could not keep pace with the numbers as announced after each roll of the ball. He therefore packed up and waited until the summer, when the croupiers roll the ball more slowly in keeping with the lazy atmosphere of August. He too failed to break the bank.

It must be noted that the croupiers take a sympathetic interest in every new system. They frequently take their day off to go to the nearest casino with roulette outside Monte Carlo – San Remo or Nice – to gamble themselves. It might be thought that years of experience of raking in the customers' money would have taught them that the percentage is always in favour of the house. But no. Hope springs eternal in their dinner-jacketed breasts.

The first real travel book about the Riviera had been written in 1896 by Augustus Hare, who constituted himself a sort of one man Baedeker. He was exceedingly critical of most of the pleasure resorts in the South of France. He approved of St. Maxime for people who did not require golf or gaiety. He dismissed St. Raphael as a beautiless and uninteresting little place. As for Cannes, he referred bitterly to the hills covered with hideous villas chiefly built by rich Englishmen 'whose main object seems to be the effacement of all the natural beauties of the place, to sow grass which can never live, to import from the North shrubs which cannot grow and to cut down and root up all the original woods and flowers. The old town is probably more full of evil smells than any other in France.'

Apart from the Villa Nevada in which the Duke of Albany had been living before his sudden death, he described most of the villas as pretentious white palaces, utterly without beauty.

He dismissed Nice as a great ugly modern town with a glaring esplanade along the sea, adding that the hotels charged the equivalent of £3 a night during the Carnival and up to £5 for a window on the route. As for Cimiez and its huge and hideous caravanserais, the Grand Hotel (twice occupied by Queen Victoria) had its view and sunshine completely spoilt by the erection of the frightful Hotel Regina.

In this connection, the Aga Khan recalls that his daily bill at the Grand was about 200 gold francs. True he was attended by his two valets, but he was living *en pension*. According to the Aga, the cost of living in the 'nineties was six times as high as it is today. In contrast to other observers, the Aga reached the strange conclusion that Queen Victoria's servants, in spite of their height and uniform, were distinctly second class, 'very different from and very inferior to the admirably trustworthy and very high-grade men whom, through the years of British rule in India, one would encounter at Viceroy Lodge or the Government House in any of the Provinces.'

In those days the cramped, primitive sleeping-car bore no relation to the very splendid luxury of the modern *wagon-lit*. The Russian grand dukes and Austrian archdukes, on the way to their villas and palaces, always had their private coaches, if not private trains. But what the Aga chiefly recalls half a century later is the solid wealth on display in jewellers' shops. 'There were none of your present-day bits and pieces of gold and silver and worthless stones made up into trumpery trinkets,' he says. 'No – this was real jewellery – great sparkling diamonds, pearls, rubies, emeralds and sapphires winking and gleaming in the bright winter sun for the eyes of the wealthiest people in Europe, whether they were financiers or landowners from England or Russian grand dukes.'

Augustus Hare, by the by, could not fail to admire Monte Carlo, though he described the gardens as being meretricious in taste and quoted an English writer as saying, 'Never anywhere was snare more plainly set in the sight of any bird. There is little in the way of amusement that you do not get for nothing here, a beautiful pleasure-ground, reading rooms as luxurious and well-supplied as those of a West End club, one of the best orchestras in Europe, and all without cost of a farthing. But the very lavishness arouses suspicion in the minds of the wary. "*Faites le jeu, Messieurs; Messieurs, faites le jeu*" is heard from noon to midnight, and the faster people ruin themselves, and send a pistol-shot through their heads, the faster others take their place.'

Hare also quoted the English historian J. R. Green as having said that the Prince of Monaco was the ruler of a few streets and 2,000 subjects, adding, 'his army rose to the gigantic force of four and twenty men, but then, as we were gravely told by an official, "it had been doubled in consequence of the war." Idler and absentee as he is, the Prince is faithful to the traditions of his House; the merchant sails without dread but a new pirate town has risen on the shores of its bay, it is the pillage of a host of gamblers that maintains the heroic army of Monaco, that cleanses its streets and fills the Exchequer of its Lord.'

Menton also received castigation from Augustus Hare. 'Once a picturesque fishing town,' he described its two lovely bays as being 'filled with hideous and stuccoed villas in the worst taste.' Artistically, in his opinion, Menton was vulgarised and ruined in spite of the deliciousness of its dry, sunny climate and its delicate flowers and trees.

Cocottes in those days had manners as beautiful as their faces and curvaceous contours, and never embarrassed their protectors by trying to meet the latter's families. Their behaviour at the gaming tables was exquisite. They never created scenes. They wore the most superb jewellery but never crossed the dividing line between the *monde* and the *demi-monde*. (Today, with modern make-up, it is often difficult to distinguish between the lady and the lady of joy, and in any event not much attempt is made to separate them socially.) Nor did they bother about banting, or flinch from the gargantuan meals of those days.

Young brides like the Duchess of Marlborough were much perplexed by the sudden realisation that there were two worlds – those of the *monde* and the *demi-monde*. At her first dinner party at the Hotel de Paris, she noted a number of her husband's friends dining at separate tables with beautiful women. When she asked who they were, the Duke was highly evasive and startled her by telling her that she must not even look at them. It took some interrogation to discover from him that, in fact, they were *cocottes*. What was still more complicated was the Duke's instructions to his young bride that she must also ignore the men, even if she knew them well, so long as they were in the company of the aforesaid ladies of joy. These beauties, and they were real beauties, were witty and cultured but, according to Victorian and Edwardian etiquette, could never mingle with women of rank.

Many stories are told of the rivalry between the leading beauties and particularly between two of them. The former Duchess of Marlborough claims that it was Liane de Pougy who took her revenge on La Belle Otero, still alive in Nice in 1956. The same story has been told with many variations about several other beautiful women of the day. The theme song remains the same – that La Belle Otero arrived at the casino one night covered with jewels. The following night, Liane de Pougy appeared in a simple white gown without a jewel, but followed by her personal maid wearing even more valuable

gems than Otero's. There is a variation even on this story –
that Liane de Pougy went into the casino followed by her
poodle wearing a coat covered with precious stones. This
sounds improbable because dogs were not allowed in the
gaming rooms. However, there are still elderly Edwardians
who claim to have seen this phenomenon with their own eyes.
One thing is certain: it was bad luck on women of good breeding and social standing to be forbidden to wear cosmetics,
whereas the *cocottes* did so with huge success. No well-bred
woman was allowed to look seductive in public. Anything
more than a touch of powder and the slightest use of lipstick
would have caused them to lose caste.

By this time American millionaires had been visiting Monte
Carlo for some years – among them Charles M. Schwab,
president of Carnegie Steel, and Pierpont Morgan, whose
nose was so cruelly caricatured by Sem, and who refused to
gamble when he was told that the maximum stake was only
£480.

1898 was an exceedingly important date in the history of the
casino. The original concession granted to François Blanc was
up and a new agreement had to be reached with Prince Albert,
who was fully aware of the vast profits being made from the
gaming tables. After protracted negotiations, the concession
was prolonged for fifty years to 1948, in return for which the
casino had to pay £400,000 cash on the nail, £200,000 on
improving the harbour for yachts and extending the tunnel
near the rock so that trains could go close to the wharves. (The
reason for this was that a tentative arrangement had been made
between the Principality and Switzerland whereby Monaco
Harbour would form an outlet for Swiss imports and exports.)
Another £24,000 had to be paid by the casino for the annual
operatic season of twenty-four performances. In other words,

each performance was subsidised to the tune of £1,000. The casino had also to take the responsibility for building new roads and keeping them up, and to agree to pay another £600,000 in 1913. Finally, the casino had to pay Prince Albert £50,000 a year plus eight per cent of the gross takings after the first million. This came to another £80,000. No wonder that he could continue to afford his costly oceanographic cruises.

Camille Blanc was the first to encourage the publication of every sort of infallible handbook on gambling which cost anything from sixpence to £24, and every week the statistics of each roulette table in the casino were on sale for the systemisers.

In those days there was little to divert the visitor from the gaming tables except the theatre-cum-opera house. Even this was in the casino and lengthy intervals between acts gave the audiences every chance of hurriedly losing money before returning to their stalls.

The tennis courts in those days were on the site of the present annexe to the Hotel de Paris. When the annexe was built the courts were moved to the roof of the Auto Riviera Garage. There were five hard courts, and the players silhouetted against the sky made an agreeable spectacle for the groundlings. Soon the entries became so numerous that further courts on the Condamine had to be laid out. These still exist and are used by the local shopkeepers.

The first women champions of Monte Carlo were Mrs. Hillyard, Countess Schulenburg, Miss Lowther, Mlle. de Robiglio, Miss Douglas and Miss Eastlake – who won three years in succession. In those days, indeed for many years, the lawn tennis players were wealthy gentlefolk. There was no question of having to bribe them to lend lustre to the tennis championships at Christmas and Easter. They stayed in their own villas or those of friends, or paid their hotel bill like anybody else. Doubtless Camille Blanc would have done what his successors were compelled to do if necessary – not only pay the fares of all the leading contestants but also put them up free at the major luxury hotels and, furthermore, give them a considerable amount of pocket money, allegedly for drinks and cigarettes. There were no sham amateurs in the golden days of Monte Carlo.

In the following year, he once again showed his prescience by inaugurating the first *Concours d'Élégance* which, like the Monte Carlo Rally and the Round-the-Houses Grand Prix Race, has been imitated all over the world. Those early motor-cars were exhibited in the morning from 9 a.m. to 2 p.m. on the terrace below the casino where they were examined by a jury. At 3 p.m. they went in procession round the gardens facing the casino, before drawing up in front of the grand-stand where the prizes were awarded. After this they circulated round the gardens again and further prizes were given for the most elegantly dressed woman in each car. From the start, the policy was never to give second prizes or third prizes. Everybody was awarded a first prize. It was either a *Prix d'Honneur* or a *Grand Prix d'Honneur* or *Premier Prix*, with a *Grand Prix d'Honneur* as the chief award. The theory was that nothing could ever be second-class or third-class in the Principality and that everybody who took the trouble to show a motor-car or to wear specially smart clothes for the occasion could go home and say that he or she had won first prize. The programme not only gave the names of the women, but also the names of their dressmakers and the names of their milliners.

It did not matter how many motor-cars were shown. There was that exact number of first prizes, and some excuse was always forthcoming for each vehicle to be placed in a category of its own so that it had to be given an award.

To ensure that the spectators were not enveloped in clouds of dust, Camille Blanc sponsored an Italian expert, Dr. Gugliemeneti, in his efforts to find a tarred road surface which would eliminate dust. It was at Monte Carlo that the first tarred road surface, therefore, was shown to the world.

A carefully preserved photographic album of the period shows the Grand Duke Serge of Russia, with the bearded Grand Duke of Luxembourg (both wearing homburg hats); the bearded King of Württemberg; the Duchess of Roxburgh and the Duchess of Marlborough, wearing huge hats and long feather boas, like my Ladies Ingram and Deerhurst; the curvaceous Belle Otero, wearing a short-sleeved black dress setting off five rows of superb pearls; the Aga Khan as a young man with a curly black moustache, straw hat and spats; that dashing young man, Lord Victor Paget, wearing a white panama; Sir Hugo de Bathe in his yachting cap; the bearded Prince Hohenlohe; Paderewski, also wearing a white panama surmounting his fluffy hair, and a huge check overcoat; Gordon Bennett and Sir Walter Ingram in bowler hat; Lily Langtry in a veil; the bearded, brisk Grand Duke Nicholas; Lloyd George in early middle age, wearing a soft grey hat; Lord Farquhar in a panama; W. K. Vanderbilt in a black stetson; Harry Vardon, bare-headed, but playing golf in tight knee breeches (before the days of plus-fours); A. J. Balfour, button-holed as usual, in a black homburg hat with Lord Wolverton; the Duke of Montrose, wearing a sombre black overcoat; Prince Kotchoubey, with his pet dachshund; Prince Radziwill, studying his polo pony; the Rajah of Pudukota in a straw hat; Lord Mar with his long white beard; the King of Sweden in early middle age; the black-bearded Duke of Norfolk; Lord Cecil Manners, reading a book as he took his constitutional; the Prince of Servia in a bowler hat; Washington Singer as a young man, wearing a stiff white collar; Lord

Nunburnholme admiring a Pekinese; the beauteous Mademoiselle de Hidalgo hurrying to a rendezvous outside the Hotel de Paris; the Prince and Princess of Braganza (she in white, as the illustrateds would say); the Grand Duke Boris in a black velvet hat; Anthony Drexel with his up-curved white moustaches; Harold Harmsworth, later the first Lord Rothermere, striding along the pavement; the white-bearded Prince of Saxe-Meiningen with his favourite collie; Prince Mirza Riza Kahn of Persia wearing a fez; Saint-Saëns himself, bearded and taking notes; the bowler-hatted Prince Albert of Monaco, with two equerries in attendance; Francis de Croisset, very debonair, with snap-brim hat; Henry Bernstein, wearing a straw hat; the Princess of Pless in white ermine; the Duchess of Sutherland in black velvet; the heavily bearded Prince of Denmark; Noilly Prat himself, small moustached, heavily overcoated; Massenet, wearing a tall black hat and a straggly moustache; Lord Waleran, bald and military-looking; Sir Theodore Brinckman, wearing a check cap and sitting on a shooting stick; the late Duke of Marlborough as a young man; Danny Maher, surrounded by admirers; Bradley Martin, carrying an umbrella; Tod Sloan, also accompanied by admirers; Madame Edwina in a huge hat; the late Earl of Rosslyn, wearing a check cap; and Gaby Deslys in a jewelled head-dress covered with pearls and accompanied by an anxious-looking, elderly beau.

Now came the first serious blow which Monte Carlo had sustained since François Blanc took over the management of the gambling monopoly. This was the French Government's decision to legalise *chemin de fer* for the first time since 1837. Roulette and *trente-et-quarante* were still forbidden, but permission to play *chemin de fer* in public in France led to the erection of casinos at various watering places such as Cannes and Nice, the first real rivals with whom Monte Carlo had to compete since the abolition of the gaming establishment at Saxon-les-Bains nearly a generation earlier.

Official French Government permission for *chemin de fer* took the country by surprise. At Cannes the first gaming rooms were inaugurated in part of the Hotel Gallia, managed by a German named, strangely enough, Smart. There were only four tables. The inaugural gala dinner, which included caviare and *foie gras*, cost 7 francs 50 centimes, the equivalent of six shillings today.

The superstition of gamblers was always extraordinary and continues to be so. The number of the cloak-room ticket, of the bedroom, of the table, the date of the month, the day of the week, the age of a child or grandchild, are only a few of the reasons why people back certain numbers. It is, incidentally, an old superstition that anybody who enters the casino for the first time and who is under the age of thirty-six should back his or her age at the nearest table on entry.

Some gamblers in Edwardian times actually employed pretty girls as mascots who charged them twenty-five per cent of their winnings for bringing them luck. So superstitious were they that the girls were not only forbidden to flirt with them but they themselves took care not to catch their eye while playing. One Alsatian beauty was reputed to have earned £3,000 during a single week in this way.

'Playing the corpse', another superstition, consisted of playing a number which had not appeared for some time, though backed by another gambler who had at last abandoned it and the table. As for the knee of the horse of the bronze equestrian statue of Louis XIV in the main entrance of the Hotel de Paris, it was touched by so many gamblers to bring them luck that it looked quite shiny. In 1950 M. Detraz, who had come from Vichy to take over the control of the casino's various hotels, had black paint put on the knee joint of the horse, not know-ing the superstition. He was quickly told, and the paint was scraped off again.

One gambler produced a match-box painted half red and half black. In it was a spider. When the spider emerged from the red side, the gambler backed red. When it emerged from the black side, he backed black. Astonishingly enough, he won.

Coral, locks of hair, skins of venomous snakes, silver images blessed by the Pope, hangman's rope, eagles' claws, rabbits' feet, imitation black cats, toy dogs, cigarette cases, even the withered heart of a bat have been used by people anxious to bring themselves luck. One rich woman used to wipe her cards with a special handkerchief before looking at them on the assumption, presumably, that this could alter the spots. Other gamblers put a spoonful of salt in the pockets of their dinner jackets to induce cards. With so many superstitions flowering in all directions it was evident to confidence tricksters that gamblers were the most gullible people whom it was their good fortune to meet.

The earliest confidence tricksters used to make the acquaint-ance of wealthy gamblers in the bar of the casino or of their hotel and confide to them that they had a particular croupier working in association with them. There was, for example, one particular croupier who used to take snuff. He was fre-quently used, quite unconsciously, by confidence tricksters who informed their victims that he could roll red or black as he liked and that he always rolled red (or black) directly after taking a pinch of snuff. The victim was advised not to stake any bet until the croupier had taken his pinch of snuff, which he did every half hour or so. In return for this invaluable information, the confidence trickster would demand a fifty per cent cut of the successful stake.

The idea was completely sound. If the croupier produced the wrong colour, the confidence trickster would tell the victim that the croupier realised he was being watched by the *Chef des Jeux* and had therefore had to roll the wrong colour, and they must wait until the next time he took the pinch of snuff. If, of course, the designated colour came up, the confidence trickster quickly pocketed his half share of the stakes and disappeared. If at the second time of asking, the croupier once again produced the wrong colour the confidence trickster disappeared – unless he thought that his victim was so gullible that he or she would try a third time.

Then, as now, November was the month preceding the build-up of notabilities coming to the South of France for the winter season, which reached its climax in February. *Le Petit Monégasque*, the journal published by François Blanc, was hard put to it to provide celebrated names before December, at the earliest. Having noted the arrival of Mr. Van Den Witten, president of the San Francisco Engineering College, the editor announced a new sartorial law about the Opera House. Women were instructed that they were to remove their hats if they sat in the first five rows of the stalls or the first two rows of the dress circle. It was added that a specially designed cloak-room had been installed.

For the first gala of the season, the only notabilities worthy of mention were the Governor-General of Monaco, the Abbot of the Island of Lerins and the Prefect of the Alpes Maritimes. Soon, however, the editor was gratified to be able to announce that the Prince Bariatinski had arrived in Cannes, whilst Lord Egerton and his wife, 'The Duchess of Buckingham', had arrived from London. It was regretfully announced that the Grand Duke Alexis had just died in Paris. The Grand Duke Alexis was the first royalty ever to visit the United States. That was in the 1870's. The rigours of the Atlantic caused the

Mayor of New York to wait nearly two weeks until the grand ducal frigate arrived.

Prince Hohenlohe Landenburg's arrival was duly noted, as was the return of Prince Albert of Monaco from a chamois shooting expedition with Duke Charles Theodore in Bavaria. Saint-Saëns, the composer, arrived next day from Paris for the first presentation of his *La Foi*. It was also announced that the Baron Bassien was in charge of pigeon shooting. Other arrivals were the Countess de Scholenbourg, by the de-luxe train from St. Petersburg, Princess Gargarine Nourdza who was flagged in at Cannes and Prince Zelle at Nice.

Cannes had also attracted Prince Louis of Orleans and Braganza, as well as Princess Pia de Bourbon. Joseph Chamberlain was due from London after Christmas. Menton had attracted Lord and Lady Wolseley and Prince and Princess Wolkowski. As usual, the King of Sweden was at Nice, where lawn tennis competitions had been inaugurated. In this event the handicaps of the various players were unknown until after the event was concluded.

The Horse Show and Show Jumping at Cap Martin were given headlines, as were the arrival of the Grand Duke Michael of Russia at Cannes and Princess Charlotte of Russia at Nice. The Duke of Cumberland and Lord Wodehouse were nominated on 1st December as organisers of the polo season, due to begin on 16th January. On the same day, an editorial article complained that the financial crisis in the U.S. in the previous two years had deprived the Riviera of its wealthy American guests, but added that the election of Mr. Taft was an augury for the best, especially as all the liners for Europe were booked until the end of January.

The sixtieth anniversary of the Emperor Franz Joseph of Austria was announced on 4th December, together with details of the local celebrations. At Nice, Princess Jourienski, the morganatic wife of Alexander II, arrived at her villa and a Mrs. Campbell-Hobson announced that she would be 'At Home' on every Wednesday from 3 p.m. to 6 p.m. during the season. Menton recorded the visit of Dimitri de Gerbertson, the Chamberlain of the Russian Emperor, and M. D'Alexeiff, the Grand Master of the Tsar's court. Horse racing and golf competitions at Nice formed other items of local interest, together with an advance announcement about the first Battle of Flowers at Monte Carlo, where the international conference on police dogs preceded the first *Concours d'Élégance*. The chief contestants were Renaults, Lorraine-Dietrichs, Mercedes and Delaunay-Bellevilles. Regattas for yachts and speed boats were also described in detail, together with the international fencing competitions.

In those days the best hotel clients were English though they formed only twenty per cent of the guests, sixty per cent being German-speaking Austrians, Hungarians and Germans. Five per cent were Americans and the rest were made up of different nationalities like French and Japanese. Hohenlohes, Hapsburgs, Radziwills stayed at the Metropole Hotel. Edward VII, as Prince of Wales, used to occupy one of the little villas at the back, now occupied by Admiral Nares. One of the richest women in the United States, Mrs. Penfield, wife of the American Ambassador to Rome, took the whole wing of the second floor, brought her own pianist and her own gigolo. Aged seventy, she took dancing lessons every day. She seldom had fewer than sixteen guests at lunch or dinner, and chicken wings were only just good enough for her Maltese terrier. Every Sunday she went on a drive to the local mountains and gave her money to the poor people from her motor-car. At her death she left everything to Catholic churches in the United States.

Another guest was Elizabeth Miller, white-haired and short,

fat as a barrel; at the age of fifty-five she fell madly in love with Sir William Orpen. The only way she could persuade the great English painter to do her portrait was to give him her Rolls-Royce. Miss Miller owned her own private lion. Deciding after a time that it was lonesome, she bought it a mate. The lion and the lioness were parked in the Villa Pergola at Roquebrune. Deciding that the local milk was not sufficiently full of proteins for them, she sent for a cow all the way from Jersey. This arrived by a separate lorry, and also lived at the Villa Pergola.

Sir Walter de Frece, husband of the immortal Vesta Tilley, and Berry Wall, also stayed at the Metropole. They invariably drank a magnum of Cliquot in the restaurant. Sir Walter founded the M.C. Club. Most people thought these initials stood for the Monte Carlo Club. In fact they stood for the Much Champagne Club.

CHAPTER 10

GOLF, MOTORING AND FLYING

By 1910 Monte Carlo and Cannes were the hub of the fashionable world from December to March. The shares of the *S.B.M.* boomed. Net profits were over a million pounds. Camille Blanc continued his lavish expenditure, realising that it always costs money to make money. The first of the beauty queen contests took place, together with dog shows, the most beautiful parasol competitions, bicycle races and a £1,500 prize-fight between the French champion and Jim Sullivan on the Condamine tennis courts.

Battles of Flowers, both on land and sea, were inaugurated, sailing regattas encouraged and no less than £4,000 in prizes given for motor-boat races when motor-boats were still in their infancy.

Suddenly this modern Garden of Eden was invaded by the serpent of revolution. The patience of the Monégasque inhabitants had become exhausted. They were tired of more and more foreigners being given jobs at the casino and wanted to have some say and share in the finances of the Principality. The Hereditary Prince was (in a technical sense) a complete tyrant and certain agitators wanted to ensure that there should be a proper budget in case the casino were abolished or the Grimaldis left the country.

News of the impending demonstrations and, in fact, of the proposed revolution, leaked out. British sailors, at the request of the Prince, were given leave from Villefranche and instructed to converge on Monte Carlo. They were told to watch the flagstaff of the Hotel de Paris, which had ostensibly laid in a new stock of wine. If a flag were hoisted they were to hurry into the hotel, open the so-called wine cases which were full of rifles and ammunition and take up strategic points to 'protect British property'. French troops were also to be on the alert.

As it happened, the hostile demonstration in front of the palace fizzled out; though many of the agitators carried revolvers in their pockets, they did not fire them. The Prince was sufficiently frightened, however, as to grant a new constitution. This consisted of seven chapters and fifty-eight articles. The Prince maintained his supreme sovereignty, but a national domain distinct from the Prince's private domain was created. The Governor-General was superseded by a Minister of State and a cabinet of three; Monégasques were granted free speech and freedom *not* to observe religious fête days, and a national council of twenty-one members was appointed with permission to meet twice a year and powers to demand that the Prince should promulgate any new law which they wanted. They were also able to discuss and criticise the health services and public works. In reality this amounted to very little because the Prince had power to dissolve the national council whenever he liked. At least, however, he was made aware of the fact that his subjects had a will of their own. Up to date he had given £560,000 for scientific research of an international character, but little or nothing to his own subjects, and there was no doubt that public opinion had been stirred by the opening of the Oceanographic Museum at a vast cost earlier in the year.

The year 1910 was notable for a special check on the visitors to the casino. Until then it had been impossible to discover the actual numbers of gamblers as opposed to the number of attendances in the casino. It was now found that the casino was being visited by 150,950 different gamblers in a single year. A simple sum of arithmetic further proved that the average loss in the casino per gambler was £8 per head (the gross receipts having been well over one million pounds). This was, incidentally, the average income tax paid in Great Britain at the time. Another cross-check resulted in the discovery that on any one given day during the winter season there were 5,767 people inside the casino, compared with only 930 in August.

Camille Blanc, brilliant impresario though he was, never made any attempt to create a summer season. It was generally regarded as far too hot for smart society who spent their June and July in Paris or London and their August on the Scottish moors, Ostend, Biarritz or the newly-created fashion resort of Deauville. And it was a sad sight in summer to see the croupiers with their rakes up in the air as distress signals to indicate that there were no gamblers at their tables. However, he induced Rougier, one of the earliest French aviators, to fly his Voisin biplane over the *Tête de Chien*, six hundred feet high and even over the sea. This was the first aeroplane flight ever made over the Mediterranean. He also persuaded Santos Dumont to attempt a flight in his dirigible for which a shelter was erected facing the Condamine. This did not prove a success. The dirigible sank gently into the harbour.

Conscious too of the growth of the motor-car industry and motoring as a pastime for the rich, he inaugurated the first Monte Carlo Rally. The origin of his idea was caused by a bet struck some years previously about the ability of a very early type of motor-car to reach Monte Carlo from Paris under its own steam. It looked like a dog-cart without shafts and the engine was started with a string wound round the fly-wheel. It had to be pushed up every hill from Paris and the whole mechanism had to be rebuilt again and again.

By 1910 the uncouth and smelly contraption of the early days had given place to a more reliable machine capable of accomplishing long journeys. But, generally speaking, cars were comfortless, roads extremely bad and travel from one country to another hedged by difficulties. The best way to overcome this, thought Blanc, was to attract public attention by means of an international competition.

The task was entrusted to the local club, the *Sport Vélocipédique et Automobile de Monaco*, and the Rally came into being in January 1911. Starting points were Paris, Boulogne-sur-Mer, Brussels, Berlin, Vienna and Geneva, and the distance to Monte Carlo had to be covered at an average speed of ten kilometres per hour (6·2 miles per hour). Twenty-three competitors started.

Little did Camille Blanc realise how this scheme for Monaco was to alter the whole concept of comfort in motoring. Most of the developments and improvements of the modern motor-car have been directly due to the influence of the Rally. Anti-skid devices, de-frosters, fog lamps, car heaters and better springing are only a few of the devices invented by motor manufacturers to improve their entry's chance in the race.

In one of the earlier rallies a French firm designed a special seat which held the driver so firmly in place that he did not have to worry about taking the strain of turning corners and could concentrate solely on driving. His performance was improved so much by this simple idea that he won the rally. Feats accomplished by these pioneers stimulated world-wide interest in motor-cars as a means of long-distance driving – rivalling the railway train – instead of being a rich man's plaything for a noisy, ostentatious journey of thirty or forty miles. The winner in 1911 was Henri Rougier, who started from Paris. His motor-car was a twenty-five horsepower Turcat-Méry, and he covered the distance of five hundred and seventy miles in twenty-eight hours, ten minutes. His motor-car was quite a novelty because it was completely closed. Nearly all the others were open tourers. He won a cash prize of £400, together with two cups and a bronze statuette.

Monte Carlo at this time was full of Daimlers, Rolls-Royces, Austins, Napiers, Wolseleys and Argylls owned by Englishmen and driven by white-capped chauffeurs. American motorists were represented by Packards, Loziers, Pierces and Wintons. It was noticeable that whereas the French, British and Monte Carlo motor-cars had number plates, the Americans had none. Germans, who were in great evidence at Monte Carlo between 1910 and 1914, drove around in large white Prince Henrys, usually with an Alsatian alongside. The Italians sported open tourers in many colours. Most French motor-cars were painted blue; the drivers dashing round corners on two wheels, relying on the klaxon, brakes and quick wits to avoid collisions, just like today. To add to the gaiety, Camille Blanc organised another Motor-Boat Grand Prix in which the Duke of Westminster's *Ursula* had a great success.

Camille Blanc's attention had in the meantime been directed to the growing popularity of golf. At that time there were, apart from the one at Mandelieu, only two courses on the Continent (at Pau and Paris), and there were not much more than four or five dozen clubs in the whole of the south of England. Arthur Balfour, however, had become an apostle of golf, and during one of his visits to Monte Carlo managed to interest Blanc in it. In his search to attract still more English visitors, Blanc looked round the rugged but beautiful neighbourhood of Monte Carlo to find a suitable site, called in a series of experts, and was informed that the only possible place was up the rocky mountain behind the casino near La Turbie. It was a very steep climb, barely negotiable by the motor-cars of that day. The countryside was dotted with vast rocks, thick scrub and the most wiry brambles. The cost would evidently be immense. Many tons of earth would have to be imported. Grass capable of surviving the heat of summer would have to be sown on the site of the prospective greens. A club-house would have to be built. The local peasant children would have to be taught the gentle art of caddying. Above all, the huge rocks dotted all over the terrain would have to be blasted away and removed by hand. The gross receipts of the casino that year, however, were nearly one and three quarter million pounds and Blanc decided to go ahead.

There are various estimates of the initial cost – from £60,000 to a quarter of a million. The true figure lies somewhere between these two extremes. When it was finally completed in 1912, Blanc, following his usual custom of attracting celebrities, invited the leading Scottish and English professionals to inaugurate it. These were headed by Andrew Kirkaldy, Willie Park, who had designed the course, and Harry Vardon.

The Mont Agel course, lying immediately below the great fortress (used by the Germans as a radar station in World War II), was perhaps Camille Blanc's greatest extravagance. It never paid its way. It never could, in spite of the many silver cups and other prizes presented to visitors and residents alike. Thirty-five years later it was entirely renovated by Henry Cotton, who was able to find a type of real grass, in place of onion grass, capable of surviving the scorching days of the Riviera summer.

In 1912, however, the drive to the course was more exciting than the drive off the first tee, and the journey back along the precipitous zig-zag route, was even more dangerous owing to the unreliable brakes of the day.

Most people have forgotten that the first Schneider Trophy

Race took place at Monte Carlo – in 1913. It was flown over twenty-eight laps of a ten-kilometre course and won by Prévost, who covered the distance in two hours, fifty minutes and forty-seven seconds. Of the other chief competitors, Garros failed to get his Moraine off the water and Weymann (the American) was flying at sixty-eight miles per hour when his oil pipe broke. From a sporting point of view this first Schneider Trophy Race was a complete failure, but it provided invaluable data for the world's aircraft designers in the forthcoming European war.

In spite of the fiasco, Camille Blanc inaugurated a flying rally in the following year. Various competitors started from different parts of Europe, but Roland Garros swept the board. He won the first prize of £1,200 by flying from Monaco to Paris in twelve hours, fourteen minutes; the second prize of £400 by flying from Brussels to Monaco in twelve hours, seventeen minutes; and the seventh prize by flying from Brussels to Monaco in two hundred and forty-five hours. The third prize of £400 was won by a pilot who flew from Madrid to Monaco in sixteen hours, while the fourth prize, another £400, went to a pilot who flew from Paris to Monaco in fifty-three hours. Two other competitors took anything from sixty-three hours to two hundred and thirty-four hours to reach the principality from the French capital. It can well be understood that the headquarters of the International Sporting Club which arranged the Rally received a crop of telegrams about false starts, returns, failures and crashes.

This was followed by the second Schneider Trophy, the contestants for which were three French pilots, two Americans, one Swiss and two English. The Swiss, M. Burri, had flown for Bulgaria in the Balkan war and was therefore one of the earliest, if not the earliest, of all war pilots. His aircraft, a Franco–British Aviation biplane with a one-hundred horsepower Gnome engine, had a trick of bouncing like a football as it half rose from the water or landed on it, the spar under the hull just lifting clear and then touching down again several times before deciding to fly properly. Of the two English competitors, Lord Carberry gave up; but the other, Howard Pixton, flying a Sopwith Float Seaplane with a one-hundred horsepower engine, won easily, lapping with the regularity of a cheap alarm clock although one of his nine cylinders cut out after one-third of the distance. His maximum speed was 92·1 m.p.h., a world record, and he completed the one hundred and seventy-two miles in two hours, thirteen seconds. After the race he was taken into the sacred enclosure of the Grand Tribune and offered a variety of champagnes. 'Mine's a Bass,' was all he said. That night Prince Albert was present at a banquet in the Hotel de Paris where the prizes were given.

Shortly afterwards he celebrated the twenty-fifth year of his reign.

War was now clearly imminent. It was said that the German visitors to Monte Carlo were never in their usual haunts when the local French manoeuvres were taking place. Italian officers had disguised themselves as workmen in order to pry out the secrets of the fortress of Mont Agel, and if one is to believe Paul de Ketchiva, the ex-croupier who wrote his memoirs, Monte Carlo was full of German generals and Italian royalty. In the meantime the Exotic Gardens were begun and the rarest cacti imported. During the War of Nerves between France and Germany in 1909 Prince Albert had frequently acted as a go-between. There were several occasions when neither side wished to lose face but were perfectly ready to accept a compromise, and he was largely instrumental in preventing war breaking out over the question of Morocco.

On 4th August 1914 he was on one of his oceanographic

cruises, but hurriedly returned to Monaco, released all the officers and men of French nationality who were recalled to the Colours, proclaimed Monaco's neutrality and, taking no chances, remained on his yacht in the harbour instead of taking up residence at the palace. This proclamation of neutrality was not particularly popular with the French under whose protection he was officially sheltering. However, he showed no objection to hospitals and convalescent homes being established in the Principality for officers and men of the Allies, while Prince Louis, his son and heir, who was an honorary captain in the Chasseurs d'Afrique, became a staff major in the 5th Army.

CHAPTER II

LLOYD GEORGE, G.B.S.

AND LES GIRLS

AFTER WORLD WAR I the social atmosphere of the South of France altered completely. No more grand dukes, no more Baltic barons, no more German princelings, no more Austrian archdukes. The Russian Revolution and the inflation of the mark put them out of business. Privacy disappeared for the remainder of the pre-war colony. No longer did the visitors confine their attention to Nice, Cannes and Monte Carlo, Menton, Cap Ferrat and Cap Martin. They discovered a whole string of delightful little fishing villages along the coast as far as Cassis. Hotels and villas sprang up like mushrooms. Nice developed into a vast boarding house.

The Château de la Napoule, just west of Nice, was a ruin when Henry Clews, the strange, brilliant American sculptor bought it immediately before the 1918 Armistice. Until his death in 1937, he spent a fortune renovating it with no other help than a master mason of the country, Jean Cossano, and his son Caesar. Clews covered the lintels, the capitals and the arches with fantastic creatures, prehistoric monsters, pelicans, scorpions, gnomes, monkeys and owls.

The Château, now open to the public at certain times of the day, contains hundreds of examples of its former owner's queer, even pornographic, genius. To judge by his work he was a cynic, a sadist and a Communist with a passion for stringing outlandish words together into one outrageous sentence. Born the son of James Clews, wealthy New York

F*

banker, he could trace his amazing artistry as a sculptor to the age-old pottery in Staffordshire owned by his ancestors. He could also scorn any suggestion of having to go out to earn a living. He sculpted for his own pleasure and became, nevertheless, the greatest sculptor the United States has ever produced.

His knowledge of anatomy was worthy of Michelangelo, but he had the bizarre mind of an Edgar Allan Poe, while his early work suggests the influence of Rodin and Whistler. He also painted water colours, while his wife's white peacocks held up the Blue Train so often that the French State Railway authorities had to make a formal demand that they should not be allowed on the railway tracks. Examples of his works are to be seen in the Louvre in Paris, in the Metropolitan Museum of New York and many of the most distinguished art galleries of the world.

His was a tortured imagination as his 'God of the Flies', 'God of the Crocodiles' and 'God of the Spiders' prove indelibly. His 'Soul of the Doctor' with its appalling sneer, and the 'Soul of the Patient', clearly resigned to frightful doom; his 'Absinthe Drinker' – a skinny little man – and his nude 'Septuagenarian' with a skull instead of the genital organs between his thighs; his passion for big bellies, hideous bodies and queer allegories make the Château de la Napoule as worthy of a visit, in a very different way, as the charming little chapel of Laghet above Monte Carlo with its little black, miracle-working Virgin and the gaudy 'Thank-you' daubs of the local peasantry.

The château deserves at least two hours of inspection. The cavernous dining-room with its fumbling inscription, 'Save me, Marie, from Gynocrat, scientist, democrat', the egg-shaped fireplace, the effigies of the Casinocrat, and of Plutocracy (showing a bloated baboo on an elephant) are only surpassed by Clews's own tomb, which bears the inscription:

If God grant me three score and ten,
I shall be ready to depart.

I shall have finished with my art
And with the ways and wiles of men.

I hope, however, to return
But not as Ouija spook before
Pures, Spiritists or Marxists or
Scientific feminists. I yearn
To come at eventide as sprite
And dance upon the windowsill
Of little folk wide eyed and still
When summer moon is shining bright.

And I shall dance with might and main
To let dear little children see
How quaint and funny I can be,
From science I shall set them free
And give them mirth and mystery
And myth and fairy lore again.

In the same funereal chamber is a tomb already prepared for
his wife. It is said that the Germans rifled Clews's tomb in the
hopes of finding buried treasure. Certainly they left the remains of an air-raid shelter behind them.

Various French savants have written critiques on Clews. So
have Americans. One of them compared him with Balzac. He
has also been compared with Toulouse-Lautrec and Dégas. In
a way, however, he is much more reminiscent of Gabriele
d'Annunzio.

Mrs. Langtry was already Lady de Bathe when she took a villa
in Monte Carlo in 1919. It had previously belonged to a

croupier. Towering on the heights above her was the palace built by Prince Mirza Khan. Near at hand was the Villa Kehelim which belonged to a Turkish general, Sheref Pasha. Among her other neighbours was the Baroness Orczy (Mrs. Montague Barstow in private life). A little distance away was the villa of Blasco Ibáñez, who wrote *The Four Horsemen of the Apocalypse*, not to mention *Blood and Sand*. This had a Moorish cinema-theatre, Valencia tiles, fountains and a garden full of Spanish plants, in strong contrast to the chintzes and yew hedges of the English villas and gardens, and the brocaded walls and Mediterranean flowers of the French villas. Mrs. Langtry was once told of the French classification of the four principal resorts of the Riviera: Cannes for a cure, Nice to amuse oneself, Monte Carlo to be ruined, and Menton to be buried in. A far better classification, also French, is the one which likens Cannes, Nice and Monte Carlo to the world, the flesh and the devil.

Among her greatest admirers was Oscar Wilde, who on one occasion slept on her doorstep waiting for her return. It was Oscar Wilde, shortly after his release from prison, who raised his hat to Edward VII, then Prince of Wales, while driving along the Promenade des Anglais. Edward VII did not recognise him, and asked who he was. When his companion told him that it was Oscar Wilde, he said to his coachman, 'Turn round and drive back.' He then raised his hat with a sweeping bow to Oscar Wilde.

The social event of the season in 1920 was the marriage of Princess Charlotte to Count Pierre de Polignac who, as her consort, was made a Prince; but the first new celebrity in Monte Carlo to flash across the headlines of the world's newspapers was Suzanne Lenglen. This lithe, hook-nosed French girl in a bandanna revolutionised women's lawn tennis the moment she stepped on to the courts at Monte Carlo. None of those long impeding skirts for Suzanne. She ran, drove and volleyed like a man, winning the Duke of Connaught's cup for the Women's Singles three times off the reel, then chivalrously leaving it to her Doubles partner, Miss Ryan, in 1922, the year in which Prince Albert died. Helen Wills and Lili Alvarez were not due to appear for another three or four years, and when Helen finally met the redoubtable Suzanne in the nearby Carlton Hotel Tournament at Cannes, she was clearly beaten.

I saw it myself, including the famous incident in which a stiff brandy was allegedly offered to one of the players, in apparent contempt of local rules governing alcoholic refreshment during the match. I also saw the spectators, who had climbed up a eucalyptus tree inside the grounds, being shaken off the branches by a zealous gendarme before the match began. Incidentally, I had the great pleasure of dancing that night with Helen Wills at the ball commemorating Lenglen's triumph. Nobody else had asked her for that particular dance. . . .

Few people would associate Cannes with anything to do with politics, but in 1922 Bonar Law was at Cannes, also Lord Beaverbrook, who was staying at the Carlton Hotel. Lord Curzon was at the Grand. While there, Lloyd George offered Bonar Law the post of Foreign Secretary. Bonar Law refused, with the result that Lloyd George dropped the idea of an immediate General Election. A few weeks previously Lloyd George and M. Briand, Prime Minister of France, agreed to attempt to reconcile the victors and the vanquished of World War I in an enduring peace. The result was that the Supreme Allied Council met at Cannes. Its object was to deal with the reparations, discuss the security pact and draw up an agenda for a future European conference. This was, incidentally, no less than the 30th peace conference since 1918. The British team at

Cannes were Lloyd George, Curzon, Sir Robert Horne, Sir Laming Worthington-Evans, Winston Churchill (as Colonial Secretary) and Lord Riddell, the proprietor of the *News of the World*.

Lloyd George stayed at the Villa Valletta owned by Sir Albert Stern. During a preliminary discussion Worthington-Evans drew breath during a long monologue. Before he could continue, a very human-sounding voice said, 'You bloody fool.' It was Sir Albert Stern's pet parrot, unobserved in the corner. The story quickly circulated and next day Briand asked Lloyd George for the loan of the parrot.

The political situation was that France wished to come to terms with the Bolsheviks because of their heavy pre-war investments in Russia. They also wished to bleed Germany to death by demanding ludicrous reparations.

On 9th January 1922 Lloyd George asked Briand to lunch at the Mandalieu golf club (it was a year later that Lord Derby founded the Mougins Golf Club with an entrance fee of £200 per member). Lloyd George also invited Signor Bonomi, the Italian Prime Minister, Bonar Law, Curzon, Riddell and Sir Edward Grigg. They undoubtedly had a very good luncheon. Afterwards Lloyd George, in high spirits, invited Briand and Bonomi to play golf with him. Neither had ever touched a club in their lives. Gaily the two Prime Ministers accepted the challenge; Riddell, Grigg and Bonar Law accompanied the trio. Surprisingly, Briand and Bonomi both managed to hit their respective balls a decent way off the first tee. After that, it was complete pantomime – Briand and Bonomi missing shot after shot, digging great divots out of the ground. Stupidly, as far as Lloyd George was concerned, no attempt was made to hold back the French reporters and photographers.

After a few holes, Lloyd George and Briand went off to tea at the Carlton Hotel, talked over the prickly question of reparations and reached complete agreement. Everything seemed set fair for the all-important restoration of conditions in which trade could flourish as it had done before the war between nations.

Next day, the Paris newspapers reached Cannes. They were full of lampoons, cartoons and bitter editorials ridiculing Briand as the tool of Lloyd George. On 11th January, after the plenary session of the conference, such alarming messages arrived from Paris that Briand realised that he had to return to face the music.

Lloyd George saw him off at Cannes railway station. 'Whatever you do, don't resign,' he said.

'I'll be back in thirty-six hours.'

Briand never returned. He was forced to resign on the spot. This was most upsetting to Lloyd George, who was certain that Briand would have fixed French opinion, especially as the German Foreign Minister was explaining the genuine difficulties of Germany at the very moment when the fateful news of Briand's resignation was telegraphed to Cannes. Lloyd George as chairman of the conference adjourned the meeting, left that night.

The only result of this conference, wrecked by a golf ball, was the agreement that Britain and France should rebuild their *Entente* and form the basis of an alliance for the peace of all nations, including Germany and Russia. Britain besought France and Italy to join in cutting down their national armaments, and that was the only end result, except that the stone plaque commemorating Lloyd George's hole-in-one was removed bodily by the angry French.

Less important from an historic point of view was the return of Diaghilev. His first visit to Monte Carlo had been in 1911, when on 19th April of that year he presented *Shahrazad*. In the same season he gave the first public performance of the *Spectre de la Rose* as well as the *Invitation to the Dance* by Weber, starring Karsavina and Nijinsky, with décor by Bakst; he also presented *Petrushka* with music by Stravinsky. During the war Diaghilev had a most unfortunate time, in spite of a tour in the United States and South America. The peace found him in Spain without a penny to his name. A contract with Sir Oswald Stoll saved him temporarily.

His ultimate salvation was provided by Camille Blanc, who invited him and his company to Monte Carlo. Here Diaghilev created *Aurora's Wedding*, *Les Fâcheux*, *Les Noces* and the *Good-Humoured Ladies*. It was to Monte Carlo that Diaghilev sent Serge Lifar, then an eighteen-year-old fugitive from Russia, to take lessons from Nijinska, the sister of Nijinsky, who had already gone mad. Lifar describes vividly his emotions on his arrival in 'Gleaming Monte Carlo'. After his first lesson he got stage fright and seriously considered escaping from the glittering loveliness of the Principality in order to return to grim and distant Russia. Ultimately Diaghilev appeared on the scene and Lifar remained with him, 'a tiny miserable chick of a boy' as he described himself at the time. So panicky was he, that he worked not only at the rehearsals of *Aurora's Wedding* but alone and at night on the jetty. There he would practise for hours while the two coloured beacons illuminated the sea and silhouetted the dark outlines of the fortress on the Rock. *Les Noces*, also in the programme, was attended at every rehearsal by Stravinsky, not merely as a spectator but as an almost hostile critic. Scenes were continuous. In a matter of minutes he would gesticulate, then take off his coat, sit down at the piano and begin singing in an ecstatic but terrible voice which carried so much conviction that no one thought it comical. He would go on like this until he was completely exhausted. Often the Prince and Princess of Monaco were present at rehearsals and sent champagne to the whole company – half a bottle per person.

A skull lies between the thighs of this famous statue
by Henry Clews.

The Aga Khan's Villa Yakimour in the hills behind Cannes. (*Joe Hollander*)

Every dawn Lifar walked up into the mountains merely to see the sun rise from La Turbie. Then suddenly he would be scared that he would be late for rehearsals, and run panting down the mountain side, to arrive long before anyone else had reached the theatre. He was only eighteen. At last the telltale rings around his eyes caused Diaghliev to suspect that he was having a series of love affairs. Cross-examining him, he discovered the truth and forbade him to go to La Turbie again.

For the next nine years the Diaghilev Company spent at least part of the year, usually during the winter season, in rehearsing the new ballets and performing them in the casino theatre before showing them in Paris, London and other capital cities. It was in Monte Carlo that Anton Dolin (ex-Patrick Keay) first joined Diaghilev.

On the surface Monte Carlo was booming, but the resources of the *S.B.M.* had been steadily drained by World War I, during which salaries had been paid to all the personnel serving in the armed forces and the cost of the upkeep of the casino had been a grievous burden. Thus it was that Sir Basil Zaharoff, the mystery man of Europe, acquired control. Zaharoff was born in 1849 at Mugla, the poor Greek quarter of Constantinople. As a youngster he did a number of odd jobs as assistant to a money-changer, a fireman and an hotel tout before joining his uncle who had a small cloth business. In 1877 he went into the armaments business as agent and salesman for the firm of Nordenfelt and earned large commissions. Nordenfelt was the inventor of the first submarine as well as of the gun called after him. Zaharoff next worked for Sir Hiram Maxim and later helped to merge the Nordenfelt and Maxim interests. Through Maxim he had his first taste of Monte Carlo.

When Maxim and Nordenfelt split, Zaharoff became an

armaments king in his own right. His Levantine genius for negotiation and intrigue won him a fortune by touring the troubled countries of Europe and selling guns and ammunition just before the start of each new war, particularly in the Balkans. His big dealing with Vickers and Krupps made him the confidant of war ministers, and in 1918 he was a millionaire, an English knight and a grand officer of the Legion of Honour. He was also adviser to Lloyd George and Venizelos. He negotiated vast loans to different countries and was a director of several international banks.

In 1918 Prince Louis had refused to take a reduction in his annual income from the *S.B.M.* Finances were chaotic. Prince Louis called on Zaharoff, who placed a million pounds at his disposal while Camille Blanc was away. His first step was to remove Camille, for various reasons which have never been divulged but are an open secret in the Principality. Zaharoff's nominees moved in. Delpierre was made president of the *S.B.M.*

Zaharoff had met him during World War I when Delpierre was in charge of French mercantile transport and aided Zaharoff in moving important consignments of Maxim guns and ammunition to the scene of the fighting. Another appointment was René Léon as managing director.

Of Zaharoff, H. G. Wells wrote:

'The picture of an Anatolian Greek overwhelmed by his riches, adorned by the highest honours France and Britain could bestow and amusing himself by running a gambling place in his declining years, displayed against a background of innumerable millions of men maimed, tortured, scalded, mutilated and killed, may be an effective indictment of our political traditions but in no sense is it a personal condemnation. Millions would have played the same game had they thought of it and known how.'

Gouty and spade-bearded, Zaharoff took a great pleasure in sitting on a sunny balcony of the Hotel de Paris and watching the gamblers going in to lose their money. He himself never gambled, always advised people to keep away from roulette, felt no pity for those fools who lost their fortunes, and liquidated numbers of pensions given by Camille Blanc to big gamblers who had been broken by the tables, in return for two months' money and a one-way ticket to Paris. His marriage to the Duchess of Marchena at the age of seventy-eight was as secret as the rest of his activities. He hated being photographed and always tried to hide his face with his hat.

In 1925 he sold his interest in the casino to certain rich banking corporations in Paris, notably Dreyfus et Cie, but kept control of the Hotel de Paris. This sale was personally effected by René Léon who had served in World War I in the same regiment as Prince Radziwill, a grandson of François Blanc and the titular head of the new financial set-up.

Small, smiling and bald, Léon was at heart a gambler himself – a very good thing for the *S.B.M.* because he was able to appreciate how the casino should be run with maximum profit but with minimum grief to the players. One of his first actions was to appoint his old friend, General Polovtsoff, to the post of President of the International Sporting Club. 'It's high time we had a gentleman in the administration,' he said.

General Polovtsoff was the son of an immensely rich Russian who lost literally millions of francs in the casino, but up to the very last day of his life still believed that there was an infallible system for winning, at both roulette and *trente-et-quarante*. As president, General Polovtsoff had not only to make the clientele of the Sporting Club as exclusive as possible but also it was his business to contact all the rich and distinguished visitors to Monte Carlo and smooth out any troubles, fancied or otherwise, which they had experienced in their hotel, the casino or the Sporting Club. He had a daily interview with Léon at 8 a.m.

Another innovation proved, oddly enough, to be most unpopular. This was the abolition of zero for half an hour every day at an unexpected moment. A bell was suddenly rung and gamblers were informed that if, during the next thirty minutes, the ball fell into zero it would not count. This gave, of course, a tremendous advantage to all system players who backed odd and even or red and black, but infuriated many others to whom zero was a favourite number. There were so many protests that this concession was withdrawn.

The next innovation was to persuade pretty English girls to go out to Monte Carlo to 'dress' the place. They had their hotel bills paid, and were given their return fare on the Blue Train, together with £2 a week pocket money. For the rest, they had to fend for themselves.

It was not until some time later that Léon introduced the first of the American Les Girls shows – with immense success. These professional beauties attracted many admirers and their whole outlook on life was delightfully personified by one of the songs they sang in the summer casino:

> Here we are in a swell hotel,
>   Swell hotel,
>   Doing quite well,
> Breaking up homes but what the hell.
> Tra la la la la.

As a case in point we can cite Betty Sundmark, who became Mrs. Dodero, and then after an intervening marriage Mrs. Shannon; and Mrs. George Hearst, who had an interim marriage to Commander Spencer, U.S. Navy. Originally she was

Xandra Rambeau, friend of Evelyn Crowell, later Day Elliot, later Mrs. Durya, later Mrs. Grayson, now Mrs. Schlosser. Two of the prettiest girls – Gay Orlova and Betty Hamilton – committed suicide.

At this point, Mme. Balsan, the former Duchess of Marlborough, and her husband became the first visitors to build a villa at Eze, the little Saracen village on top of a cliff two miles from Beaulieu. The work was completed in twelve months by six Italian stonemasons who crossed the frontier every Monday, returning to their womenfolk only on Saturday nights. The architect was Duchêne, who had designed Sunderland House in London. The cost of the gardens must have been fabulous. The grounds were precipitous and the earth was always being washed or blown away. All bulbs had to be dug up and replanted every year. Called Lou Sueil, it saw many distinguished guests, including the Duke of Connaught who spent all his winters before the outbreak of World War II at his superb villa on Cap Ferrat.

The Riviera was indeed as full of royalty and near-royalty in the middle 'twenties as it was in the old days before World War I. The King and Queen of Denmark, those inveterate cyclists, the King of Sweden, a still more inveterate lawn tennis player, the Crown Prince of Japan, the Maharaja of Kapurthala, all paid visits. Later on the guests included a certain Polish ambassador who recalled to Mme. Balsan his encounter with Goering. 'In Poland,' said the Count, 'we have so many poachers that our game preserves are sadly diminished.' Snorted Goering: 'Take it from me, Excellency, you need only shoot two or three as I have done and you will have no more trouble.'

Another guest was Serge Voronoff of monkey gland fame. Lord Curzon spent a fortnight at the villa. Lord Curzon, the great patrician, is remembered for his haughty retort, 'My pilasters are alabaster,' when someone else had referred to his marble pillars. On the last day of his visit he turned to Mme. Balsan.

'Then it has been worth the sacrifice!'

'Sacrifice?'

'Yes, to give up being "the beautiful Duchess of Marlborough" and all that it meant.'

'But of course, George, I have never regretted not being a Duchess any more.'

Curzon just stared at her disbelievingly. Sacha Guitry, owner of a villa at Cap d'Ail and still married to Yvonne Printemps, was among the other guests who included Charlie Chaplin, Sir Philip Sassoon, Edith Wharton and Elsa Maxwell.

Sir Winston Churchill was certainly the most distinguished visitor to Lou Sueil. He used to dictate during the morning and paint in the afternoon. His departure on these expeditions was something to see. The easel, stool and parasol having been assembled, together with the brushes and canvases, he finally selected his Hat of the Day, filled his cigar box and sallied forth with a detective whom the British Government insisted on providing for him.

Lady Oxford and Asquith, when a guest, had a habit of slipping notes to her hostess and sending them in to her with the breakfast tray. Willie Vanderbilt, who brought the first racing car to the United States, was of course a regular guest, being Mme. Balsan's brother. Lord Berners who had a harmonium installed in his Rolls-Royce, Lord Balfour and Suzanne Lenglen all came to know the villa, which must have been one of the very last to be built on the Riviera for the winter season rather than for the summer months.

By now a number of small holiday resorts along the Riviera, notably Juan-les-Pins and Cap d'Antibes, were attracting a healthy number of visitors for the summer season.

This vogue, though usually attributed to the late Frank Jay Gould, owes some of its success to Edgar Baudoin, a small hotelier who had noticed a few people bathing at Nice in June. Raising a certain amount of capital, he started the casino at Juan-les-Pins in the summer of 1924. At that time it was a small, unpretentious, attractive seaside resort. Three years later, Gould, holidaying at the nearby Lutetia Hotel, lunched in the restaurant of the casino and was immediately fascinated by the *hors d'œuvre*, which still have an international reputation. They included stuffed sardines, stuffed onions, stuffed *courgettes*, wild rice, *ratatouilles*, quenelles of celery with horse-radish sauce, red and green pimentoes with anchovy sauce and onions stuffed with currants, among other savoury dishes. Being a great gourmet, he was persuaded to invest fifty million francs in the casino, then in financial difficulties.

Gould belonged to the sensational generation of American millionaires. His father, a former watch repairer, built up a railway empire. He was a strict man and it was not until after his death in 1892 that Frank Jay Gould was able to see life. He married three times and was divorced twice. For ten years, he sued practically every member of his family, collectively and individually.

After acquiring control of the Juan-les-Pins casino, and building the Hotel Provençal, he descended upon Nice, where he bought the Palais de la Mediterranée. His 'palace that the Caesars could not have built' was in direct competition with the Casino de la Jettée. When the depression hit the U.S. and then Europe, he leased both his casinos to an Anglo-French syndicate. In the meantime, he had bought the Hotel Majestic in Nice for thirty million francs. He also acquired a hotel in Cannes and blocks of flats in Monte Carlo and Menton. One of his innovations was to supply soap in every bedroom of the French hotels which he owned. This was followed by all the other big establishments. During most of his active career, Gould lived at the Villa Semiramis, near Cannes. This too he sold. He never returned to the U.S. after his departure in 1913. His three wives were Helen Kelly, Edith Kelly and Florence Lacaze. His sister, Anna Gould, first married Count Boni de Castellane and later the Duc de Talleyrand.

Over a period of years before his death at his Juan-les-Pins villa, he liquidated most of his holdings, including the Juan-les-Pins casino. He was known as the sad millionaire. And no wonder. For the last ten years of his life he was bedridden.

René Léon now decided to profit by the new craze and create what neither François Blanc nor Camille Blanc had ever attempted, a summer season. He embarked simultaneously on a series of very ambitious projects – the building of the Country Club and the summer casino together with a gigantic swimming pool and an hotel, at the cost of one and a half million pounds. Both the Country Club and the Beach Hotel were across the Monégasque border in France, which added considerably to the expenses. But when completed, the huge turquoise-blue swimming pool looked exactly like a Hollywood film set with its white chairs and gaudy parasols, an orchestra playing rumbas, waiters bringing long cool drinks, and sunburnt young men in trunks flirting idly with pretty girls in the briefest of bathing dresses. Originally known as the Rubber Beach, it had been Elsa Maxwell's extravagant idea when she was appointed to the management, to cover the pebbles with huge sheets of crape rubber. Unfortunately she did not realise that sea-water was a corrosive until the flood of interested inquiries from manufacturers who had received advance news of the project made it clear that she was attempting the impossible.

In 1923 Elsa Maxwell celebrated her fortieth birthday at

Monte Carlo. In previous years she had visited Mary Garden, the famous operatic singer, who was regarded as quite eccentric, because she chose to spend her summers there instead of Biarritz or Deauville, and was practically the sole occupant of the Park Palace Hotel.

Elsa Maxwell's story is that Prince Pierre de Polignac, having noted her success in making the Lido fashionable, offered her 10,000 dollars a year, paid quarterly, if she would help to popularise the Principality. Her first suggestion was that a summer season should be inaugurated by creating proper bathing facilities, a summer casino, and international lawn tennis matches to take place after Wimbledon. This last-named idea never matured and indeed, when asked to comment on Elsa Maxwell's version of her contribution to Monte Carlo's summer season, René Léon smiles discreetly but offers no comment.

Among Elsa Maxwell's other recollections are those of King Gustav of Sweden, who always took a sidelong glance at his opponent's cards at the bridge table if he had half a chance, and also sputtered rather disagreeably when he spoke. He did, however, do a great deal for lawn tennis, and was as starry-eyed as a girl on her first date, when invited to lunch with Susanne Lenglen and Henri Cochet. When Elsa wanted to start luncheon because Lenglen and Cochet were nearly an hour late, King Gustav would not hear of it. 'There are fifty kings and emperors,' he said, 'but there is only one Lenglen and one Cochet. I can wait. They are the aristocrats and I am the commoner today.'

It was unfortunate for René Léon that these vast outlays should have been approved only two years before the international slump of 1930–31. In the meantime much hay was made in the remaining sunshine, though a recrudescence of local unrest occurred in 1929 when the National Council of

Monaco was dissolved no fewer than four times. Revolvers were fired (though only in the air). Prince Louis was publicly hissed at the railway station, and not only a London butcher with the princely surname of Grimaldi but also the Marquis or Chabrillon, who renewed his demands in 1950 on the death of Louis II, claimed the throne. On the tennis courts Henri Cochet won the Men's Singles in 1928 and 1929, the Women's Singles being won by Eileen Bennett and Betty Nuthall.

Following the example of Camille Blanc in always looking for some fresh attraction to divert rich men and public attention to Monte Carlo, René Léon instituted the Monte Carlo Grand Prix, the world's first Round-the-Houses Race. Popularly and justifiably known as the Race of the Thousand Corners, it attracted the cream of the world's racing motorists, among them the then unknown Caracciola in a Mercedes, who came in third to a couple of Bugattis driven by Williams and Bouriano.

The world slump did not do so much harm to Monte Carlo or Cannes as might have been expected. Film stars like Charlie Chaplin and Gloria Swanson; millionaires like James Hennessy, the Duke of Westminster and the Aga Khan; statesmen like Clemenceau and Venizelos; crowned heads like the Kings of Sweden and Denmark; authors like Phillips Oppenheim, Baroness Orczy and Somerset Maugham continued to frequent it. Night clubs like the Knickerbocker, starring Indefatigable Charlie, sprang up in all directions and made fortunes for their owners. Those were the days of Jennie Dolly, Madame de Bittencourt, Sir Warden Chilcot's *Dolphin*, the Duke of Sutherland's *Sans Peur* and the Grand Duke Dimitri, Jean Gabriel Domergue, Jean Jane Marmac, Commodore Beaumont, Jimmy Walker, Maurice Chevalier, Schiaparelli, Drexel Biddle. Gertrude Lawrence was photographed wearing pearls on her bathing dress. The Paramount Pasha of Marrakesh accompanied by the Grand Vizier played golf at Mont Agel. Phillips Oppenheim watched Ronald Colman and William Powell playing the fool in the swimming pool. Peggy Hopkins Joyce appeared daringly in 'slacks' (actually the earliest of the beach pyjamas), which were not at first regarded as correct clothing. On the tennis courts could be seen Bill Tilden, Brugnon, Cilli Aussem – the King of Sweden's regular partner, – Dr. Prenn and the first Englishman to win the Singles for many years, Bunny Austin; wonderful whoopee, but where are they now?

Over at nearby Cap d'Antibes almost everyone was a celebrity, such as Fred Cripps and his wife, the former Duchess of Westminster, Princess Faucigny-Lucinge, formerly Miss Baba d'Erlanger, in her white silk pantaloons and tight white silk bootees, the lovely Marquise de Casa Maury and her husband, Lady Cunard always in a white dress, Mrs. Somerset Maugham, Lord Inverclyde, Willie Rhinelander Stewart, Otto Kahn, Mrs. Benjamin Guinness, Lady Erroll or Michael Arlen.

Another was Bernard Shaw. Like others, in past years I had seen photographs of him and his beard romping in the warm waters of Italy. But little did I expect ever to bathe with him.

Mr. Shaw was staying in seclusion at a small hotel four miles away. I learnt that he bathed privily at eight in the morning and sometimes in the evening. My curiosity thus whetted had to be wetted too. I must bathe with Bernard Shaw.

A taxi-cab to the hotel was simple. But on arrival it was announced firmly that Mr. Shaw refused to see interviewers. I was told that Mr. Shaw had taken seven rooms in the hotel. I was told that Mr. Shaw was writing a film with seven acts and an epilogue. I was told that Mr. Shaw was on holiday. I was told that anyone who wanted to see Mr. Shaw had to write him a letter to which he might or might not reply in undue course. But something had to be done about bathing with G.B.S. and then came the inspiration – just a note: 'Are you too sunburnt to be seen?'

Two minutes later footsteps could be heard, and the great man appeared. Was he in a Norfolk jacket? He was not. Was he in white flannels? No, again. He was in a camel-hair dressing-gown and his beard. A minute later we were on the way to the private bathing beach attached to the Château des Enfants.

'Sir Oswald Mosley and his wife are here,' I said. 'It seems a bit incompatible, don't you think – a Labour man like that?'

'Not a bit,' was the reply. 'I am a Socialist myself. Who wouldn't keep and enjoy four thousand pounds a year if it were offered him?'

We walked on.

'What about your going to America to stay with the Fairbanks?'

'There's not a word of truth in it.'

I went on talking.

'Michael Arlen is down here. Didn't you say he was the only Armenian who never sold you a carpet?'

'I? Certainly not. I have read nothing he has ever written. I told him when I met him here that I have read nothing since Sir Walter Scott. I had, of course, just heard of his name. But he has great charm, I find, and a gift for friendship.'

It was a fine warm evening. Mr. Shaw walked with a springy step, chest bared to the breeze. I hastened to keep pace with him. 'Have you been in the casino yet?'

A horrified grunt was the only reply. The answer I gathered was that Mr. Shaw had not. And had no intention of doing so. None. Casinos were pretty stupid places. The people were the same.

I told him that in America they had been wondering how much I had been paid for persuading him to appear in his original talking-film interview. 'You should have got thousands, of course,' said Mr. Shaw.

By this time we were at the rock pool. And then I realised I had left my bathing-dress behind. However, as far as I could see, Mr. Shaw had done so, too.

A moment later, the camel-hair dressing-gown, which looked like a friar's cowl, slipped to the ground, disclosing Mr. Shaw in a pair of diminutive white cuts. His chest was pinkly sunburnt; his white beard was ruffled by the gentle breeze. As he stood contemplating the peacock blue of the Mediterranean, forty feet below, he spoke again.

'A young woman told me about a fool-proof dive this morning,' he said. 'All one had to do, she said, was to hold oneself rigid, arch the body, hold the hands above the head, and dive in. I did. Fool-proof? I received a tremendous buffet on the face when I struck the water, I was never so outraged in my life.'

A moment later he clambered down to the diving-rock, eighteen feet above the level of the sea. For a second he poised in his short white cuts, and then positively hurled himself forwards and outwards. There was a loud splash; a moment later he and his beard reappeared swimming strongly on his back towards the setting sun. I followed, but was rapidly outdistanced.

Cannes in the meantime answered the challenge of Monte Carlo and Antibes and Juan-les-Pins with the erection of the Palm Beach Casino at the far end of the Croisette. Specifically designed for the hot summer, it had high ceilings, an adjacent swimming pool, open windows in all directions and a general atmosphere of cool luxe. Grand galas marked its opening with such celebrities as Maurice Chevalier, then at the height of his reputation, as cabaret stars.

Polo was encouraged, with the Duke de Gramont as president, and the Duke of Westminster as a typical member. The Mandalieu golf course was kept open throughout the summer, however parched the fairways.

As for the Duke of Westminster, he was very restless. One day his yacht, the *Cutty Sark*, would be in Cannes harbour, the next it would be gone – nobody knew where. Occasionally he would play golf at Cagnes with the indefatigable Mrs. Satterthwaite, the lawn tennis player.

He was a great gambler, concentrating on *trente-et-quarante*. At one time he held the record for winning seventeen maximum coups on black.

Fritz Kreisler also liked a gamble at *trente-et-quarante*, although his wife disapproved. On one occasion he had put forty gold louis on red. After they had doubled up six times, he was about to take them off, when his wife appeared on the scene. He had his back to the table as usual. He knew of her disapproval of gambling, and did not like to admit that he was in fact playing *trente-et-quarante*. To his agony, his winnings kept on mounting up. When his winnings had accumulated 1,280 *louis d'or*, black turned up and he lost the lot.

Lord Beaverbrook never gambled. He had always preferred to sit in a comfortable chair in the gaming rooms, where he was quickly surrounded by the various notabilities present. In the old days it would be H. G. Wells with his piping voice, Lord Castlerosse, who was born right out of his generation, and should have been a Regency buck (he was always in magnificent plumage, with a huge expanse of white waistcoat, and outsize cigar), Lord Horne, and Leslie Hore-Belisha, later Lord Hore-Belisha.

Lord Iliffe and Lord Kemsley would arrive in their yachts.

Lord Iliffe never gambled, and Lord Kemsley would only play at the three-louis table.

I remember once sitting next to him and the ex-King of Portugal, who was eating a plate of chicken sandwiches at the *chemin de fer* table – a somewhat unusual sight.

Chaliapin was a great gambler, like most Russians. On one occasion, he was with General Polovtsoff, still the President of the International Sporting Club.

'Why,' he asked, 'do we follow this barbaric habit of putting soda in whisky? Let's drink it straight.'

As he spoke, Berry Wall ambled by with a pretty American girl. Berry Wall pointed out Chaliapin to her.

'Who is Chaliapin?' she asked loudly.

Before Berry Wall could answer, Chaliapin said to General Polovtsoff:

'I like these children of nature. They are very savage of course.'

Introductions were effected. Said Chaliapin:

'You do not understand my name – it is Chaly-Apin.'

Said the girl:

'Oh yes, you sang rather well in *Don Quixote*. You know, you could do quite well in Hollywood.'

CHAPTER 12

WAR AND THE GAMBLERS

A SERIOUS BLOW was inflicted on Monte Carlo by the French Government in 1932. This was the legalisation of roulette and *trente-et-quarante* in all French casinos which had sufficient financial reserves to meet any run against the bank. Until then, Monte Carlo had a monopoly of both games. Italy followed suit, and roulette was made available not only at the Lido in Venice, but also at San Remo, just a few miles across the border.

The reason for this was that under René Léon's instructions, the Monte Carlo casino had introduced '*tout va*' – in other words, real baccarat – thus openly flouting the agreement with the French Government in 1907, whereby roulette and *trente-et-quarante* were made exclusive to Monte Carlo on the understanding that '*tout va*', the only alternative to *chemin de fer* and *boule* in the French casinos, was left severely alone.

François André and the other casino chiefs were incensed by this flagrant infringement. They informed the French Government that unless they were allowed the right to introduce roulette and *trente-et-quarante*, they would close their establishments.

The revenue from the casinos and the de luxe hotels which depended on the patronage of rich gamblers was so considerable that the threat succeeded. No longer was it necessary to go all the way to Monte Carlo to hear the prohibitive cry, '*Rien ne va plus*'.

1934 was the year of the Communistic Popular Front manifestations, and also the year in which gold once again appeared on the gaming tables. It was a sensation. Posed photographs (the casino never permits real photographs to be taken inside the casino) appeared in the newspapers of the world, showing the scene on the 5th February 1934, when a single table in the Sporting Club was provided with gold coins instead of chips and plaques for the first time for many years. René Léon had given a very large order for eighteen-carat gold *jetons* to the French Mint, but had been told there would be a delay of four and a half months before delivery. This did not upset the wizard of Monte Carlo. He immediately bought up the whole float of American gold dollars in France and as many more as he could acquire from England. They were all five-, ten- and twenty-dollar gold coins.

There they jingled on the green baize tables. Piles of real, heavy, ringing yellow metal instead of the usual bone or plastic plaques. It was like the first Technicolor movie after years of black-and-white films. The minimum stake was five dollars.

Most of the gamblers who won took their gold coins away with them; not that René Léon minded. He had made an excellent commercial deal with the Bank of France and the Bank of England and it actually paid him when the gamblers did not change their gold dollar pieces back into francs. On the other hand it meant that the brief reappearance of gold instead of plaques came to an end in a matter of months.

Among the visitors that year were the King of Sweden, the King of Denmark, King Christopher of Greece, Princess Hohenlohe, the Aga Khan and Sir John Simon. 'Indefatigable Charlie', alias Karl Heinz von Schwedler, was at the peak of his popularity as a night-club entertainer. (In 1941 he reappeared in the night club as a German intelligence officer in plain clothes.) The usual crop of American Les Girls appeared on the scene but one of them, Freda Jones, was gravely disappointed.

'What men care about here,' she pouted, 'is gambling. We girls got a real shock. We went some place to dance, and believe it or not, we had to pay the men for dancing with us! It's unbelievable.'

Thereafter the casino promised free dancing partners for Les Girls.

Kreisler was a distinguished visitor, coming all the way to Monte Carlo to hear a single performance conducted by Strauss. Lily Pons came, but not to sing.

That year the Round-the-Houses Race was won by Caracciola. Owing to the oily surface of the roads, only two of the competitors finished. Prince Bira made his first successful appearance in Continental motor racing by winning the Rainier Cup. As for the Rally, D. M. Healey won more prizes than any other competitor. On the tennis courts Baron von Cramm won the Singles for Germany. The Grand Prix was another clean sweep for Germany – von Brauchitch (Mercedes) and Kautz (Mercedes) . . .

The harbours of Monte Carlo and Cannes were full of yachts with illuminated gang-planks at night, decks gay with lanterns and the soft strains of dance music. Chaliapin sang Boris Goudunov and walked off in the middle of the performance although the King of Sweden and Princess Juliana of Holland were in the royal box. René Blum sponsored the Russian Ballet. Fritz Kreisler backed in maximums. An English bookmaker, having studied the roulette tables, was heard to observe: 'Thirty-seven runners and all trying! No, thank you.'

An English manufacturer who had invented a new type of rake for the croupiers and was given a trial order, lost £500 which was removed with his device. Rachmaninov gave concerts, like Kreisler. Berry Wall appeared on the scene with his famous chow.

How far escapism is a source of happiness is a problem. But

the gambling in the Sporting Club and the two casinos became more intense than ever.

The major event of the winter season of 1936 was the arrival of Mrs. Wallis Simpson, shortly before Edward VIII's abdication. In order to throw off the reporters, she drove in a highly zig-zag way across France, by way of Evreux and Vienne, before reaching the Provençal-style, monkish villa of the Herman Rogers' at Cannes.

Here she was virtually besieged for weeks by newspaper correspondents and photographers with long range cameras. And yet, within three years, the greatest event of the decade had so lost its drama that when the Duke of Windsor was in Palm Beach Casino at Monte Carlo, he was actually jostled by people wanting to get past him to the *chemin de fer* or the dance floor.

The South of France, once described as a sunny resort for shady people, has always been a magnet for ex-royalty. Apart from the ex-King of England, there have been the ex-King of Portugal, the ex-King of Spain, the ex-King of Yugoslavia, and the ex-King of Egypt – not to mention the ex-Emperor Bao Dai. These are only a few of the out-of-work monarchs who have sought the gay life of the royal playgrounds between Menton and St. Tropez which they knew in happier days. Nearly all the glamour has departed from them.

One day, the Emperor Bao Dai was minding his own business in the bar of the casino at Cannes, attended by three members of his ex-imperial entourage. Said a spirited English lady of title to Eric Forrester, the barman, 'I won't sit at the bar with all those Chinese. Kindly get rid of them.' Said Eric: 'I am sorry, I cannot do anything.' Said the lady of title: 'Send for André (François André, who runs Cannes), because if you don't get them out of here, I will take my big yacht away.'

André appeared a few minutes later. Eric Forrester repeated

the demands of the English lady of title in French, including her threat to remove her yacht. The lady did not understand French. André smilingly nodded his head up and down like a mandarin, and said in French: 'Let her take her big yacht away.' As the ex-Emperor was at that moment about to leave the bar, everybody was happy.

André is a great Anglophile. Let there be two English dukes and an English earl at Cannes, and it makes the season for him, irrespective of their inability to spend the money of fat French industrialists or Indian, Arabic or Persian potentates and oil kings. He is insistent on dinner jackets wherever possible. There is no one at Monte Carlo who can so personally control the casino and hotels in the impresario way adopted by André.

In 1938 the Duke of Windsor came over to Monte Carlo from the Château de Croye near Cannes which he had leased. Unlike his grandfather Edward VII, he always came in the summer. By now, the summer season had easily surpassed the winter season in terms of popularity, though the amount of money staked on the green baize tables was less than in the winter. Visitors during July, August and September were younger and therefore had less money. Visitors during the winter have always been older, therefore better off, and have gambled more heavily. In which connection one can point to another aspect of gambling – that really serious gamblers only play *trente-et-quarante* or baccarat as opposed to *chemin de fer* or roulette.

The gross profits of the casino that year were no less than one hundred and eight million francs in spite of Hitler's sinister rise to power. The Men's Singles were won by Puncec (Baron von Cramm being in disgrace); the Women's Singles falling to Madame Jedrzejowska.

Two sports which were to become internationally popular were intimately associated with the Riviera in the late 'thirties.

True, Christopher Mackintosh had the temerity to try out the possibilities of water ski-ing on an Adriatic cruise from Venice to Istanbul a short time previously. But the first time that it proved really successful, with specially wide water skis to take the necessary weight, was at Cannes. It was in effect an adaptation of the Norwegian principle of ski-joring, but applied to a motor-boat instead of to a horse-drawn sleigh. As soon as it proved practicable, it was developed to a point where waterskiers, both men and girls, succeeded in jumping several feet out of the water and still maintaining their balance when they came down to the surface again, several yards away.

The other sport was under-water fishing.

Another innovation popularised in Monte Carlo was the fashion of wearing white dinner jackets. The only difficulty was that the wearers were sometimes mistaken for stewards.

Many thousands of people, feverishly anxious to have a final fling at Monte Carlo before the imminent European war swirled over them, made the summer season the gayest on record, in spite of whispers from late revellers about columns of troops on the march which they had met in the small hours of the morning between Cannes and Monte Carlo. There were strange tales of spies being put ashore at Cap Martin and Cap Ferrat. There were rumours about German military intelligence officers in mufti at the casino. The Crown Prince Umberto was among the distinguished visitors. A sensation was also caused by the prolonged stay in the Hotel de Paris of two Spanish noblewomen with a suite of servants, all of whom disappeared after twenty-four hours except for the sauce chef and chauffeur. For nearly a year the average bill for food and wine for the two women was £32 a day. This was surely beyond the two people to consume, and it was generally believed that certain people were being secretly harboured in the suite for military or political reasons.

On the day in August 1939 when Russia announced her Non-Aggression Pact with Germany, there was very nearly pandemonium in the Principality. The hotels and villas emptied in a matter of hours.

Came 10th May 1940, and hectic attempts were made by English residents, including Somerset Maugham, to escape before the Germans drove south. At least three novels have been written about the two coal boats which were put at the disposal of the 'Foolish Virgins' and ultimately reached England after a certain amount of discomfort to the crowded passengers.

Then the real blow fell – real as far as Monte Carlo was concerned. Italy declared war on France, and within a fortnight of Mussolini's stab in the back, Italian troops overran the French rearguard at Menton, which still shows a number of scars, and entered Monte Carlo.

Prince Louis hopefully enough stood on his rights as the ruler of a neutral sovereign state, claiming that the Italians (and later the Germans) had no authority to cross his boundaries in uniform. Needless to say, the Italians paid not the slightest attention to this, and sent for the Minister of the Interior to arrange for billets for their men. The Minister, who was married to an Englishwoman and had secreted the British consulate's Union Jack in his own apartment for safe keeping, protested as strongly as the Prince. But it was of no avail. The long lines of olive-green troops entered Monte Carlo to the tumultuous cheers of hundreds of the Italian populace. The streets were lined by Italian girls and young men waving the Italian flag.

Numbers of the English residents after investigation were sent to a temporary concentration camp at Sospel, where they remained for anything from twelve days to three months.

This minimum of twelve days was accorded to an old lady who had falsified her age for so long that she felt in honour bound to claim that she was under seventy although, in fact, she was an octogenarian. The senior Italian officer refused to believe her, but after a series of spirited protests, agreed to satisfy her honour by carting her off to Sospel.

Came the fall of the Vichy Government.

The first of the German occupation troops to enter the principality were the Gestapo, who installed themselves at the Hotel de Paris. Strangely enough, and despite their reputation, they proved much milder than the O.V.R.A. They were followed by the headquarters staff of a complete German Panzer division, which occupied the Hotel Metropole. These supplied their own food and their own canteen. General von Kohlermann, a Bavarian, surprised the management by insisting that his officers should eat exactly the same food as the men and those members of the hotel staff who were hired to clean the rooms. In addition, there were two batteries of German coastal defence troops who installed themselves along the coast and barbed-wire defences at all the strategic points. But there is little doubt that the German troops in Monaco behaved with extreme correctitude. Proof of this is given by the acquiescence of the German officers to the insistence of the casino authorities on wearing civilian clothes when gambling in the casino.

At last came the landings of the American troops along the coast between St. Tropez and Dramont. Unfortunately for Monte Carlo and the rest of the Riviera east of Nice, the Supreme Command decided to allow that section of the Riviera to fall into its hands like a ripe plum when the right moment occurred. Instead of proceeding along the coast to the Italian frontier, the American troops drove up the Rhône Valley towards Lyons, to link up with the British and American armies driving south-west from the Normandy beaches.

The food situation in Monte Carlo was acute. All that the

Government could do was to arrange for the issue of one litre of liquid, containing barley and a local root called *rutabaga*, which even pigs dislike, to each member of the population. This was distributed at the luxury hotels and restaurants such as the Metropole and the Café de Paris. Time passed on. The American troops showed no sign of working their way along the coast. Then small bodies of troops, of never more than company strength, infiltrated along the Riviera. Out-bluffed, the Germans made no attempt to hold Nice or Monte Carlo, and it was real joy for the Monégasques to see them hiring taxis to escape. Then, on 3rd September 1944, two slightly hilarious American soldiers appeared on the Place d'Armes asking in broad Yankee accents where the hell they were.

Their appearance caused delirious excitement. The Government made tremendous plans for a triumphant march past of the American troops. Unfortunately, the American commander had been instructed not to proceed beyond the French border, and decided to do what neither the Italians nor the Germans had done – to recognise the neutrality of Monaco. He therefore ordered his troops to halt a kilometre or two away from the boundary, and the celebrations went off at half-cock.

Even after the Liberation, Monte Carlo was very badly off for food. Bridges could not be rebuilt overnight; roads could not be repaired in a matter of hours. To add to the general confusion, the American military authorities suggested that Monte Carlo should be made a leave centre for no fewer than twelve thousand American troops. The Monégasque Government courteously pointed out that there was not that number of rooms available, and that in view of the congestion in the hotels and boarding-houses and private dwellings, only twelve hundred visitors could be accepted. The Government also suggested that their honoured guests should all be officers. The

American authorities replied tartly that (a) Monte Carlo would be well advised to accept private soldiers and non-commissioned officers, because these could be suitably controlled, whereas officers were less inclined to discipline, and (b) it was not worth the American army's while to send in military police, canteens, Red Cross outfits, and all the other paraphernalia for a mere matter of twelve hundred men. When the Monégasque Government repeated that its capacity for welcoming American troops was limited to twelve hundred beds, Monte Carlo was put officially out of bounds to American troops.

Hectic weeks passed, during which special squads of demolition experts removed the barbed wire and other fortifications from the tiny Principality. Expert bomb-disposal parties removed no fewer than six hundred mines moored along the two-mile stretch of Monaco. Many of these were rendered harmless within a matter of yards of the famous Rubber Beach. But one mine exploded in April 1947, killing four workmen who were busily cleaning up the approaches to the luxurious swimming pool for the 1947 International Diving Competition.

Numbers of British army officers stationed in Italy entered Monte Carlo from the east, but the American military police frequently detected them and, announcing that Monte Carlo was out of bounds not only to U.S. troops but also to all Allied troops, forced them to return.

The social history of the Riviera since 1919 is inextricably bound up with two men, François André and Nicolas Zographos.

Zographos was the greatest gambler of all time, head of the Greek syndicate which put Monte Carlo completely in the shade where baccarat was concerned. On one occasion, he won nine million francs on two cards. He always claimed there was as big a difference between a good baccarat player and a poor one as between a scratch golfer and a man with an eighteen handicap. According to Zographos, the most dangerous opponents were the ones who took drugs. Full of confidence they would double up when winning, in contrast to most players who double up when they are losing and decrease their stakes when they are winning. He once said, 'There is no such thing as luck. It is all mathematics. There are three kinds of cards – good cards, bad cards and indifferent cards. You must play them according to what they are. That is not a contradiction. You may have luck for an hour or two, even a day or two, or even a week. There was the time when seat Number Two was winning continuously for eight days. It was terrible for me. There was only one thing to do. I persuaded the management to put away the biggest chips of all and have only the ten-*mille* chips. That made my opponents think a bit when they had to push a whole mountain of chips on to the table. Indeed, it was that which saved me. Psychology, my dear Charles. To be a gambler like me, you have to have a very strong heart, literally. It is all a question of your heart. If you get excited you either show it by flushing, which means that your heart is in a bad way; or you go pale, which means that your stomach is queasy. That also affects your brain and consequently your card sense.' Zographos tapped his forehead. 'After all, I have played against the whole world, and I know. That is why I, myself, gave up playing cards at baccarat for over a year because I found it was beginning to affect my stomach'.

In comparison with Nicolas Zographos, the gaming-house keepers of San Francisco, Alaska and New York; the Irish rake-hells who fleeced the English peerage during the seventeenth and eighteenth centuries; and all the people who were supposed to have broken the bank at Monte Carlo, were mere pikers. Incidentally, to break the bank in a casino before the war did not mean that the gambler had won more than £4,000, for that was the sum with which each roulette table started every session.

By 1939 Zographos according to the French newspapers, was worth ten million pounds. This was probably too high an estimate. But even accepting a figure of *two* million pounds as his fortune, it is fantastic to realise that the vast bulk of this was earned from the green baize tables, before being salted away in good English, American and Swiss securities.

His early years are as wrapped in mystery as those of the late Sir Basil Zaharoff. He was particularly reticent about his association with Greek shipping, but admitted that he had an interest in this form of enterprise during World War I; and it was not really until 1919 that his trail could be followed with any degree of ease.

It was in 1920 that the historic moment arrived when Zographos settled down at the middle seat of the baccarat table and said quietly, '*Tout va*'; in other words, 'The sky's the limit.' Unquestionably, he was the finest card player in the world, even though he handed over the baccarat banks to his nephew to play the cards for him.

Through the nineteen years during which he held the fort against the richest gamblers in the world, he never once lost his temper nor showed any signs of impatience. As he said, 'If I am winning, the others are losing, so it is tactless to look happy. Also, it is bad policy to look sad if one is losing.'

Alfred Capus once observed, 'If there were such a thing as an intelligent machine, it would have to be constructed exactly like Zographos.' When he entered the casino during his playing days he was as formal as a bank manager; and he gave a correct 'Good day' to all the casino staff. Previously he had lunched off a grilled cutlet and fresh fruit, together with a glass of mineral water. He probably had bathed as well. In Deauville he always stayed at the Royale. At Cannes he had a yacht.

At ten o'clock in the evening after the first session of play he would leave the casino for his hotel, and then return after midnight when the big game was about to start. Many a time in the boom years I have watched him play. On the last occasion there were sixty people clustered round the oval table behind the brass railings. Twenty of them were gambling on either side of the small Greek with his haunted eyes, high forehead and imperceptible fatigue. He had won on both sides of the table five times consecutively just before I arrived, and as I stood and watched, he did it four times more. In front of him were a pyramid of white oval 'biscuits' worth eight hundred pounds each; three feet of oblong red and blue eighty-pound 'biscuits' neatly packed on the green baize table; and a flood of transparent discs worth eight pounds each. In all, there was thirty thousand pounds in front of him, of which eighteen thousand represented his winnings that afternoon.

Zographos never smiled when he played, and seldom talked. His sole mannerism at the table was to put his hand on his hip while the croupier raked in the money. But his gaze flickered all round the table. Not (as he told me afterwards) that anybody ever tried to cheat at the big table, but quite often the croupier himself did not rake in or pay out the exactly correct sums of money represented by the chips; and to prevent any unpleasantness Zographos always made a point of making up any deficiency when the occasion arose. Only once did he ever touch alcohol at the table. That was when a fat French industrialist won twelve million francs from him in the space of twenty minutes. On that occasion Zographos had one glass of iced champagne and promptly won it all back.

The biggest loss that Zographos ever had over a period of a week occurred in 1928. On that occasion he lost no less than thirty-six million francs. True, the exchange was one hundred and twenty-five to the pound. Even then, the sum was £288,000. 'Well, you see,' Zographos said deprecatingly, 'Monsieur Citröen, the Aga Khan, and Mr. James Hennessy were staking between them five million francs on each hand ... The largest number of times I have ever won on both sides of the table is twelve, and on one side of the table, nineteen. It is, of course, humanly possible for the bank to be broken at each session, but I do not think it will happen. The advantage of the banker in drawing his second card after the player's gives a tiny, but definite advantage. But the main difference is that the players double up when they are losing and hedge when they are winning. It is only human nature, but there you are. I will put it another way. The bank plays baccarat as though it were contract bridge, weighing up mathematically every chance. And let me tell you it needs the brain of a very good accountant to assess immediately the amount of money being staked on either side of the table and then to work out mentally whether it is worth drawing a third card. But the players play baccarat, naturally, as if it were poker. I could put it even better. The bank plays with cards; the players play with money.'

Numerous syndicates, however, often with large capital behind them, have been completely wiped out at various casino towns. Having seen the success of Zographos at Deauville and Cannes, they thought that they were on a certain winner. They were wrong. Notably a syndicate at Biarritz.

Zographos himself did not believe in luck in any shape or form. 'There is no such thing as good luck or bad luck,' he once said. 'If you think you know of any particularly lucky card-holder, just you bring him along to the baccarat and you will see what you will see. What people call luck is merely an established fact seen through the spectacles of after events. If a girl marries a rich husband she is not lucky, she is intelligent; because if she had not married him, someone else would have done so.'

After his retirement from active play he attracted unconsciously a great deal of admiration. For although he knew that thousands of pounds of his own money were being wagered all the time, he would never once go over to the baccarat table and see how things were going. That must have taken self-control. No, he always stayed there talking to a group of people, usually the chief celebrities in Cannes, because they always searched him out, fascinated by his philosophy and romantic life. It was another of his good qualities that he always advised his friends to keep away from the green baize tables. 'You are bound to lose,' he would say. 'Why throw your money down the drain?' When, occasionally, friends of his (who shall be nameless because they are well known in England) started to get into deep water, he invariably rescued them. He has also been known to refuse to allow their cheques to be cashed – cheques which would enable them to continue playing against the bank. For he would see that anxiety or wine or both was militating against their playing their cards well that evening.

Zographos's wife, who survives him, believes in luck. This used to be an amusing topic of argument between the two of them. Frequently she played against her husband's own bank, but seldom with success. It is recorded that on one occasion shortly after they were married he found her playing *chemin de fer* at one of the twenty-five louis tables. He went and sat beside her for a moment. 'Buy the shoe,' he said suddenly when the current bank had already won ten times. She bought it and ran it four times. 'Pass it now,' said Zographos. She did so. It died on the next hand. And so it went on for an hour, with Zographos giving exactly correct advice every time. As they

left the table, Mme. Zographos said, 'How on earth did you
know just when a bank was going to die and just when it was
going to run?' 'But, my dear,' replied Zographos, 'don't you
realise that I know *all* about cards?' 'But why did you not tell
me before and help me?' his wife pouted. Zographos just
smiled – so the story went – and passed on into the big
baccarat room where play was due to begin.

He had many warm English and American friends and yet
led the fugitive life of a gipsy. Above all, he was a philosopher
and a fatalist. He was also an excellent *raconteur*, his best story
being the one about the American who returned to Ohio after
a visit to Deauville. 'What is this game called baccarat of which
we read so much?' his friends asked the American on his return.
The latter scratched his head thoughtfully, and then replied,
'Well, I guess I don't quite understand it, but I will try to tell
you what happens.' He took a deep breath and continued,
'There is a big room with several people who never look as
though they had ever been in love with anybody, standing
round a green baize table with a number of chairs, on which
the actual players are sitting. In the middle is a small dark
Greek, and in front of him whole piles of red and white
chips. Also in front of him is a wooden box with a lot of cards
in it. First the little man gives a card to the man on his left; then
he gives one to the man on his right; then he gives one to himself. Then he repeats the performance. He looks at the man on
the left enquiringly, who grins and says, "*Non*"; then he does
the same to the man on his right, who laughs and also says,
"*Non*". The little man does not change expression at all. He
picks up his two cards, which are face downwards, and turns
them over, and pushes them out into the middle of the table.
Whereupon the croupier, who sits beside him with a wooden
shovel, says "*Neuf*", and everybody says "Damn".'

Then there was the story about the gambler who had asked

whether he should draw on a six when he had given his opponent a six. Zographos told him that it was the right thing to do because it was half a point in his favour. Unfortunately the man did not realise that Zographos meant that he should only do this when his opponent asked for a card and was given a six. In consequence, he lost thousands of dollars by always drawing on a six, even when his opponents had not asked for a card. When finally asked why he kept on making this mistake, he said, 'Oh, Zographos told me always to draw on a six.'

According to Zographos, Sir Winston Churchill used to gamble at four tables simultaneously, but never for more than four hundred francs and never for less than three hundred francs, with a cigar in his mouth and a whisky and soda in his hand. 'Once at Maxine Elliott's, I spent three hours with him. He asked me what I thought about the French, English and Italian armies. I replied that some men have courage and no physique; some have physique and no courage; some have both courage and physique. That is the English Army, and I told him that in my opinion it would never be beaten.'

Zographos died in 1953.

He had, in the meantime, handed over the card-dealing, first to his nephew Frangopoulo, who was not a great success, and then to his cousin Georges Eliopulo. He had seen Georges playing *chemin de fer* in Paris, decided that he was a brilliant gambler and suddenly remarked one night, 'Would you care to play cards like me?' Georges said, 'Like you? I'd love it.' So, forgetting his job in the commodity market of Paris, Georges began his present fabulous pasteboard existence.

Born at Hubli near Bombay while the British Raj still flourished in India, he carries an English passport and was thus jailed in the St. Denis prison by the Germans during the war. He had passed his school days in Smyrna which he hated so much that when, after a nightmare that he was back in class,

The Begum Aga Khan and M. François André. (*Photo A. Traverso*)

Somerset Maugham on the terrace of Villa Mauresque, his Cap Ferrat home. (*Joe Hollander*)

Viscount Rothermere's Villa Roc Fleuri at Monte Carlo.

he woke to find that he was merely in prison, he sighed with relief. Following an apprenticeship at the Cercle Haussmann in Paris, Georges was avid to take the big bank at Cannes. During the first fortnight, he had the unprecedented luck of winning ten consecutive *coups* on both sides of the table at the start of his bank. His other records include losing eighteen consecutive *coups* on one side, and winning sixteen consecutive *coups* on one side, and losing £280,000 in one day. Of this, £55,000 was won by the Marquis de Soto and £50,000 by Ilhmy Hussein Pasha, a kinsman of ex-King Farouk.

Like Zographos, Georges Eliopulo remains entirely impassive on the surface. 'Yes,' he says, 'I am very calm. But then I am lucky. My pulse is only fifty-nine to the minute instead of the usual seventy-two.' He needs a minimum eight hours' sleep, lunches off a couple of boiled eggs at 3 p.m. in the afternoon, unless he is playing golf, drinks very little. Golf and bird-watching are his chief relaxations, particularly bird-watching. At Cannes he appears in December and holds the fort until the end of the Cannes Film Festival in April. He has had many tilts with Jack Warner and Anatole Litvak, among others. 'Jack Warner always animates the table,' he says. 'Sometimes this is good for me. When he wins he whistles. Darryl Zanuck also plays heavily. Anatole Litvak is a very steady gambler, like Charles Feldman. Stavros Niarchos plays sometimes. But money means nothing to him, nor to Onassis, who never gambles. Just before Zographos died, he asked Onassis how much he was worth, knowing that he was earning at least thirty thousand pounds a day. Onassis said simply, "I do not know at all. I have no time to count." '

Ex-King Farouk played against Eliopulo only three times and won five million francs. He preferred to deal his own cards at *chemin de fer*. On one occasion an Englishman won £4,000 from him and died of heart failure in his chair.

Some of the statistics of the big table are almost incredible. When gambling is high, more than £650,000 is wagered in a day. There are two sessions – at 6 p.m. and midnight. The average *coup* amounts to £20,000 and there are 160 *coups* (or deals) per session. According to Eliopulo, he was invited to go to Las Vegas to start an open bank as at Cannes and Deauville, but a special emissary reported back that the gambling there was far too low to make it worth his while. So he never went. That, anyway, is his story and he sticks to it.

One of his happier memories was when American Jack Mackeon, having won the equivalent of a million dollars, put all the notes into an open umbrella, closed it, put the rubber ring round the top of the spokes, and drove to Paris. At the Restaurant Fouquet, where he got out, it was raining and blowing hard. He opened the umbrella . . . the Champs-Elysées was suddenly white with scudding banknotes, not all of which were retrieved.

What would happen if Eliopulo went sick? 'A man of steel never gets a virus,' he says firmly. One can only presume, however, that the big game would cease. He has no deputy. Since 1946 he has paid one million pounds in taxes to the French Treasury. There is no escape. After each session the special Custom and Excise police examine and count all the torn scraps of paper, each of which represents a *coup*. Eliopulo pays $1\frac{1}{4}$ per cent on each winning *coup*, his opponents being relieved of this unkind tax. After one particular good day, he paid no less than £5,000.

Dark, good-looking, fifty-ish, Eliopulo is married to the current bridge champion of France. He never plays cards with her. Her usual stakes are five francs a hundred.

François André is a most remarkable person. Reaction being always the operative factor in life, it is not surprising that in his early days he was employed by an undertaker in Paris. He measured people for coffins; he took orders for funeral wreaths; he did everything that a bright young undertaker's assistant should do.

His father was a brewer on a very small scale in Marseilles. André himself began his career as a *plongeur* – in other words, a dish-washer – in a brasserie in the same town. But he had a friend who was the son of a man who made a fortune as an undertaker in Paris. This was Monsieur Couronne. Young François was a very intelligent boy. His friend's father hired him; but the association lasted for only three months because the time had arrived for his military service. This he thoroughly enjoyed, and learned to play cards, at which he rapidly became expert.

During two days' leave in Paris, he met a charming modiste and fell in love with her. When his service came to an end, he proposed to the girl, with whom he had corresponded since he first met her. They married. In order to keep the wolf from the door, young André sold postcards on the Boulevard like any René Clair hero. Then a former army friend of his, named Bidasse, secured him a job in a gaming club as money-changer, going round with a leather bag turning clients' cash into chips. This lasted for a brief period. Whereupon André borrowed 400 francs from his wife and purchased the monopoly for running a tiny *petits-chevaux* game at Deauville. The prizes consisted of candy, dolls and similar articles.

During this period he realised the public taste for gambling. With the profits from the *petits-chevaux*, young André started a gaming club in the Rue de Courcelles. It was the first time that a gambling club had ever admitted women. This was not surprising. By law, mixed gambling has never been allowed in Paris. Every week or so he was raided, but he carried on. His audacity in evading the law – when he succeeded in doing so –

brought in more money than the fines cost him. Soon people began to talk about him.

Money was rolling in, and we next find him at Ostend shortly before World War I. That was in the days when Ostend almost justified its now unjustified title of 'Queen of the Foreign Watering Places'. With the exception of Monte Carlo, Cannes and Nice, it was the most fashionable seaside resort on the Continent.

André was manager in 1914. Instead of applying for a commission, as a man of his experience might have done, he rejoined the army as a private and refused to take officer rank. He served right through the war in the front line, winning the Croix de Guerre and the Médaille Militaire. He was also mentioned in dispatches several times. When the war came to an end, he was a senior sergeant. He had also been wounded twice.

At this stage Cornuché, the man who invented Deauville, took him under his wing, and rising from a modest position, André proved himself invaluable. So much so that when Cornuché died, André automatically became managing director of the companies controlling Deauville and the Cannes casino.

Gambling was now at its height. The English and the Americans came over and left fortunes in the *cagnotte*. André expanded right and left. He took a view about La Baule. He wanted to squeeze out Biarritz, and decided that when the season came to an end at Deauville he would divert the rich gamblers to this village in southern Brittany and also to Pau, where he built a casino. At La Baule he not only built a casino, he erected two hotels and started a third. Contrexéville was another of his speculations. When 1929 dawned, André, the ex-assistant funeral undertaker, was worth an impossible sum of money. 'Everything was going far too smoothly,' he said. 'I could not really sleep at night because of it all. I used to tell my wife that it could not last – that it was all far too easy. I did not actually pray for more obstacles to surmount, but if I had, my prayer was certainly answered. The slump suddenly arrived, and within eighteen months nine-tenths of my fortune had completely disappeared. . . .'

André is tall for a Frenchman, with a greying moustache and an admirable smile. He speaks with his eyes. He sees behind his back. His knowledge of politics, finance and literature is only equalled by his ability for controlling the casino. He has a number of peculiarities. He never goes to bed before 6 a.m. He never gets up later than 10 a.m. He has a horror of cheese. Even if the President of the French Republic was sitting down to dinner with him and a Camembert was placed on the table, you may be sure that André would go up like a rocketing pheasant and not return. André prefers his own home-cooking to that of any hotel. Another of his characteristics is that wherever he goes he takes an umbrella with him. Even at Cannes, in the height of August, you will see a morose gamp in his hand. Every year his friends give him umbrellas for Christmas presents. They know that they are a secret passion with him. He is also very fond of panama hats. He is odd, too, about his clothes – in fact, the despair of his wife. He will finally be persuaded to order a dozen suits at a time, but when he has had all his fittings he will return to some old suit which he has worn for years.

André has never drunk a cocktail in his life. He is practically a teetotaller. Also, he eats very little. He has a country place called the Château des Pins, run by his wife. But when he is on the job in Deauville or Cannes, he is in complete control. He tastes the food in the restaurant. He curses a dilatory *chasseur*. He replaces a fuse. He chooses the cabaret, and placates a ruffled gambler. He is everywhere at the same moment.

Today André believes that rich Americans are much more sophisticated and cultured than they used to be, but do not feel so much pleasure in spending their money because of a guilt complex. This seems somewhat strange when we think of the Vanderbilts, Drexels, Van Alens, Astors and other leading Americans such as Willie Rhinelander Stewart, Laddie Sanford and Jay Gould who lent tone to the South of France over thirty years ago, and more. Listen to him, though: 'The rich in America have gained immeasurably in self-confidence in the past thirty years,' he says. 'Europeans used to joke about them, but it would be absurd to do so now. In culture, charm and good manners, they are the equal of any Europeans and perhaps their masters. Americans no longer feel uneasy in the presence of titled or wealthy Europeans. Often it is quite the reverse.'

But he admitted there was a slightly sad side to this picture. 'The Americans usually have more money than anyone else – except the Indian princes – but they seem to get less genuine pleasure out of it. They have acquired acute social consciences since I first knew them. They have a tremendous dread of being described as playboys or of having their photographs in the newspapers doing something a little foolish. They have become what the English used to be. With less money, the English do not worry so much about their responsibilities any more.'

According to André, movie stars are far more subdued than their predecessors of thirty or even twenty years ago. 'Today it is the movie stars who try to act like aristocrats,' he said, 'and the aristocrats who act like movie stars.' He disclosed that the biggest spenders at Deauville are invariably the legion of Indian maharajahs who were bought out when India became independent, trading their elephants and ivory palaces for cash. 'Their money is all tax-exempt,' said the shrewd old man who has seen millionaires come and go, 'and there is plenty of it. But I predict that in a generation most of it will be gone.'

CHAPTER 13

HARRY PILCER,

JULES AND PIERPONT MORGAN

THE BEST KNOWN BARMAN on the Riviera today is Jules, the big dark Monégasque in charge of the Carlton Hotel, Cannes. Jules was born in Monte Carlo and is another champion of the theory that the climate has altered enormously since he was a boy; fifty years ago, he claims, the normal temperature in summer was anything from 90° to 100° in the shade. Today it is nearer 85°. As a youngster he was always sent away by his parents during the hot weather, when Monte Carlo was as dead-and-alive as Nice, the local inhabitants lazing around doing no work at all, living on the money they had made during the winter season.

Jules' earliest recollections are of being given a gold louis, as a normal tip, for calling a carriage when he was a young *chasseur* at the Hotel de Paris. Another early recollection is of Count von Zernsdorf, who married a Hohenlohe and used to light his cigarettes with thousand franc notes, then worth fifty pounds. Young Jules would try to put his foot surreptitiously on them before they were burnt. Sometimes he succeeded.

Those were the days of incredible wealth. The Mantacheff brothers, each of whom had a reputed income of £25,000 a day from their Silesian oil wells, were regular clients. One of them, Dimitri, was six feet six tall, a giant of a man with an appetite to match. He would eat a complete baby lamb or two large chickens at a sitting. A greater gambler than the Mantacheffs was the bearded Russian Estekieff, whose chief peculiarity was to drink a full bottle of chianti at every meal. He lost eight million gold francs in the casino and was ultimately given a small pension. Prince Orloff, another regular, gave his name to that famous dish consisting of saddle of veal truffles, fresh cream, mushrooms and *foie gras*. Prince Poliakoff was a tremendous gambler.

Jules later on became barman in the Sporting Club at Monte Carlo, where he frequently made temporary loans to gamblers. He was always repaid with interest. His scattered memories of those days include the beautiful South American, Mme. de Bittencourt, another famous gambler; Berry Wall and his big floppy ties, his chow, and his wife who received a Legion of Honour for work with the Red Cross; Phillips Oppenheim, florid and bushy eyebrowed, who came from Guernsey every year to write his annual thriller about the casino; Lady Mac-Carthy, who fascinated Jules by her taste for a tomato juice cocktail hotted up with a full teaspoonful of tabasco sauce; and, particularly, the Hon. Mrs. Ronnie Greville, who had taken him into her service as a second footman in her London home during the summer season to improve his English.

Later Jules left Monte Carlo for the Carlton at Cannes. He knew that it would normally take at least five years to build up a really smart clientele, but fortune smiled on him. One day Lord Brownlow, Lord Castlerosse, Lord Beaverbrook, Lord Cholmondeley, Mr. and Mrs. Herman Rogers, Mr. and Mrs. Sidney Allan, Major King and, above all, the Prince of Wales came to his cocktail bar. Jules was made.

In that summer of 1930, the Carlton would normally have been closed, but the rain was so appalling in June and July all over northern France that the management decided to shut the Royal Hotel at Dinard and re-open the Carlton at Cannes on the 5th August. That was perhaps the first official recognition at

Cannes of the summer season, now so much more fashionable than the winter one. Today, the Carlton Hotel bar has a staff of sixty-eight in the summer and from it are served 3,000 drinks an hour from noon onwards. Not surprisingly, Jules has had offers to go to the U.S., notably Miami, where a three-year contract of $25,000 a year was handed to him for signature. He did not accept. Later, he was selected to dispense drinks at the Château d'Horizon on the occasion of the wedding of Aly Khan and Rita Hayworth. No Cannes Film Festival would be complete without at least one cocktail party under his aegis. His special clients include Jack Warner, Darryl Zanuck, Prince Pierre de Polignac (the father of Prince Rainier), the Duke of Devonshire, Lord Derby and Signor Agnelli, the tall dark proprietor of the Fiat motor-car concern.

Another legendary character of the Riviera is Harry Pilcer, the American-born stage dancer who partnered Gaby Deslys at the height of her fame before she died tragically at the age of twenty-nine. Harry must be rising seventy, but his sleek, black hair belies his age. In spite of all his other triumphs and activities as permanent stage manager for François André at Cannes and elsewhere, he lives with his memories of Gaby, dead over forty years ago. He still carries, next to his heart, her cancelled passport of 29th April 1916, which describes her as having blonde hair, blue eyes, chestnut eyebrows, perfect nose, round chin, oval face, milk-white complexion, age twenty-nine, height five foot six inches.

His first appearance with her on the Riviera was at Monte Carlo in 1911. They had met two years previously at the Folies Bergères, New York, which Ziegfield had transformed into a roof garden from the previous Fulton theatre. Jake Shubert was Gaby's impresario. Minerva Coverdale was Harry's partner. Gaby was engaged for the Winter Garden. Here Gaby took one look at Harry. 'Zees iz ze boy I weesh to dance wiz,' she said succinctly and asked him round to the St. Regis to talk terms. She already had a dancing partner.

Harry had temporarily to refuse her suggestion, being already booked for another New York show. When it flopped and he saw huge posters all over New York drawing attention to the beauteous mistress of King Emmanuel of Portugal, he teamed up with her, and invented the Gaby glide.

When the show closed two years later, they did a double act at the casino in Beau Soleil, half a mile from the Monte Carlo casino, having driven there by car from Paris by way of Cannes and Nice. The journey took a week. At the Hotel de Paris, Monte Carlo, where they stayed, Senhor Unzue, a South American millionaire, presented Gaby with a cask full to the brim with twenty-dollar gold pieces (Harry still has one as a keepsake). Gaby was only mildly impressed. In those days she wore a seventeen-string pearl necklace, each pearl the size of a small grape, says Harry proudly.

The other beauties of the day were La Belle Otero, Cleo de Merode - very slim, with her hair parted in the middle - Lan Telinar, who disappeared later off a yacht in the Seine, Mrs. Langtry and Liane de Pougy.

When Gaby and Harry danced in the Restaurant des Ambassadeurs at Cannes for the first time, he could not believe his eyes when at one table he saw the King of Sweden, the King of Denmark and, of course, the King of Portugal. 'Don't forget to bow to the royal table before you start your act,' he was told, 'and don't forget to bow to the royal table before you bow to the public when you have finished your act.'

Later on, Gaby and he became estranged. Teddy Gerard took her place as Harry's partner in the revue *Rouge et Noir*. Gaby was furious. She went backstage, entered Teddy's dressing-room during the dress rehearsal and cut up all her clothes.

Harry talks of nothing but Gaby, unless really pressed to

change the conversation. This dark, lithe, monkey-faced man still carries a blazing torch for her. His experiences immediately before and during World War II were hair-raising, but quite unimportant to him compared with the Vicar of Brixton's helping to ban a bedroom scene which he played with Gaby at a London theatre, visited night after night by the young Prince of Wales.

Having gone by train with Serge Lifar and Anton Dolin to Paris, Harry walked from the French capital to Vichy after the German occupation, hitch-hiked his way to Irun on the Spanish frontier and finally made his way to Portugal and thence to the United States. Within three months of the war being over, he was back in Cannes. Apart from his obsession about Gaby Deslys, he can talk freely of the house in Kensington Gore, bought for her by Gordon Selfridge, of the Dolly Sisters, and of Mrs. Langtry.

Another old timer with a fund of memories is Sheila Wallace, daughter of the British Consul in Nice at the turn of the century. As she says, everybody on the Riviera had hoped that Edward VII would return after he came to the throne. He never did. It seems that shortly before the coronation a queer incident occurred. A senior gendarme, on retirement, opened one of the olive-wood souvenir shops which were all too frequent at the time. He was in a café at Nice when he overheard three men talking in the Corsican dialect, which he fortunately understood. They were planning the assassination of Edward VII during the Coronation procession. They were to have a window in Piccadilly, and would be met at Dover by anarchist agents. The ex-gendarme took down their descriptions, and went off to the police station.

For the next month Mrs. Wallace's father, the Consul, was most mysterious about the people who came to the consulate at all hours of the night. Then, of course, the Coronation was

postponed because of Edward VII's attack of appendicitis, and
many undesirable characters were caught on the coast when
trying to slip across. Not long afterwards the olive-wood shop
was burned down. Revenge?

Mrs. Wallace recalls the annual visit of the Duchess of Saxe-
Coburg-Gotha to the Château de Fabron at Nice. On arrival,
she always sent the lady-in-waiting and lord chamberlain to
call on the Consul. Various royal relatives visited her, such as
Princess Beatrice of Battenberg and Princess Ena, afterwards
Queen of Spain. The royal pew at Holy Trinity, the English
church, was usually full up. On one occasion, Princess Ena wore
a hat trimmed with fresh white gardenias – very dashing, in
those days.

The Empress Eugénie came to Nice in her yacht *Thistle* in
the winter of 1902–3. 'Father took her a book about her Scottish ancestors, of whom she was very proud,' recalls Mrs.
Wallace; 'I and my governess went to the harbour hoping to
see her. She was an old lady all in black, with striking eyes.
She gave us (just one governess and one little girl) the lovely
révérence often mentioned in accounts of her. This seemed to
include us both and yet be for oneself.'

In those far-off days members of the large English colony
had vast villas, to which they brought English servants. They
passed the winter only among the colony, completely ignoring
the town. No casinos for them! Mrs. Wallace recalls an
elderly Englishman with a large villa at Carabacel, who took
round the plate in church in faultless morning dress. In the
spring he returned to England and did it all over again. There
was a collection of elderly ladies who sang in the choir, and
helped at parsonage parties, as if in an English village, but
wore the most regrettable hats. Then there were others. It was
often remarked of couples that 'they' had known 'her' with
someone else. (Where was the clearing house? Paris?) Many

young men in Nice society were said to be the illegitimate sons of the famous. Nor was this, probably, slander.

One season there arrived a foreign lady who claimed to be Russian royalty, complete with white bearskins, hounds, and an old retainer who called her 'ma Princesse' at frequent intervals. Afterwards, she was said to be bogus, and a spy.

Mrs. Wallace recalls the Duc de Pomar, who gave very nice parties in a big apartment. Earlier, he had written lurid novels, such as Passion and Fashion. By this time he was a very kind host, plump and white-haired. His mother became Lady Caithness, châtelaine of the house now called Castle of Mey, the property of Queen Elizabeth, the Queen Mother. She was obsessed by Mary, Queen of Scots, dressed like her, and thought that she was her reincarnation. Indeed, she obtained special permission to spend the night at Holyrood, and next morning produced a ring which she said Mary had given her: it was not very attractive – heavy gold set with rather small stones, including rubies. Lady Caithness insisted on being buried at Holyrood. Her grave can still be seen in the ruined chapel grounds.

In those days there was no summer season. From May to October everything shut down, and the local inhabitants lazed through the heat. The only sign of life was the satirical play at the local theatre, entitled Sin d'Estiou. It mocked the rich winter visitors, the theme being, 'Nobody is here except ourselves, so we can let our hair down.'

There was one small bathing place, which scarcely anyone used, the sea being regarded as a feature of the landscape and nothing more. Apart from that, there were supposed to be octopuses in the neighbourhood and the town rubbish was taken out for a couple of miles in a steamer once a week and dumped in the sea. Next morning there was always a fringe of orange peel along the beach.

Those were the days when Princess Daisy of Pless confided to her diary that 'common people with money who have no position in their own countries turn down their noses at Nice and say it is common.' People sure of themselves like Princess Daisy found Nice very central, being between Cannes and Monte Carlo, with Cimiez particularly healthy and charming. Those were the days when Princess Daisy described Prince Arthur of Connaught as 'such a nice boy' on his return from presenting the Order of the Garter to the Emperor of Japan, and she herself, accompanied by Lady Randolph Churchill and the Duchess of Marlborough, made so bold as to attempt to motor from Cannes to Avignon. 'We soon ran out of essence, or whatever the stuff is called that makes the motor go,' she recalled. 'I think essence is a most inappropriate name for a substance that smells so horribly.'

Those were the days at Mandalieu Golf Club when the flying dance was invented. Four men linked arms. The ladies put an arm round their men's necks, while the men held their partners around the waist with their free arms. They then began to revolve faster and faster like one of the figures of the Lancers, until the ladies were lifted off their feet and flew round – their trains parallel with the floor. Lovely to watch, but dangerous to try.

Those were the days of Ogden Goulet, that well-known American banker whose fine yacht competed so often with the Duke of Westminster's *Flying Cloud*; of the Maharajah Duleep Singh, who called himself King of Lahore, and who became too friendly with the Russians and had to sell his jewellery because his pension was stopped by the British Government; of George Gapon, the Russian nihilist priest, who escaped after the first abortive Russian Revolution, had the effrontery to go into the Monte Carlo casino dressed as a Rumanian bishop, and gambled at the same table as one of the grand dukes (his body was found months later on the outskirts of St. Petersburg); of the defeat of the English Conservative Government and the rapid return after the General Election of a series of cabinet ministers and twelve Members of Parliament who lost their seats and came back to console themselves in the sunshine of the Riviera; of Pierpont Morgan who had three yachts, all called *Corsaire*.

The first was 165 feet, the second was 205 feet, and the third was 320 feet.

He wanted everything to be exactly the same in *Corsaire III* as in *Corsaire I* and *Corsaire II*. But the carpets were no longer obtainable when *Corsaire III* was fitted out; so he had the pattern set up on the looms again and specially woven for him. They were thus literally unique and cost him a fortune.

Those were the days of Mado Taylor, and 'Charlie' Brighten, and the sisters Gui, and La Pomme and La Japonnaise, and Yvette Laurent, the close friend of the Grand Duke Dimitri; of Princess Ghika; when it was permissible to go into the *Salles Privées* in polo clothes at a time when the *Salles Privées* were smaller than the present bar in the casino.

CHAPTER 14

VILLA LIFE AND BARRY DIERKS

DURING THE WAR OF 1939–45, properties belonging to English and Americans automatically fell into disrepair. However, the estate agency firm of John Taylor was able to remain in operation under French direction. As far as English owners were concerned, arrangements were made through the Treasury and a neutral country to transfer funds to France for up-keep expenses. In this way many properties were kept going by faithful gardeners and old retainers.

During the occupation by the German army, some of the best villas were chosen by the German staff, and one found the curious and rather galling situation, from the British point of view, of these people enjoying the amenities of some beautiful properties at British expense. However, thanks to the vigilance of everybody concerned, very little furniture or valuables were lost. In one case, a German general was persuaded to replace a broken teapot as if the affair had been an ordinary seasonal rental.

Alas, estates on the coast were in some cases badly damaged by bombardments, ironically enough from Allied warships or aeroplanes later in the war.

After the end of the war, owners started with amazing rapidity to put their properties in order. This was a very busy time for the firm of John Taylor, assessing damage, putting in claims and supervising repairs.

Since World War II, there have been many changes, not

all for the worse. Many of the larger estates have inevitably been broken up into smaller units, and the largest houses converted into very fine flats. This is a sad but universal trend. One of the first to go was Lady Trent's Springlands in Cannes. It was followed a few years later by the equally famous Villa Fiorentina belonging to the Princess Karageorgevitch, who was American born. Her granddaughter, Atalanta Mercati, married Michael Arlen in Cannes. Other properties which were split up into smaller units were Lord Cheylesmore's Villa St. Priest, and Lord Brougham's Villa Eleanore. However, these losses were other people's gain, and today well-to-do people enjoy the really lovely apartments thus formed, and some charming, but of course much smaller, villas have been constructed in the parks which retain their beautiful trees, statuary and fountains.

On the other hand, there are still some large estates in private ownership, although not always in the hands of the original owners or their families. One of the best known of these at Cannes is the Villa Sansovino. This property is now in the possession of M. Adrien Thierry, French Ambassador. Madame Thierry was a de Rothschild.

One of the outstanding examples of family tradition in these parts is the record of the Norman family. The Hon. Lady Norman, daughter of Lord Aberconway, who inherited the Château de la Garoupe estate from her mother, has now restored this lovely Cap d'Antibes property to its former magnificence. In fact, it now gives enjoyment to more people than ever before, as new houses have been built since the war. Lady Norman and her family are amongst the oldest and most respected landlords in this part of France.

Lady Burton, whose property, the Château de la Croe, was known as the Château des Rois because it was occupied successively by the Duke and Duchess of Windsor, King Leopold of the Belgians, and the Queen Mother of Italy, is the widow of Sir Pomeroy Burton, once well known in the newspaper world. They built the château between 1930 and 1932, having had to buy land from eighteen different owners, mostly peasants, to make up the present park. The property is now in the possession of Mr. Stavros Niarchos, the Greek shipping magnate. It is certain that he will keep the place up in the best tradition.

Amongst other permanent residents on the Côte d'Azur are Mme. Bezancon de Wagner, better known as Maggy Rouff, who has a lovely villa at Cannes; Picasso, who has a large and comfortable villa in the best residential district at Cannes; and M. Thorez, the French Communist. The Aga Khan and Aly Khan, Jack Warner and André Dubonnet all put tremendous store by their properties and thoroughly enjoy them.

One more famous villa which has changed hands is the Château de Garibondy just behind Cannes, where Queen Victoria once stayed. Its original owner was a great English character – Miss Amy Paget, who died in 1947 aged ninety. She passed the whole of the last war at her château, and fearlessly flew the British flag for all to see throughout the Occupation.

The Germans were far too polite to ask her to take it down. She always employed Russian menservants over six feet in height. Two of these are still on the property. The present owners are Mr. and Mrs. James Douglas, charming Americans.

Says Mrs. Montague, proprietor of the family estate agent business:

'I can only add that our job here is a most fascinating one from the point of view of the different people we meet, of all nationalities. We deal with a mixture of persons, stretching from peasants to multi-millionaires. Often the former are harder bargainers and more tenacious than the latter. We never know who is going to drop into our office next, and on this coast, especially in the summer, the garments worn are no indication of the size of the pocket of the person involved. We try not to slip up in this respect.

'We have a great variety of property for sale – from the famous camel that stands with its keeper between Juan-les-Pins and Cap d'Antibes to the loveliest of villas. We once offered the camel to Mr. Claude Swinden, the London industrialist. The price was reasonable and the takings from people being photographed on its back were excellent. He answered by telegram: "Close if you can secure Zsa-Zsa Gabor as keeper." Mr. Swinden had always admired that camel, but unfortunately we were not able to secure Miss Gabor.

'One more story – about a certain millionaire who wished to rent a palace for the summer season a few years ago. Price was no object. He was on the top of the world, as apparently he had secured a world monopoly in the sale of a certain essential part of ladies' apparel. Nothing was good enough – nothing was big enough. Finally, the disappointed agent drove the magnate back to town. The latter suddenly let out a yell of joy from the back of his vast car. "There it is!" he thundered, "I'll take it!" Our excited representative said, "Where?" "There, you fool, can't you see?" cried our magnate, indicating one of the largest and most famous hotels on the coast. He returned home a disappointed man.'

For more than half a century, owners of estates at Cap Ferrat and elsewhere spent a fortune on creating superb gardens which form an integral background to the actual home. Maryland, frequently visited by Edward VII, was distinguished by its floral trout streams – a stream of forget-me-nots tumbling down little gullies and spreading out into pools with wide banks of dark purple iris forming the edges of the 'stream'. A high wall festooned with rosemary, pergolas covered with roses, cypress and olive groves, oleanders, olives, Japanese medlars, double red daisies, Chinese plum trees, almonds, mandarins, orange trees and a pool, but *not* a swimming pool, gave it a character all its own. Maryland belonged to Muriel Ward, daughter of Edward VII's host at Tranby Croft. She sold it for £15,000 to Carl Fridt, a Belgian who renovated it and sold it to M. Birgitt, a major stockholder in the Hispano-Suiza company.

Leopolda, originally on the property of King Leopold of the Belgians, but not built during his lifetime, is a thousand feet up on an isolated spur of the hillside, which seems to have slipped down from the Estorels, with a ravine between it and the Middle Corniche and a deep gorge to the east. It was originally built for the Comtesse de Beauchamp, who bought the property, on which were two peasants' cottages. One was renovated as a guest house in Provençal style. The other was enlarged with a library connected by a semicircular colonnade. It had four terraces, a Spanish garden, a Moorish tea-house, olive trees, twin pools (not, again, swimming pools). It was then almost completely rebuilt by Ogden Codman. Today it belongs to Signor G. Agnelli, the head of the Fiat motor-car company, and the garage contains a fabulous selection of personal motor-cars, such as Bugattis, Bentley Continentals and the like. It also has a real swimming pool.

The Villa Primavera, on a small promontory between the arms of Cap Ferrat, was built by Sir Laurence Phillips, and was one of the few which escaped the floods of 1927. Echiniums as big as trees, paved walks and cypress arches made it different from the others.

Mon Brillant was built for Lord Wemyss in 1909 on the Marseilles side of Cannes. It specialised in wistaria, Japanese ivy and sunken terraced gardens.

Champfleuri, in the Californie section of Cannes, was built

to the instructions of Mme. Vagliano. Groups of old cork trees, a path of marble squares, a vast sloping lawn with a stream running through it, the Dutch garden, the Fountain garden, a hanging garden, and tame flamingoes in the Japanese garden gave it an air of distinction. Her husband could well afford it. He was a partner in the Greek Syndicate.

Sainte Clare le Château belonged to Edith Wharton, the writer. Its round tower justified its title of Château. Surrounded by ramparts so ancient that the French Government nominated them as a national monument, it contains a rock garden with better tropical plants than the one belonging to Prince Rainier at Monaco.

The Souleiadou, on the point of Cap Ferrat where the cliffs are 200 feet high, was built for the Vicomtesse de Breteuil. It has a Provençal loggia, a partly colonnaded south front with a deliberately large number of pine trees.

On the eastern edge of the bay of Eze is Isoletta, built by Mrs. E. O. H. P. Belmont, better known as Mrs. W. K. Vanderbilt, between the railway and the sea. The garden is on the edge of the Mediterranean and therefore subject to the mistral.

The Villa Rosemary, originally built to the design of Arthur Cohen, was named for his daughter, now the wife of Major Paley-Johnson, who is in direct line to the succession of perhaps the most unusual baronetcy in the world – that of New York City. It was built by Harold Peto, the architect who preceded Barry Dierks. Later it was sold to Sir John and Lady Ward, and then bought by Carl Fridt, who changed its name to La Palladienne, and was asking £65,000 for it in 1956. This sounds a great deal, but it would cost at least £150,000 to build a similar villa today.

It is, incidentally, a pity that these historic villas with semi-historic names should have their nomenclature changed by new owners. It is something like the cities of France and

Belgium where important streets have their names altered, to the irritation of householders and shopkeepers along them, as an inexpensive way of paying a tribute, instead of hard cash, to some retiring politician or successful general.

La Mortola, where Queen Victoria stayed, is a classic villa. The Via Aurelia once went straight through its garden. Before Sir Thomas Hanbury bought it, it was known as the Palazzo Orengo, and Machiavelli was supposed to have slept there. Sir Thomas first approached it by boat, and was fascinated by the square keep and the watch tower. The original owners were in permanent danger from the Corsairs. It was, however, the gardens which became the pride of that part of the world.

Villa Fanfarigoule, built by Sir Allan and Lady Johnston above La Napoule, specialised in lavender hedges, mimosa, heliotrope and old oil jars filled with rosemary. The main entrance was at the back, with the living-rooms on the ground floor opening out on to the veranda.

Lord and Lady Forres turned an old, terraced lemon-farm, way back behind Menton, into the Villa Mont Agel. Villa Fiorentina has wistaria flowing over the steps, and a vast water garden. It was built by the Princess Karageorgevitch high up behind Cannes, with lovely cloisters at the foot of the garden. The house is massive. The marble hall is entered from the porch through a fine grill, then ascends two storeys with a colonnaded gallery on three sides above, from which the room opens out. The dining-room and drawing-room on the ground floor open off the hall. The salon and yellow boudoir look out over the garden with its brilliant flower beds, cedars and cypresses.

Ralph Curtis of Boston[1] built the Villa Sylvia. The entrance

1. When Lord Harris asked Curtis in a condescending way whether he had ever met the Vanderbilts, the demure reply was 'No. You see they were still Vanderbuilding when I left New York.'

is from the road on the first floor, with the main marble staircase leading down to the hall and reception rooms, each interconnected. This was another Peto house on Cap Ferrat, with gardens full of banana trees, lemon groves, and orange groves. Once again, the pool was not for swimming.

Les Bruyeres, built for the Duke of Connaught at Cap Ferrat, has lawns planted with eucalyptus trees, wide grass walks, mimosa, dwarf cypresses, and old jars of creamy earthenware from ancient oil mills, full of geraniums. It now belongs to M. Forgeot, one of the owners of the Hispano-Suiza company. The ducal gardener still works there.

Villa Cypris at Cap Martin was the property of Mme. Donine. It had a colonnaded garden house, vast cloisters, sunken gardens and an Arab pergola. Nor must one forget Villa Youke, the home of Prince and Princess Troubetskoy. The Princess is the sister of Frank Stranahan, the international golfer.

Villa Biggozi at Antibes belongs to the chief shareholder in the Simca automobile company. The exterior is Italianate. Inside, the visitor can guess that it was designed by an engineer, so efficient is its lay-out.

La Vigie, not to be confused with the hideous villa of the same name overlooking the beach at Monte Carlo, became the property of a French arms manufacturer – M. Rozet-Fourneyra. When he died, he left it floor by floor to his three children.

The Villa Yakimour, up behind Cannes, takes its name from the telescoping of the initial letters of the Christian names of the Begum and the Aga Khan, with the French for love as good measure. The present Begum (the third), *née* Yvette Labrousse, was born on the far side of Marseilles, but met her husband in Cairo, marrying him later in Switzerland. The villa is set in the most beautiful grounds. Having passed through the tall green iron gates, the visitor sees in the distance a flight of wide shallow stone steps flanked by cypresses leading to a dazzling white villa with the usual green shutters. The steep drive between the lemon and orange trees ascends to a terrace from which there is a superb view of oleanders, petunias, roses, palms and mandarin trees. There is also a splendid swimming pool with sliding doors across the middle. These can be closed in chilly weather, transforming it into an indoor swimming bath with specially heated water. The Duke of Edinburgh has swum there more than once. Doves flutter around the top of the pink and gold tiled roof. In the dining-room stands the Aga Khan's golden trophy of the Paris Grand Prix

In 1943, three men, masked, hooded and armed with tommy guns, robbed the Begum of £200,000 worth of jewellery in a daylight raid. She, her husband and her personal maid were intending to motor to Nice airport to fly to Deauville. Barely two hundred yards from Yakimour, a strange car was drawn across the road. The three men jumped out, slashed the tyres of the Aga Khan's motor-car, threw open the door and produced revolvers. One snatched the Begum's jewel box as it rested on her knee, another of the trio said: '*Soyez gentils.* Allow us to get away.' The Aga Khan called out: 'Hi – come back. You've forgotten your tip.' One of the men rushed back questioningly. The Aga Khan handed him a number of *mille* notes. '*Merci,*' said the man as he ran back. It took four years and a number of strange developments before the three men were tried and convicted of the theft. In the meantime, part of the loot had been mysteriously returned to the police.

The most attractive villa on the Ile de Ste. Marguerite was built for his English mistress, Miss Howard, by Napoleon III, as recompense for his marrying the Empress Eugénie. Today the Grand Jardin, as it is called, is owned by the Danish sculptor, Viggo Jarl.

The Château de l'Horizon was originally built for Maxine

Elliott, who spent the last ten years of her life there, forgotten by the public, though not by Sir Winston Churchill and Sir Anthony Eden. They held many secret conferences there with the French and Italian Foreign Ministers before the Japan and Munich crises.

Towards the end of her days, Maxine Elliott grew monstrously fat, and spent all her time playing backgammon by the side of her swimming pool.

Daisy, Lady Warwick, friend of Edward VII, built the Villa Grevillea, which is still in the family. This is unusual. The local estate agent can expect to sell any given villa two or three times in twenty-five years. Lord Brook, heir to Lord Warwick, spent his honeymoon there in July 1956.

Of the Americans still at Cap Ferrat, there are Messrs. Strong and Munroe, who own respectively the Villa Kawaroc and the Château St. Jean. Cecil Singer sold his château to a rich Egyptian, who promptly tore it down. The late Mabel Ball owned the Sorrentina. Her gigolo shot himself at the gates of the villa. Isadore Duncan came over frequently from Nice, but never had a villa at Cap Ferrat. Jean Cocteau rents a local villa from its American owner. He has a yacht too.

The average rental of a villa is £100 a month, with another £100 for staff, unless a mere cook and maid suffice. The Grand Hotel, Cap Ferrat, which is closed in February, October and November, offers another method of living close to the villas of such celebrities as Somerset Maugham and Prince Rainier.

Of the 200 villas on Cap Ferrat only half are in French ownership. The remainder belong to Englishmen, Belgians, Swiss, Americans and a few Italians. Before the war there were dozens of American proprietors, most of whom came for the winter season. Since World War II they prefer to pay their visits in the summer.

Times have changed with the cost of living. Between the wars, Lady Ward, the wife of Sir John Ward, came with eighteen servants; the late Arthur Cohen brought more than a dozen, like the Duke of Connaught. The Aga Khan alone maintains a pre-war staff. In 1939 cooks cost £2 10s. 0d. a month. A maid's wages were £1 5s. 0d., a gardener received £2 a month, while a *femme-de-ménage* (charwoman) was paid 30 francs an hour. Present-day prices are £30 to £40 for a good cook, £25 for a maid, and £40 for a gardener (all found), with 150 francs an hour for a *femme-de-ménage*. With social insurances and accident insurance in addition, a staff of seven, including gardeners, now costs £300 a month, if available. Men who before the war would have been footmen are now in the building trade, or work in garages or are employed in light engineering firms, while their wives, who would have been domestic staff before the war, live at home and do some light charring.

The rise in the cost of train fares and air fares precludes any possibility of foreign villa owners bringing their own staff from home. Coal incidentally costs £20 a ton, and it requires at least eight tons to warm a villa during the winter in the South of France.

To build a small villa nowadays costs anything from £10,000 to £20,000. This would be limited to four bedrooms and a dining-room, two bathrooms, servants' quarters, a garage and perhaps two thousand square yards of land.

The biggest villa on Cap Ferrat has an estate of 90,000 square yards. Owned by M. Marnier, of Grand Marnier, and known as Les Cèdres, it once belonged to King Leopold. The Marnier family comes in relays throughout the year.

Le Clos – the most ancient villa – is now the property of Roderick Cameron, who owns a good amount of the Hospice section of Cap Ferrat. Though an American by nationality, he was Australian born, the son of Lady Kenmare by a former marriage. Claudette Colbert rented Le Clos in 1954, and in her practical French-Canadian way repainted the previously indecipherable name of the house with her own charming brushwork. It is a real Provençal *mas* – in other words, a regional farm-house, but now most luxurious with four bedrooms and bathrooms, and a beautiful patio under a terraced vine canopy.

Villa Iberia, Prince Rainier's snuggery at Cap Ferrat, is in pinkish-white stucco, facing north over its own little harbour. It dates back to the 'eighties, but its previous connotation does not delight Princess Grace, and it was put up for sale after the wedding.

Villa Cuccia Noys is regularly rented by the former Mrs. Herman Oelrichs, now Princess Lichtenstein. It is the property of Henry Stuyvesant. Earl Blackwell, the remarkably good-looking founder of Celebrity Service, leases the Villa de St. Hospice, a pinkish, melon-coloured villa facing due south.

Apart from all this, Cap Ferrat rejoices in a delightfully naïve statue of the Virgin to commemorate the saving of a number of sailors; and a vast quarry from which all the stone for the Monte Carlo casino was dug. Alas, this is surrounded by a gigantic 'Camping' in the summer, which very much spoils the amenities of the Cap, just as Mandalieu suffers between June and October – shades of the Grand Duke Michael who died in 1930, but without the same pomp and ceremony as his father, for whom a Russian battleship was sent all the way from the Baltic, with searchlights playing over the Mediterranean, while the state barge slowly transported his Grand Ducal corpse to the gangway.

The Villa L'Olivette belongs to Princess Ottaboni. It has vast ceilings, vast sofas, vast rooms, vast carpets, vast furniture and vast black marble floors. When guests arrive, they are confronted with tables all set for canasta, backgammon and bridge, but there is no real garden. The Grand Duchess Marie, the last practising grand duchess in the South of France, is a frequent guest of Princess Ottaboni.

A special road was built at huge cost to the Villa L'Olivette and the Villa La Pausa, once the property of Mlle. Chanel, and now the property of M. Reves, the rich Dutchman who is responsible for the Continental publication of all Sir Winston Churchill's books. Sir Winston paid him several visits with his easel and paint brushes after resigning the Premiership. The villa lies up behind Roquebrune, the charming little hill-billy town where Van Meegeren, the most fascinating picture-forger of all time, practised secretly before 'discovering' all those Vermeers which completely deceived the experts for so long.

Another famous villa was the Rosmarino at Menton, built by the Duke of Sutherland in 1911, and used as a leave centre by King Albert I of Belgium in the 1914–18 war. A more recent villa at Menton is L'Annonciade. Built in 1936 for President Tardieu, it now belongs to Mme. Vaudable, owner of Maxim's restaurant in Paris.

Villa Egerton, built by the Baron of that name, is now the property of Lord Iliffe. Lord Rothermere inherited Roc Fleuri at Monte Carlo from his father. Then there was L'Oiseau Bleu at Menton, built for Gina Palerme, the queen of the Folies Bergères, who designed her own blue marble bathrooms. La Lomas was the property of Sir James Dunn at Cap Ferrat; Sir James died in 1956, leaving twenty-six million pounds.

At Monte Carlo, the Villa Paloma, property of Mrs. Hudson of Hudson's soap, has been famous for years. The Bastide at Beaulieu was the property of the late Lord Salisbury. Queen Victoria visited him frequently. After World War II it became the headquarters of the Admiral of the American Fleet in the Mediterranean.

The Villa Mereze at Eze-sur-Mere is the property of Princess Antoinette, sister of Prince Rainier, to whom Grace Kelly was introduced almost immediately after her arrival at Monte Carlo for her wedding.

The drawing-room is long and narrow, very chintzy, with Regency furniture. The general colour-scheme is red and white – the national colours of Monaco. It leads into the dining-room, which has Napoleonic furniture. Here one gets the feeling that one is almost eating in the nursery. It is all so unpretentious. Like other properties, the Villa Mereze lost many trees as well as its flowers and bushes during the catastrophic spring of 1956.

Villa Les Glaieuls at Cannes, the property of the former Lady (Mortimer) Singer, shows comparatively few signs of having been occupied consecutively by Germans, Poles, Italians and Royal Air Force. Even its cellar of fine wines was untouched – thanks to the enterprise of the gardener, who painted 'Danger de mort (transformateurs)' on the cellar doors. The Germans at first tried to call his bluff and told him to open the doors. The gardener bluffed it out. He said that if this were done everybody within four kilometres should be given half-an-hour's warning to clear out. So the Germans left it alone.

One of the visible after-effects of the German occupation was that several of the chairs in the beautiful salon were marked by the salt water from the wet bathing dresses of the officers as they came straight in from the swimming pool. Some of the stone vases in the garden had also been wantonly shot off, but the tulips and the palm trees, the judas trees, the roses and the wistaria, and the swimming pool itself, remained unscathed – like the honey-coloured villa itself.

The most spectacular villa in the neighbourhood belongs to Mr. Joseph Goldman, and was successively occupied by various military units of different nations. At the very top of

Super-Cannes, it is called Domaine de la Croix des Gardes. The villa itself – 'villa' is now a totally inapposite name for any of these fine houses which have none of the tin-pot, cheap-jack, tawdry construction with which the word is usually associated – is almost literally stuffed with treasures which miraculously escaped looting.

It is surrounded by the most beautiful lawns, hundreds of cypress trees, beds of tulips, rose gardens and rock gardens, lemon trees and olives, cork trees and umbrella pines. The setting is more Hollywood than anything that Hollywood has ever produced. One can look over the blue sea to the rocky outline of La Napoule Bay, to the Islands of Lérins and even, at dawn, to Corsica. It is a villa to end villas. You feel at any moment a *corps de ballet* will suddenly appear on the beautiful lawns in the first act of a musical comedy.

The only visible trace of the Germans is that, for some unknown reason, they shot off the noses of the various nude statues in the grounds. The red paint which they daubed on to the more intimate parts of the anatomies of the statues has, of course, been removed.

The values of villas on the Riviera are difficult to ascertain. The French Income Tax authorities, knowing that the French dislike paying more to the Inland Revenue than is strictly necessary, have a habit of assessing villa owners and villa tenants on the basis of The Scene of Exterior Richness, to use the exact English translation.

It is safe to say, however, that many a villa is rented at £400 per month.

There is always great competition among millionaires to buy land or villas at Cap Ferrat or Cap d'Antibes. These are regarded as the two most desirable places on the whole of the Riviera. In contrast to the old days, however, a villa is leased not so much for its superb gardens as for its swimming pool. Barry Dierks, the American architect from Pittsburg, son of the local agent for Steinbeck pianos, has had a greater effect on the Riviera's mode of private life than anyone. Having taken his degree at the Carnegie Institute of Technology and then studied at the Beaux Arts in Paris he became, to everyone's surprise, assistant cashier in the firm of Choillet. The general manager was Eric Sawyer. The two men became partners in 1925, and set up as architects and gardening experts on the Riviera.

Their first job was the rebuilding of the Villa Mauresque, a Moroccan style house which Somerset Maugham wanted re-modelled, at Cap Ferrat. It is still somewhat Moroccan in appearance, but Barry Dierks improved the interior, increased the size of the windows to make them real french windows, and enlarged the rooms.

The Villa Mauresque was originally built for an archbishop of Nice in the early nineteenth century. It was because he had been Bishop of Algiers that he chose this North African style of architecture. There were various shrines in the grounds, and it could only be reached by mule track.

Renovated by Barry Dierks in 1925, it now has a square indoor patio open to the sky, where Somerset Maugham (Willie to his friends) can dine in the summer and lunch in the winter. There are cloisters around it. Maugham's workroom is on the top floor, reached by a narrow wooden staircase. Deliberately it has no view over the Mediterranean, because this would be too distracting. Instead, its windows face over the rockiest part of the gardens. One window is unique. It is a picture painted by Gauguin on glass, bought by Maugham from his cabin in Tahiti.

The interior of the workroom is austere, L-shaped. The octogenarian author writes at a table, not a desk, facing a wall covered with books. The dining-room, formerly full of Marie Laurençin pictures (one of them – incredibly – a portrait of Maugham), is now hung with the works of Toulouse-Lautrec, Matisse, Monet, Rouault and Pissaro. In the big drawing-room are Renoirs, Utrillos and a Graham Sutherland, but not the portrait of the author, which hangs in the Tate Gallery. The gardens have had two casualties; the first was when the Royal Navy lobbed shells into the grounds and tore through the best eucalyptus tree in 1944. The second was the 1956 disaster, when the snow and frost and gales ruined the gardens for at least three years. Maugham spent hundreds of pounds in paying tree experts to lop off dying or dead branches to conserve the remainder of the trees. He was truly upset, and went every morning around his estate at 9 a.m. accompanied by his head gardener and a secretary with a notebook. The swimming pool is cut out of the live rock.

The next job for Barry and Eric was the erection of their own home. The Villa Trident is built on top of a tiny peninsula at Théoule ten miles from Cannes, with the sea on three sides – hence the name. The centre of the villa is a loggia out of which open the library, dining-room, bedrooms, bathrooms, offices, spare rooms and dressing-rooms. The flat roof, tiled, is pure white. Each floor has its own terrace, the villa being built on the side of a cliff. The bedrooms are furnished with particularly large cupboards. The villa was in exact contrast to all the other villas on the Riviera.

Built for the winter season, which can be cold and windy, the rest had old-fashioned sculleries, black passages, a maze of stewards' and housekeepers' rooms, practically no bathrooms and frequently with only one entrance to the gardens. A typical example was the aforesaid Villa Sansovino, built for the late Lord Derby. To make it tolerably habitable in the summer it had to be gutted. Walls were ripped out, bathrooms were

Joan Fontaine, Aly Khan and Elsa Maxwell at Monte Carlo.

The Château Clews at La Napoule. (*Joe Hollander*)

installed. Outside loggias and terraces had to be added; an atmosphere had to be introduced, enabling guests to feel at home in bikinis in the drawing-room. Like other villas re-modelled by Barry Dierks, it had to be simplified and opened up with marble or tiled floors instead of wooden floors, which attracted insects. Windows and mosquito nets had to be de-signed so that they could slide into the walls. Wallpaper was supplanted by paint. Ceilings had to be raised where possible.

Another job was to build the Villa L'Horizon for Maxine Elliott, already mentioned. The style is Palladian. In the grounds a full-sized Olympic Games sea-water swimming pool was constructed – thirty-three metres long, hanging right over the sea, with a chute into the sea. The villa contains twelve bedrooms and twelve bathrooms, every bathroom facing the Mediterranean. Although built between the railway line and the sea, no sound of the railway trains can be heard. Barry built the villa on a raft of cinders, thus creating a zone of silence, as he had learned in school at Pittsburg.

Among his other well-known villas are the Villa Le Roc, built for Lord Cholmondeley, where Garbo is often to be found nowadays; Ferme St. Antoine at Mougins, built for the late William Burton; Sou le Vent, a very lovely property on the end of Cap d'Antibes; and Villa Houzée, Cap d'Antibes, for Mrs. Jan Boissevain, well known on the American stage as Charlotte Ives. Villa Hier nearby is a reconstruction and now one of the finest properties on the coast, with an outdoor sea-water swimming pool which can be heated to summer tem-perature all the year round. He also built several lovely small villas on the Garoupe property for the Norman family; Villa Zero on Cap d'Antibes for Sir Duncan Orr Lewis, Bt.; Pibon-son built for the late Lady Rothermere; Les Couloubriers for Jean Prouvost; Le Sault for Miss Dickie Fellowes Gordon, which she shares with Elsa Maxwell; Sagitta built for His

Excellency M. Corbin, Ambassador of France in London at the outbreak of war; Ad Astra built for General Catroux just before the war; Les Orangers bought by the late Sir Alexander Korda, just before his death; the Reine Jeanne, a magnificent property on the Cap Benat near Hyères belonging to M. Paul-Louis Weiller; a number of luxury bungalows on a lovely property just above the Monte Carlo beach; and finally a charming small residence near the Palace built for H.S.H. Prince Pierre de Monaco, father of Rainier III.

Villas on the Riviera vary in size and magnificence even more than the so-called cottages in smart American seaside resorts. Some of the villas are real palaces. Some have been turned into hotels, others have been transformed into apartment houses, like the Villa Kasbeck. Battlements worthy of a *Schloss*, turrets reminiscent of a château, do not prevent an edifice from masquerading as a villa. By and large, the Dierks architectural style is primarily Palladian, with a leaning away from the local Provençal architecture to that of Greece and southern Italy. Owners of existing villas who started to follow the new fashion and were spending the high season on the Riviera instead of leaving their villas bolted and barred from May to December, suddenly found that their homes were almost uninhabitable in July and August. One visit to the Villa Trident-Miramar, and the services of Barry Dierks were almost invariably requisitioned.

Better still, the socialites following the sun, the strawberries and the Duke of Windsor (then Prince of Wales), commissioned Barry Dierks to build new villas anywhere from Menton to St. Tropez. One of his most successful achievements was the villa he built at Antibes for Mrs. Sidney Allan, the Listerine heiress. It remains the perfect combination of a private house in Paris and a Riviera home. With its eight master bedrooms and a similar number of master bathrooms, a dining-room to seat forty people, eighteen staff rooms and six more bathrooms for the servants, double walls with a space between them to insulate the interior from damp, heat and cold, its loan was gratefully accepted by General Eisenhower as his personal leave centre during the latter part of World War II.

In contrast is the little Provençal farmhouse owned by Colonel Eric Dunstan and transformed by Barry Dierks into one of the most delightful homes on the Riviera. It has its own trout stream, melon patch, vineyard, vegetable gardens, cows and potatoes and ornamental gardens. Eric Dunstan claims to be the most contented man in the world. No wonder.

Barry Dierks does not mince his words when describing the architecture of some of the better-known villas, but does not like to be quoted. Another home he transformed was the Villa Lou Viel, in which Mrs. Wallis Simpson sought sanctuary, with her friends Mr. and Mrs. Herman Rogers, whilst the abdication was taking official form. Once the property of the monks of Lérins, it has been restyled completely as a typical Provençal home. Jack Warner's Villa Aujourd'hui is completely modern. Built on a site which Barry Dierks describes as being about the size of a grand piano (in fact a quarter of an acre), it gives the visitor the impression that he is on a yacht; just as Onassis's famous yacht, *Christina*, suggests that he is in a private house ashore. In the Villa Aujourd'hui, the guests can sit on any chair in a wet bathing dress, without doing any harm. It looks out over terraces, pine trees and lawns of Australian grass.

Lord Beaverbrook's villa, in contrast, has lawns of blue verbena. Built originally for Captain Molyneux, the dress designer, it has been lent to Sir Winston Churchill, Mr. R. A. Butler, and many other distinguished people during its owner's absence.

CHAPTER 15

CANNES FILM FESTIVAL

ONE OF THE MOST BRILLIANT FORMS OF PUBLICITY ever conceived was the Cannes Film Festival.

The original plan had been to inaugurate it in 1939 from 3rd to 17th September. The European war intervened. The idea was resurrected in September 1946. There was no American interest in the Festival, unless one counts the arrival of Errol Flynn in his yacht. His papers were not in order. He had to retire ingloriously to Monte Carlo.

The British Government took a different view. The aircraft carrier *Colossus* appeared on the scene with the late Sir Duff Cooper, British Ambassador in Paris. He laid a wreath on the war memorial. A detachment of the Argyll and Sutherland Highlanders made a spectacular entry to the cries of, '*O la la, les kilts et les bagpipes!*'

In 1947 Grace Moore, covered with jewels, and Eric von Stroheim represented the U.S.A.; Russia, Poland, the Argentine, Brazil, Bulgaria, Egypt, France, Hungary, Mexico, Luxembourg and the U.S.A. sent films. Ray Milland was voted the best actor of the year for his performance in *Lost Weekend*, whilst Michèle Morgan was awarded the title of the best actress. There was no Cannes Festival in 1948, largely because Hollywood claimed that it was not ready to show any recent movies.

The following year, the Festival was held, not in the casino as heretofore, but in the vast new Festival Palace, erected on the site of the Cercle Nautique. It has wonderful acoustics and sliding seats available for people suffering from either emotion or boredom. The walls are draped in mauve and yellow velvet. Elsa Maxwell represented Variety. The first prize went to *The Third Man*.

There was no Cannes Festival in 1950.

The Russian and Polish entries for 1951 were not nominated until a week before the official opening. They were allowed to take part; whereupon the Russians protested at a Swiss movie which they regarded as anti-Stalin. The head of the Soviet delegation was Nicholas Semenov, Vice-Minister of Cinematography. A reporter asked him:

'Are you happy to come to Cannes with the Russian delegation?'

'I am happy.'

'What do you think of foreign films?'

'There are good foreign films, but technically, and above all in colour, the Soviet Union has a comfortable lead.'

'What do you think of Cannes?'

'Very pretty, but Yalta is much more southerly.'

The chief American contribution in 1951 was Harold Lloyd in *Mad Wednesday*. Fifty movies were shown. The Russian talkie about liberated China was banned by the committee, but the Soviet representatives were given a prize for décor and a special award for four documentaries. The Russians abstained from the Cannes Festival of 1952. Tunis, Madagascar, Cuba and the Saar participated for the first time. Mack Sennett was present on this occasion. Somebody asked him what he thought of a blonde nearby. He said:

'She's a nice pretty girl. But then they are all nice pretty girls. The place is lousy with them. Look at that one there,' and he pointed to the phenomenal physical edifice known as Gina Lollobrigida. 'Have you ever seen such a figure? But I would never have given her a job as one of my bathing beauties in the old days. Not when I had girls like Bebe Daniels to choose from.'

That year was notable for Orson Welles winning the first prize with *Othello*. The 1953 Cannes Festival got off to a good start with a gala dinner for forty-two guests, given by the Aga Khan. At his table were Orson Welles, Prince and Princess Christian of Hesse, and Sir Bernard and Lady Docker. Among the Hollywood representatives were Edward G. Robinson, Kirk Douglas wearing a beard and jeans (he was tipped 100 francs by a French yachtsman for lending him a hand with his dinghy), Lana Turner scooping garlic sauce into her fish soup, and Mel Ferrer. As usual, there was a scene about the showing of a movie. This time, the American contingent resented the Spanish film *Bienvenido, Mr. Marshall*. The head of the selection committee, Jean Cocteau, with Abel Gance and Edward G. Robinson, refused to withdraw it.

Gary Cooper received forty-eight love letters before breakfast on the day of his arrival. There was another scene about another film – *The Wages of Fear* – which was allegedly anti-American. It won the Grand Prix. Such was the feeling about Charlie Chaplin at the time that the whole Hollywood contingent threatened to withdraw if he appeared on the scene. In 1954 the Russians had a change of heart and sent entries. Their delegation paid a call on Picasso at Valoris; after which they drank champagne with the local Communist mayor. Lollobrigida made a personal appearance to support her *Bread, Love and Dreams* movie. The Russians walked out because of a Swedish film. The Japanese won the Grand Prix with *The Gates of Hell*, a costume movie of the twelfth century.

The following year, 1955, there were Bulgarian, Polish, Czechoslovakian and Rumanian entries in addition to the more usual quota. A Yugoslav movie was withdrawn at the request of the German delegation. The Grand Prix was awarded to

Marty, the first American movie to be successful for some years. Britain sent *A Kid for Two Farthings*, entered independently by the late Sir Alexander Korda.

Nowadays, the Cannes Film Festival takes place a fortnight after Easter Sunday. The only occasion when the date has been altered in recent times was in 1956, when it clashed with the wedding of Prince Rainier and Grace Kelly, who had made a personal appearance at Cannes to support *The Country Girl*, and thus met her future husband.

Such is the public interest in the Cannes Film Festival, which has almost completely supplanted the Venice Film Festival, that the Riviera needs no other publicity. The French Government made an annual grant of the equivalent of £80,000 for it. 'Why should we dip into our own pockets,' François André gently asks, 'if publicists offer their services?'

At the 1956 Cannes Film Festival, the stars of thirty-three nations disported themselves. As usual, there were international complications about the showing of films by one country which were said to be likely to cause offence to other countries.

In all, there were forty-five full length movies and forty shorts, presented by such countries as Sweden, Egypt, Japan, Brazil, Bulgaria, Mexico, the Belgian Congo, Hungary and India, apart from the better-known movie-producing countries like the United States, England, France, Germany and Italy.

One film critic wrote wistfully: 'Miles of film are being unspooled, though the rich sands skirted by the warm Mediterranean are only twenty yards away. Here we must defy the siren lure of oleanders and cypresses.'

Susan Hayward was given the award for the best acting, in *I'll Cry Tomorrow*. The Grand Prix was awarded to *The Silent World*, a French under-water film. The Russian version of *Othello* was voted the best production. There was a special jury prize for *The Picasso Mystery*, and *Red Balloon* was voted the best documentary. American and British movies were almost completely ignored. One oddity was the showing of ten minutes of *I, Claudius,* the never-completed picture of Robert Graves' best seller, as a strange tribute to the late Sir Alexander Korda.

The most glamorous film star, who caused a scene, was Diana Dors. She announced that the British film company sponsoring her appearance refused to pay more than half the costs of her hotel and other incidentals. This was ultimately smoothed out.

Cannes has always been a great place for romance and honey-moons. In 1956 ex-King Peter of Yugoslavia and his beautiful wife Alexandra spent a second honeymoon there after years of rift. It was, incidentally, Peter's grandfather King Alexander of Yugoslavia, who was assassinated at nearby Marseilles, while the newsreel camera man imperturbably shot the whole scene including the immediate slaughter of the murderer by the Garde Republicain.

Queen Alexandrine of Denmark, a regular visitor to Cannes, still tells the story of her courtship there. King Christian of Denmark had invited her – then the Grand Duchess of Meck-lenberg-Schwerin – to go for a sail round the Ile de Mérins. She accepted. As they approached a reef the King said peremp-torily, 'When I say, get ready to jump – you must jump.' A moment later came his royal command. Obediently, though clad in a blue jersey skirt, white blouse, white boater and white sand shoes, she jumped. Said King Christian, 'I will not come back until you say yes,' and sailed off a few yards. Two minutes later the Grand Duchess waved her hand in capitulation, 'And that's how I became Queen of Denmark,' she says with a reminiscent smile.

Ex-Queen Elizabeth of Greece – sister of Ex-King Carol of

Rumania – was a permanent resident of Cannes. In her opinion nearly all royalty had incredibly vulgar minds with an inclination to chamber-pot humour. She blamed this weakness on the race of English nannies who for the past century have ruled the royal nurseries of Europe.

One of the last of the royal nannies still operating is Miss Kathleen Churchill-Wanstall who not only brought up Princess Charlotte of Monaco, but also Prince Rainier and his sister Princess Antoinette. She is now in charge of Princess Antoinette's three children – Bitsi, Buddie and Baby – at the Villa Mereze two miles out of Monte Carlo. Miss Churchill-Wanstall is a formidable figure in spite of her seventy years and even now Princess Antoinette claims to be scared of her. There is no doubt that her three high-spirited youngsters can be cowed by a single glance, and indeed they are inclined to remain tongue-tied all the time that Nannie is in the room.

CHAPTER 16

THE GOLDEN GREEKS

FOR TEN YEARS after the war, the Riviera saw an ever-growing visitation from the U.S., Great Britain and other foreign countries, including Germany. French socialites claim that Cannes, Monte Carlo and the other royal playgrounds are socially insupportable in July and August. Certainly the growth of 'campings', the transformation of villas into boarding-houses and the nose-to-tail procession of motor-coaches, with all that this connotes, from one end of the Corniche to the other, has popularised the South of France in the most literal sense of the word. September has become the fashionable month in the summer – with January, February and March as the winter season for the older, and therefore richer, visitors.

Hollywood has in recent times sent most of its leading actors and actresses to the Riviera where autograph-hunting is still in its infancy and a touch of European polish can be readily acquired. Many of them paid their first visit as a result of the Cannes Film Festival and then renewed their acquaintance between pictures.

A further touch of colour has been provided by the Golden Greeks, as Onassis and Niarchos have been nicknamed.

Aristotle, son of Socrates Onassis, was born in Smyrna. His father had become a well-to-do tobacco merchant, and young Aristotle was brought up in a tense atmosphere. When the Turks recaptured Smyrna from the Greeks in 1922, two of his uncles and several other relations, including a first cousin, were massacred; another died of shock; an aunt and her baby died in a church set on fire by the Turks. The sixteen-year-old Onassis was himself saved from untimely death by the American Vice-Consul and allowed to migrate to Athens. Here the remnants of the Onassis family had to start from scratch all over again. His father being in the position of having to support not only his wife Penelope and his four children, but also four widowed sisters-in-law and seven orphan nephews and nieces, it was decided that 'Ari' – short for Aristotle – should go to Argentina, whence, with good luck, he would be able to help his family; the Greeks having a strong sense of family unity.

To gain entry he was compelled to falsify his age on his passport, claiming to be twenty-two instead of seventeen. He arrived in Buenos Aires with sixty dollars. His first job was that of a switchboard operator with the United River Telephone Company. In order to send back money to his family, he limited his sleeping hours to three out of the twenty-four and went into the tobacco business, specialising in the importation of Macedonian leaf tobacco. Such was his success that he made 100,000 dollars within a few years on a five-per-cent commission basis. He then started his own cigarette factory. His astuteness as a business negotiator was recognised by the Greek Government after he had successfully concluded a commercial agreement with the Argentine Government. The Greeks rewarded him for this by appointing him Greek Consul at Buenos Aires.

Then came the great depression with a slump in shipping which caused vessels to be laid off all over the world. Onassis, who had always been passionately fond of boats since he had sailed toy vessels in his uncle's bathing establishment in Smyrna, decided that the phenomenally low prices asked for good cargo vessels in 1932 would not remain long at that level.

He came to London, whence he went to Canada with an Ithacan marine consulting engineer. Here he negotiated the purchase, at £5,000 apiece, of six cargo ships out of the several that were laid up in the St. Lawrence River. Of these, he bought two straight away, naming them *Onassi Socratis* and *Onassi Penelopi*, after his father and mother. That was in 1932. These two ships were the first of a fleet which is now considered to be one of the greatest – if not the greatest – of all the independent fleets in existence.

So well did he succeed with them thereafter that in 1936 he was able to order his first tanker in Sweden, which he named *Ariston*. This tanker was the largest ever built in Sweden, thus making Onassis a pioneer in tanker construction.

Came the war, and Onassis bought and sold ships until in 1946 he ordered five super tankers from the Bethlehem Steel Shipyards, and later on dozens of others in Germany and France. The tankers he ordered with Bethlehem Steel were the biggest ever ordered at that time (27,000 tons). Then he was the first to order tankers (in France this time) of 32,000 tons; and he kept up his lead by being the first to get into the 47,000 tons group with the giant tankers *Tina Onassis* – named after his wife, Tina (short for Athina, after the Goddess Athene), daughter of another famous Greek shipowner, Mr. Stavros Livanos – and *Al-Malik Saud Al-Awal* (47,000 tons), named after King Saud of Arabia, and flying the Saudi Arabian flag. Mrs. Onassis is the sister of Mrs. Stavros Niarchos.

Soon afterwards, Senator McCarthy, then in his heyday, drew public attention to a dusty obsolescent 1916 law, introduced in World War I to prevent Germans from buying American ships. This Act forbade any vessel flying the United States flag from being owned by a foreigner. A long legal dispute culminated with a settlement, not a fine, of seven million dollars. Following the settlement, they are now in a trust in favour of Onassis' children, Alexander and Christina, both of whom were born in the U.S.A., and are therefore American citizens.

Small, dark, with a slight American accent and American idioms – like 'boloney' – imposed on his native Greek intonation, Onassis talks slowly when making a point and very fast indeed when he becomes really excited and interested in what he is saying. One of his proudest moments was when he was made a free citizen of Ithaca, the home of Ulysses, hero of Homer's *Odyssey*.

The captains, officers and seamen of the Onassis fleets include no fewer than three hundred Ithacans. One of his chief passions is history, particularly Byzantine Greek, classical Greek and Minoan Greek.

When in the mood, he will pick up a guitar in a tavern and entertain his friends quite uninhibitedly. He is an accomplished linguist, speaking fluently (besides Greek) English, French, Spanish and Italian, some Portuguese and Turkish, and a little German and Swedish. He spends a great deal of his time travelling. He seems to be constantly on the move, usually by air, but he enjoys nothing more than relaxing every now and then on the shores of his beloved Mediterranean. Monte Carlo, which reminds him so much of Greece and the beautiful suburbs of pre-1922 Smyrna, is thus a spot after his heart.

In 1956, Onassis placed another order for giant tankers in Japan. As with his other ships of the same type, he insisted on the best possible accommodation for officers and men. Tonnage under his control is in the neighbourhood of one million, five hundred thousand. He has, however, sold his whaling fleet to the Japanese. His latest interests are Greek airlines, and the construction of ship-repairing yards in Greece.

Many sensational stories are told about Onassis' arrival at Monte Carlo. The truth is that he was fascinated by Monte

Carlo ever since his first visit as a child. When not long ago he discovered that the former Winter Sporting Club, close to the casino, was derelict, he offered to buy it. Told rudely that it was not for sale or even for renting, he asked for a reason, but was given none. He thereupon acquired enough shares in the company to acquire control, at a cost of 500,000 dollars.

This automatically enabled him to acquire the premises he wanted. Some people say that originally Onassis had been led to believe that he could fly the Monégasque flag as an alternative to the Liberian and Panamanian flags on his ever-growing fleet of tankers and whale catchers. This, they claim, is the real reason why he decided to start operations in Monaco where income tax does not exist, before he discovered that only 40,000 tons of Monégasque shipping is permitted to fly the local flag; after which, according to the treaty with France, all ships must carry the French flag and be subject to French taxes. The explanation Onassis gives personally for installing the offices of his operating agency *Olympique Maritime* in Monaco, is that Monte Carlo is not only beautiful, but also central for his European interests in Genoa, Marseilles, Athens and London. Monte Carlo, only half an hour by motor-car from Nice aerodrome, is indubitably well placed.

His interest in the company controlling the casino and the top hotels is in his own words 'highly relative'. This is because of the old-fashioned power of veto which Prince Rainier can exercise on so many matters, including the approval of the directors of the *S.B.M.*, even if appointed by stockholders. There is certainly no question of his *Olympique Maritime* evading taxes. As an operating company, its profits are taxed all over the world.

Onassis and Prince Rainier see little of one another, although Onassis informed Prince Rainier that the yacht *Deo Juvante*, on which the Prince spent his honeymoon, was for sale at an attractive price. What annoys Onassis is the newspapermen's habit of describing him as the uncrowned king of Monaco.

Said Onassis to a newspaperman in the summer of 1956: 'Like all residents of the Principality, I owe devotion to its Sovereign Prince. It is all nonsense that the Prince and I started off as pals and then fell out. Whoever heard of a simple resident of a country being a pal of its sovereign?'

Onassis' yacht, *Christina*, is the partial realisation of a youthful ambition of its owner. 'I want to be an admiral,' he told his parents in Smyrna where he sailed a toy boat. It is always the biggest vessel in the harbour of Monte Carlo, dwarfing even Sir Bernard and Lady Docker's *Shemara*.

Originally a Canadian frigate, it was so rebuilt that it would have been cheaper to have constructed a brand-new vessel. The general impression is that it is a home and not a ship. On the foredeck is a swimming pool, which can be converted into a dance floor, covered with a red and green reproduction from the Palace of Minos at Knossos, Crete, showing men playing the bull-baiting game. This leads into a lounge with oyster-ribbed silk velvet hangings. Real Chinese lacquered tables, Florentine inlaid side-tables, a map of Greece and the Aegean in Sienna marble and lapis lazuli are other features, like the lapis lazuli fireplace. The cocktail bar has whales' teeth handles on the outside so that the guests can keep steady on their stools in the event of a swell. On the top of the cocktail counter is the equivalent of a miniature railway, except that when the button is pressed it is not railway trains, but a series of miniature ships of all rigs from earliest history up to the latest tanker, which are set in motion. Earlier than Noah's ark, for example, is a tiny effigy of Jonah being towed by a whale. There is also a representation of the *Kon-Tiki* balsa-wood raft. A gyroscopic long-playing radiogram and a tape-recording machine are other attractions in the cocktail bar, which is stocked with every possible liqueur. There is also a magnetic map showing where the units of the Onassis fleet are sailing at any given moment, rather like the device at Scotland Yard which at once shows the whereabouts of any police car. Nearby is a children's room with a toy hurdy-gurdy, and frescoes of La Petite Madeleine.

The illusion of the yacht being a complete home is heightened by the circular staircase with onyx- and gold-plated banisters, proceeding from the ground floor – one should say the main deck – up to the dome parallel with the bridge. Each of the main cabins is named after a Greek island. The biggest is called Lesbos. There are in addition the Ithaca suite, with its pink marble bathroom, washstand decorated with a gilded dolphin, and gold-plated shower bath. There is a complete set of gold hairbrushes. The Chios suite has a motif of green marble.

In the dining-room the table can expand to take twenty guests; the chairs have wicker backs. The drawing-room is wainscoted. Among its treasures is a jade Buddha, the hands and head of which move up and down at the slightest motion. Queen Elizabeth and the Aga Khan are the only two other people who have a similar treasure. The armchairs are in muted pink, contrasting with the pearl-grey carpet. Onassis' personal suite is also wainscoted, with full bookshelves. In the corner are gold-scabbarded swords presented to him by King Saud of Arabia. Near them are five rifles and shotguns, a harpoon and a Portuguese swivel hand-gun. Mrs. Onassis' bathroom has a Sienna marble washstand and a sunken bath decorated with a mosaic of blue flying fish, also a Minoan motif. Rock crystal lampshades and solid gold hairbrushes catch the eye in the dressing-room.

The kitchen is twenty yards long. This is not too large for a crew of thirty, ten stewards and the occupants of the nine double guestrooms. The table silver is a faithful reproduction of the discoveries of Sir Arthur Evans in Crete, another proof of the great fascination for Onassis of the maritime civilisation of Crete, the earliest Greek civilisation. An oddity is that the men's lavatories are all blue, and the others are all pink. The tablecloths are priceless.

All this sounds perhaps as being ostentatious beyond words. In fact, Onassis' taste is impeccable. There is no garishness. It would take a connoisseur a week to examine and appreciate every item of furniture.

There is no doubt that the two brothers-in-law 'Ari' Onassis and Stavros Niarchos thoroughly enjoy their friendly rivalry. First one, then the other, orders larger tankers, buys into other businesses quite outside their shipping interests, and acquires a bigger and better yacht or villa.

When Onassis bought control of the Monte Carlo casino and its hotels, Niarchos bought ten thousand shares in the Ritz Hotel, Paris. Niarchos in the meantime owns the largest private sailing yacht in commission – the *Creole*, a 699-ton schooner capable of seventeen knots.

What is most intriguing is that just as Onassis is a free citizen of the most seamanlike island of Greece – Ithaca – so Niarchos comes from Sparta, the most military part of the mainland. Actually, his parents were wealthy mill owners in the Piraeus, and it was the need to acquire larger vessels to bring the grain that caused Niarchos to go into shipping.

At the outbreak of war, his family had a fleet of fourteen with an aggregate dead weight of 100,000 tons. These were handed over to the British Government, while Niarchos himself served in a Greek destroyer on convoy work in the Atlantic. At the end of the war, eight of the fourteen still remained. With the insurance money of the others he bought a fleet of T-2 tankers and sailed them under the flags of

I

Panama, the United States, Liberia, Greece and Great Britain. He also ordered the construction of twenty ships, aggregating 640,000 tons, the biggest being a 46,000-tonner, at a total cost of thirty-six million pounds. Then came his *Spyros Niarchos*, the fifth largest ship in the world. This, in the meantime, is being dwarfed by Onassis' 100,000-tonner, which he ordered in July 1956.

It was Niarchos who provided the *Agamemnon* for Elsa Maxwell's royalty cruise of the eastern Mediterranean, and the *Achilles* for the cruise of her Dukes and Duchesses and other cultured and beautiful friends. Said Niarchos to Maxwell: 'You can have it for nothing. I've not hired it. I merely bought enough shares in the company that owns it.'

Among his previous employees has been Lord Milford Haven. Prince Alexander of Yugoslavia is still on his payroll. In 1954 he paid four million dollars to the United States Government in settlement of profits earned by his ships. This caused him no pain. Not long ago, he bought the broodmare Segula for 126,000 dollars. He started a string of race horses in England headed by True Cavalier, which ran in the 1956 Derby and Cesarewitch. He gave £80,000 to the Louvre in Paris to save the Puirforcat silver collection for France.

Like Mrs. Onassis, he likes St. Moritz, and is said to have acquired a major interest in this *de luxe* Swiss winter resort. His normal year consists of winter in St. Moritz, two months in the U.S.A., two months in his Claridge's hotel penthouse in London, and four months in the Mediterranean, either on his yacht *Creole* or in the magnificent Château de Croye at Antibes.

The astonishing Lady Docker, another leading yacht owner on the Riviera, was born Nora Turner.

In a series of articles on her early life, she said that after her father's death, her mother ran a small hotel unsuccessfully and she herself, after various adventures in Birmingham and London, sold lampshades in a departmental store.

She was twenty when she married one of the directors of Henekey, the London chain of wine and spirit shops. This was Clement Callingham. At his death she was left £177,500. Shortly afterwards she married the sixty-nine-year-old Sir William Collins, the Cerebos salt king. He died within a year, leaving her £955,500. In 1949 she married Sir Bernard Docker, the multi-millionaire. It was not until then that her scintillating, mercurial, controversial, unpredictable personality made its real impact on the public.

Nora Docker thoroughly enjoys being a millionairess.

'My father could not even afford a mantle over the gas flame,' she told a reporter in a revealing moment. 'I want to give other working girls a target to aim at.'

She has a quick temper, and caused an international stir when she slapped the face of the official physiognomist at the casino following a strange scene between herself, Prince Jean de Faucigny-Lucinge and her husband. Whereupon she and her husband were officially barred from the Sporting Club, and Sir Bernard filed suit for £10,000 damages. Before the case could be heard, Prince Jean had given up his presidency of the company controlling Monte Carlo, as a result of a personal dispute between him and Prince Rainier over raising a new loan from the French banks.

Another time that Lady Docker hit the headlines was when her husband, following questions in the House of Commons, was fined £312 10s. for a currency offence. On later occasions, Sir Bernard was removed from the boards of the Midland Bank and B.S.A., the vast Birmingham undertaking of which the Daimler motor-car company is a subsidiary. In the latter case, it seemed that the reason for Sir Bernard's dismissal was his wife's expense sheet, including a bill for £7,000 worth of clothes. In the meantime, Lady Docker had uttered the immortal apophthegm: 'Mink is too hot to sit on,' which was why she had zebra-skin seats put in her last Daimler model. Undoubtedly, her sextet of gold-plated Daimlers had created tremendous publicity all over Europe.

In Monte Carlo, according to columnist Arthur Helliwell, who partnered her on the dance floor: 'People clapped and jeered at us when we started to dance.' Helliwell is also on record as saying that Lady Docker had £20,000 worth of dresses on her yacht *Shemara* 'apart from her furs and jewels'. Pink champagne, caviare, and the more humble gins and tonic provide a background to her life aboard the *Shemara* for which, she says, her husband was in 1955 offered £600,000 in dollars.

To a tax-ridden country like Great Britain, Lady Docker has provided undiluted entertainment for nearly a decade. Her tantrums in public, her appearance on television, her presence at a gangsters' party in Soho, her championship at marbles, but above all the way she revels in her wealth, laughs at austerity, divests herself of all inhibitions; behaving in fact with all the flamboyance of the grand duchesses in Edwardian times, makes her front page news wherever she goes.

There was the time, just before the Kelly-Rainier wedding, when she wrote an official letter of protest to the Prince because the casino's night-spot had been booked solid by the bride's mother for a private party. There was the time when she was subjected to the slow handclap and cries of 'Sit down!' when she delivered an impromptu speech at the charity ball in aid of the Variety Artistes Ladies' Guild and Orphanage. There was the time when she stalked out of the plush Café de Paris in London because Mrs. Bessie Braddock, the portly Labour M.P., wore day-clothes when introducing Marlene Dietrich.

Marlene Dietrich herself is an addict of Cannes, Antibes and Monte Carlo. She was at Antibes just before the outbreak of

World War II, and managed at the last moment to get Rudy Sieber, her husband, an American passport and thus enabled him to reach New York.

Maria, her daughter, was at that time still full of puppy fat as we swam together from yacht to yacht off the Garoupe beach.

Dietrich never gambles, in spite of the publicity story, released in July 1956, that she had been refused admission to the *Salles Privées* because of her black Oriental trousers. She was currently making *Monte Carlo Story*.

CHAPTER 17

TROUBLE IN PARADISE

WHILE EVERYTHING WAS BOOMING at Cannes, Nice, Juan-les-Pins and the other Riviera resorts in 1955, Monaco was seething with unrest and financial worries. Things had come to a head with the arrest in July of M. Liambey, the founder and principal director of the *Société Monégasque de Banque et de Métaux Précieux*. This did nothing to end the stream of speculation and rumour that had been coming out of Monaco ever since the announcement by Monte Carlo radio that the Government of Monaco had, in the interests of public credit, 'taken the necessary measures to safeguard its own interests and those of depositors' in the *Société Monégasque de Banque et de Métaux Précieux*. This was the first hint of the bank's difficulties, although it was suggested that they might be connected with its heavy investments in the Images and Sound group of companies which controls the Monte Carlo commercial television and the Europe Number One commercial radio and television station in the Saar.

The preliminary inquiry carried out by members of the Monaco National Council, the nearest approach to a parliament in the Principality, demanded the immediate suspension from office of three of Prince Rainier's household, all of them connected in various ways with the financial affairs of Monaco. In the next few days it seemed that the issue ceased to be financial, and became frankly political, with an incipient clash between the Prince and the National Council.

One of the men concerned, M. Crovetto, resigned soon after the National Council's first interview with the Prince; but the other, M. Solamito, who, as well as being Privy Councillor to the Prince, was also chairman of the Radio Monte Carlo Broadcasting Company, and M. Pierre Rey, chairman of the *Société des Bains de Mer*, were apparently still in office.

A fourth man, M. Raoul Pez, chairman of the Television Monte Carlo Company, and of the *Société Monégasque de Banque et de Métaux Précieux*, had apparently no official position in the royal household but was said to be a personal friend of the Prince. The delay provoked the members of the National Council to further protest, and late on Sunday night, 3rd July 1955, a brief and enigmatic communiqué was issued announcing that Prince Rainier had requested the members of his cabinet and entourage to resign 'in order to ensure the maximum of impartiality and objectivity in the examination of the situation created by certain financial engagements undertaken by the Public Treasury.'

Meanwhile, the accountants who were carrying out the expert investigation of the bank's affairs had made an interim report, according to which the financial situation of the bank was said not to be as serious as at first rumoured. The interim report showed a deficit in the bank's affairs of about 700 million francs (£700,000) which, it was stated, might be reduced by a more exact valuation of the assets. The next day an announcement from the Monaco Government stated that it had been decided to guarantee the repayment of deposits in current accounts with the bank, this decision having the unanimous approval of the National Council.

Then the political aspect of things again flared up, when the Government found it necessary to issue a communiqué stating that M. Crovetto and M. Solamito had been relieved by the Prince of their functions, 'whether as public servants or as agents of the reigning Prince, in all affairs both public and private.' It was evidently in response to certain rumours that the retirement of these men might not be so total or permanent as had at first appeared.

The same day, the Minister of State, M. Henri Soum, who was at one and the same time the head of the Monaco Government and the chief French representative in the Principality, denied that the *Société Monégasque de Banque et de Métaux Précieux* was a State Bank. He pointed out that the Government had deposits in other Monaco banks as well; this, he said, was a normal Treasury operation, and never had anything to do with the investment of funds in private companies. Asked whether there was any question of criminal proceedings, he replied that this depended upon the findings of the investigating committee, which were likely to take a long time to be made known.

Two days later, however, a Government communiqué said that, after studying the interim report of the three investigating experts, the Minister of State had, on the instructions of Prince Rainier, brought an action against M. Liambey in the Monaco court. This made necessary an order for his arrest, but, as he was living in France (at Cap Ferrat), extradition procedure would have to be resorted to.

M. Liambey, who was then sixty-seven, had a heart attack on being arrested, and was taken to the prisoners' wing of a hospital at Nice. Reports said that charges made against him in connection with the crisis in the bank's affairs included fraud and abuse of confidence. It seems that the three experts drew attention, in their report, to the total of 420 million francs entered on the bank's books as 'anonymous loans'. Asked about this, after his arrest, M. Liambey is reported to have said: 'I am not the only one responsible.'

A new factor was added to this already mysterious story by

reports that Aristotle Onassis, the Greek ship-owner who is the majority shareholder of the *Société des Bains de Mer* in Monaco, was intending to come forward and help the bank out of its difficulties. Onassis declared, however, that neither he nor his company had any connection with the *Société Monégasque de Banque et de Métaux Précieux*, and denied the reports that had been circulating.

In May, the National Council of Monaco, consisting of eighteen members elected for four years, which helps to govern the Principality under the authority of the reigning Prince, held a session to consider the 1956 budget, and outlined what appeared to be a major constitutional reform.

The lines of this reform were included in a report of the finance committee, which recommended strengthening the power of the National Council. Without waiting for the reforms promised by the Prince last year, the National Council voted a seven-point action calling for the adoption of several resolutions that should, according to the motion, receive the Prince's approval without delay.

The National Council wanted to be informed of, and to decide on, the public finances in all their respects, which meant not only receipts and expenses, but the whole national wealth and all the economic or financial undertakings of the State. It also wished to receive monthly from the Government a complete and precise note of the constitutional reserve, of the state of the Treasury, and all the various accounts affecting operations that fall outside the annual budget.

The Council called for a complete budget estimate for 1957 to be presented to it in October 1956; it required to be consulted about international negotiations, and to be able to set in action and supervise the contracts made by the State with various monopoly companies.

Another sensation of the 1956 season was the arrest of three Americans who came to Monte Carlo with the avowed intention of making a fortune at the crap table in the *Salles Privées*. The plan was simple enough – to switch the dice. Unlike gaming hells in the United States, gamblers are not compelled to roll up their sleeves before they throw the dice.

The three men were Jason M. Lee, a naturalised American born in Korea, Arif Shaker, a Lebanese, also naturalised American, and Philip Aggie, born in North Dakota.

Jason Lee, a round little man with grey hair, was a born gambler, like most Asiatics, and frequented the various gaming houses of Hong Kong. He proceeded by way of the United States to Tangier, before arriving in Monte Carlo. His first visit was purely a reconnaissance, to see what dice were used in the casino. They are, in fact, green or red, transparent, with the numbers marked in white. The American firm of Wills in Reno, who made the dice specially for Monte Carlo, stamped the actual words 'Monte Carlo' around the top of the figure 1.

Having had a good look at the dice, Lee sent Philip Aggie off to the United States to have similar ones made for his personal use in the casino. The firm of T. R. King & Co., 1035 Olive Street, Los Angeles, produced 200 dice at a total cost of 220 dollars, as exact replicas of those used in Monte Carlo. This done, Aggie, who was accompanied by Shaker, flew to Tangier, where Lee was awaiting them. Off they went to Monte Carlo, where they stayed at the same hotel. Lee rolled the dice; his two accomplices, though pretending not to know him, always backed his throws.

On the first day (a Sunday) they actually lost £5,000. They returned on the following day. Lee started to win. In a few minutes the trio had won back £3,000. The inspectors, however, had had their attention drawn to the impertinent number of times in which seven appeared on the first throw. One of the inspectors made a sign to the croupiers, who withdrew the dice which had just been rolled by Lee, and ostentatiously handed him two genuine dice.

They realised the game was up, and left the casino at full speed, collected their luggage from the hotel and separated.

In the meantime, the inspectors discovered that two of the green dice used by Lee were exactly like the genuine ones, except that the L in Monte Carlo was printed a trifle differently. They also discovered, of course, that the dice were loaded very adroitly, making sure that either 6 and 1, or 3 and 4, would end on top when rolled.

Lee and Shaker took a taxi to Nice; Aggie disappeared. The Chief of Police at Nice was warned on the telephone by his opposite number in Monte Carlo, and the three men were arrested just as they were buying their air tickets back to Tangier.

Shaker's suitcase, when examined, produced some interesting finds. They included nearly 200 dice, some of which only had the numbers 6, 4 and 2, each one having 4, 5 and 6 on the opposite side. Others had only 6, 3 and 2 on one side, and 2, 3 and 6 on the other.

When questioned, Shaker said:

'Yes, it is quite clear. These dice are faked, and you found them on me. But who put them there? It is for you to prove that I knew they were in my possession, and I have nothing to say until I see my lawyers.'

His two companions adopted similar tactics.

All three were charged with embezzlement by trickery at gambling, to use the exact translation from the French. The difficulty was lack of proof that the three men had already had time to victimise people in France. It was necessary, therefore, to send them to Monaco for trial.

Jason Lee received a sentence of one year. Three months

later, his son appealed to Prince Rainier for his release on the grounds of ill health. Prince Rainier granted it.

In this connection, it is interesting that René Léon had a grandiose scheme in 1949 of inviting thirty of the top Texan and other American gamblers who frequented Las Vegas to Monte Carlo, all expenses paid. He reckoned that if they gambled at the same level as they did in Nevada, the casino would be sure of at least £400,000 a year net profit.

Prince Louis of Monaco agreed that it was a splendid idea, and told René Léon to go ahead. Léon returned to the United States and raised over two million dollars for his plan.

Unfortunately, Prince Louis died before he had time to sign the document which Léon wanted. This was to the effect that, if he died, his heir, Prince Rainier, should not be allowed to exercise his power of veto. So the whole scheme fell through.

CHAPTER 18

THE DOLLAR PRINCESS

IT MAY BE SUPPOSED that if the Victorians and Edwardians had been conversant with modern slang, they would have described the high-days at Monte Carlo as a 'riot'. In the proper sense of the word, and despite the opportunities for gangsterism which the Principality has always offered in the presence of so much wealth, there never was the slightest suggestion of riotous behaviour at Monte Carlo, apart from minor incidents, until April 1956, when the eyes of the world were focused on That Wedding.

Symbolic of the clash between the methods of the old world and the new was the outcome of Prince Rainer's betrothal to Grace Kelly. This had its inspiration in an apparently chance visit which Cardinal Spellman, Archbishop of New York, had paid to Monaco a few years earlier. Ruling princes are considered to be ageing when they have passed twenty-five. For at least seven years before the Wedding, influential residents of Monaco (including many tax-free minor million-aires) had been worried by the fact that their Prince was apparently satisfied with a succession of unattached girl friends, and showed no sign of settling down with a consort who would in due course provide him with an heir. Rumour, that if the Prince did not produce an heir in the direct line this would result in the Principality passing to the control of France after his death, always proved stronger than fact. The truth was that at any time the Prince could have adopted a son or daughter – presumably one of the children of his sister, Princess Antoinette. The problem was strongly put to Cardinal Spellman, who combined all the efficient energy of his American birth with the prestige of a Prince of the Church. He was quick to appreciate the critics' point of view, and was naturally anxious to ensure the preservation of almost the last reigning Catholic family in Europe.

On his return to the United States, Cardinal Spellman looked around for a suitable adviser to send to Monaco in the triple role of parish priest of the fashionable Church of St. Charles, private chaplain to the Prince, and adviser on affairs of the heart. His choice fell upon the man who turned out to be the most colourful figure in the subsequent matrimonial mêlée – Father Tucker. Since he was without any experience of traditional court circles in Europe, having spent many years in a poor Irish parish of New York, it was generally felt by the rich and rather world-weary internationally-bred society of Monaco that the Cardinal's choice was – to say the least – somewhat over-stimulating.

Father Tucker burst upon the Principality and the Prince like a bomb. It was not very long after his arrival that it became clear that the ultimate aim and object of his mission was to ensure that the Prince should be wedded to the Right Girl. And with due loyalty to the country of his birth, he decided that the Right Girl could probably only be found in the Right Country.

So it was that, on location at Cannes for Metro-Goldwyn-Mayer in 1955, Grace Kelly met the man who was to become her husband amid the greatest matrimonial hullabaloo of recent times. From their different points of view, the Prince was as immediately attracted to Miss Kelly as was Grace to the Prince. It had been for some time current gossip in Hollywood that, for Miss Kelly, love and marriage went together like a horse and carriage; so there was no question of a fate worse than death. The Prince, keenly self-conscious of the criticism of his subjects at his single, though not entirely loveless, state of life, immediately realised all the advantages of romance and respectability which Grace Kelly so competently combined in her exceedingly charming and beautiful personality. When she left Monaco in the summer of 1955, the Prince could hardly wait for the visit to the U.S.A. which he had planned in the winter of 1955–6 in order to pop the question, not only to Grace but to her somewhat exacting Papa and Mama, Mr. and Mrs. Kelly in Philadelphia.

When Miss Kelly, Mrs. Kelly and Mr. Kelly all said 'Yes', the Prince was exceedingly cock-a-hoop, but with typical Grimaldi egocentricity, entirely overlooked the fact that this alliance would create a world-wide sensation, not because it presaged the wedding of the hitherto practically entirely un-known Prince of Monaco, but because it involved the crown-ing of one of the Queens of Hollywood – and one under contract to M.G.M. at that.

When he went around in Monte Carlo in the past, practi-cally nobody took any notice of Prince Rainier. Occasionally a stray photographer would take a few pictures of him fondling his pet monkey in his private zoo, and his court photographer would take some shots on birthdays and other anniversaries. So that when Miss Kelly's ship with all her friends and rela-tions aboard dropped anchor off Monaco in April 1956, and she was escorted ashore by her delighted fiancé, His Highness was astonished and not a little put out to be confronted by a battery of some 600 cameras focused upon him and his future bride by a vast cohort of photographers representing the press of the whole world. As they came into sight, Miss Kelly's features were totally obscured by a 'queen size' cartwheel hat, and the Prince's face, though exposed to view, was hardly more photogenic than that of his bride, since he was seen to be scowling mightily. Despite the most painstaking contortions, the assembled 600 cameramen were quite powerless to obtain the photograph which their 600 million readers all over the world demanded of the bride being handed by the bridegroom on to the shore of her new domain. It had also started to rain which, as frequenters of the Riviera know, always happens at any moment of personal crisis along the Mediterranean.

It soon became evident that His Serene Highness had lost all his serenity as far as publicity was concerned, and had no intention of giving the cameramen a chance. He had given his Palace at Monaco over to the Kelly family while he went to live in a villa further up the coast until after the cathedral ceremony. Nothing was seen of the happy couple again until the afternoon of the following day when the Prince was due to motor Grace back to the Palace from a picnic in the mountains, driving his own car. Again the watchful 600 faced a complete failure of their mission as the car came into view travelling at breakneck speed towards them. More of Miss Kelly's face could now be seen rushing towards them, but not really enough as she was wearing a very large pair of sun-glasses. In this moment of impending crisis, a French photographer attached to the *Match* team decided to make the supreme sacrifice on behalf of his colleagues. In a flash he hurled himself full length in front of the advancing car. The Prince was forced to bring the car to a dead stop and the screech of the brakes was almost drowned in the simultaneous clicking of the 600 cameras.

That was on Friday afternoon. The Prince and Miss Kelly's next public appearance was timed for ten in the evening on the following Sunday, when they were to attend a great gala reception at the International Sporting Club which had been decorated for this evening at the cost of £10,000. All the top wedding guests and most important people on the coast had

Château de la Croyë, the property of Stavros Niarchos.
(*Edward Quinn*)

Princess Grace and Prince Rainier.

been invited, and the bill was to be footed by the *Société des Bains de Mer* (chief stockholder, Aristotle Onassis) as part of their wedding gift to the Prince and the future Princess. On the morning of Saturday, an edict went forth from the palace that the Prince had banned all photographers from this function and that they would only be allowed to occupy an open stand, placed on the wrong side of the entrance to the Sporting Club. Meanwhile it rained all day Saturday and when ten o'clock on Sunday evening arrived, it was still pouring down. A force of police almost outnumbering the photographers had taken up their position between the press stand and the entrance to the Sporting Club, with the result that when the Prince and his bride arrived, they were entirely invisible to the photographers through the forest of policemen, even if they had not been out of range from their position on the stand. While the junketings were going on inside, a mass meeting of wet and angry photographers was held in an adjoining café at which it was decided to give the 'happy' couple the warmest reception of their lives when they should emerge in the early hours of the morning.

Then it was that Monte Carlo became a 'riot' in the real sense of the word. As Grace Kelly preceded the Prince into the car, the great crowd of cameramen forgot all about photography and rushed towards the car shouting, booing, hissing and giving G.I. whistles. The police cordon was entirely disorganised. Individual scraps broke out between photographers and police. Slowly crawling its way through the mob, the car eventually disappeared round a corner into a side turning and the last glimpse of Miss Kelly showed her with her face buried in her hands.

Perhaps she was realising for the first time that a Princess's part is not all rose petals.

By next morning it had become evident that the fury of the

photographers had been reinforced by that of the internationally famous stars at the Great Gala the night before. Many of them had travelled from far places to appear on this occasion, leaving valuable engagements behind them. Most of them were providing their services on an honorary basis.

Monte Carlo was shaken to the core, and next morning even the hitherto imperturbable Father Tucker abandoned his customary open press conference in the vestibule of the Hotel de Paris. Rumour had it that he was talking to the Prince. What he said is not known, but it resulted in a complete change in the Prince's attitude. From that moment onwards the photographers were warmly welcomed in the radius of the royal smile which had miraculously replaced the scowl of the preceding few days. The arrangements for allowing only two photographers at the civil marriage and four at the wedding in the Cathedral were hastily abandoned and in the immortal words of Father Tucker, 'the boys were given the run of the joint'. By this time, Father Tucker was also in need of some friendly help from the press, since he had delivered a sermon in the Church of St. Charles on the Sunday morning during which he had suggested that the Prince's marriage was entirely dictated by love of his people, leaving in the minds of the congregation the impression that devotion to Grace was not the prime motive.

In this new atmosphere of peace and reasonableness, everyone settled down to enjoy themselves at last. The rain stopped, the sun came out, and Monte Carlo – apart from the enormous crowds – started to look like its old self again. Rumours that Grace Kelly might change her mind at the last moment were scotched by the smooth carrying through of the civil marriage, and they presented themselves radiant and happy-looking for the first time in the royal box at the Opera for the Grand Ballet performance, in which Margot Fonteyn, who had flown from England, was to appear. In the little gilded theatre (commonly regarded as the masterpiece of Garnier, the famous nineteenth-century architect) the most glittering crowd of modern tiaras had assembled. Uniforms were blazing with orders, women were scintillating monuments of bejewelled excitement. As they took their seats, one rather modest-looking little man in white tie and tails, without a medal of any kind, could be seen threading his way to his stall. This was Onassis, who, in the words of an American newspaperman, 'could have paid cash for the whole lot on the spot without bothering to ring up his banker in advance'.

Of the ceremony in the Cathedral, nothing much need be said. Once matters fell into the orderly hands of the Papal Legate, everything went off without a hitch under the spell of the time-honoured liturgy with which all the actors are so familiar that no rehearsal is ever really necessary.

Their memories and mementoes safely packed, the wedding guests had nearly all left Monte Carlo by the week-end, leaving Jean Broc, the manager of the plush Hotel de Paris, to heave the biggest sigh of relief in the whole of his career. The traditional peace and quiet, the dignity and discretion of its atmosphere had never been so shattered before. Even as the waiters and chambermaids finished pocketing tips of a size which they could never hope to touch again, they too echoed their Manager's sigh of relief. '*C'est la guerre*,' they murmured, '*mais ce n'est pas Monte Carlo*.'

Reaction to any international event depends a great deal on one's position in life. Nothing could be more different than the account of the wedding in an English glossy and that in the trade journal of Fleet Street.

Jennifer, in the *Tatler*, referred ecstatically to the:

'white lilac, lilies, and lilies of the valley, massed in profusion, decorating the Cathedral at Monaco for the recent marriage of Prince Rainier III, Sovereign Prince of Monaco, and Miss Grace Kelly, daughter of Mr. and Mrs. John B. Kelly of Philadelphia.

'This has been a truly fairy tale wedding which has touched the hearts of millions throughout the world. Miss Kelly, now Her Serene Highness Princess Grace of Monaco, was one of the most beautiful brides I have ever seen, entirely serious and dignified throughout. There was a hush as she walked up the aisle on the arm of her father, wearing her quite exquisite parchment tinted, pearl embroidered lace and satin wedding dress. She was followed by two little pages in parchment satin suits. Her child bridesmaids wore primrose organdie dresses with wreaths of yellow flowers in their hair, while the older bridesmaids or maids of honour, headed by her sister Mrs. Davis, wore primrose organza dresses with hats to match.'

She went on to say: 'The bride and her retinue arrived first, as is the custom if the bridegroom is a ruling Prince. Prince Rainier, who wore a most picturesque uniform of light blue braided trousers, a black jacket with touches of red and yellow and gold braid, on which were numerous orders and decorations, walked up the aisle accompanied by his Lord Chamberlain, Comte Fernand Caillard d'Aillières, his aide-de-camp Col. René Séverac, and the two priests, Father Francis Tucker, his private chaplain, and Monseigneur Gilles Barthé, Bishop of Monaco.

'A guard of the Prince's company of Carabiniers, in red, white and blue uniforms, with their light blue helmets trimmed with red and white plumes, took up their position each side of the aisle and at the Elevation sounded a fanfare of trumpets.

'The music, with the singing of the choir of a hundred voices and the soloists, was magnificent, and very moving throughout the wedding ceremony and Nuptial Mass.

'The male guests wore full evening dress of white tie and tail coat. Besides the ministers and officials, who wore full dress uniform, the uniforms of the representatives of over twenty countries with their orders and decorations added to the brilliant scene. Foremost among these was the tall upright figure of the Queen's representative, Maj.-Gen. Sir Guy Salisbury-Jones, Marshal of the Diplomatic Corps, who was accompanied by Mr. W. B. C. Weld-Forester, the British Consul at Nice.

'Among other guests at the wedding were the Earl of Dudley sitting with the Earl and Countess of Dumfries, who wore a pale pink coat and little hat to match, Lady Diana Duff Cooper, who had a pale blue picture hat with a grey and white striped dress. Dame Margot Fonteyn, wearing a small hat with her silk suit, was accompanied by her husband, H. E. Señor Dr. Roberto E. Arias, the Ambassador for Panama in London.

'Also present were Mr. and Mrs. Onassis, Mr. and Mrs, Arpad Plesch, Ava Gardner, the Hon. Mrs. Reginald Fellowes. Mrs. Cornelius Whitely wearing an enormous shocking pink velvet hat with her dress to match, and Mrs. Robert Rea of Philadelphia in a luxurious pale blue satin coat over a dress to match, with a pale blue organza hat and lovely jewellery. She was accompanied by her husband.'

The *World's Press News* was more down to earth:

'If it was dignity he wanted, he should have arranged a quiet wedding,' wrote the special correspondent.

'In the words of one British photographer three days after he had arrived in Monaco for the Grace Kelly wedding: "This is a carve-up."

'It was almost worse than that. Photographers or journalists wishing to know what was going on were simply referred to *France-Soir*, *Life* or *Paris-Match*. The Pool was just that. There was no attempt to distribute seats, no attempt at equal treatment. It was a carve-up on the part of those papers who were in a position to send representatives to Monaco weeks before the wedding in order to get their hands on the few seats which were going and on most of the facilities.

'Protests against the whole set-up began to pour in, and twelve days before the wedding, Jean Mercury, who organised and was responsible for the press house, told correspondents that he had heard that there were complaints. He said that the best way to deal with problems was for journalists to contact the presidents of their associations who would then bring the complaints to his notice. But he also intended to place a complaint book in one of the large halls. This called forth some raucous laughter and a cry of "half a dozen".

'The press house itself cost £5,000. It contained a general room where journalists could ask questions and obtain more or less useless information. There was a photographic service where old photographs were sold at thirty shillings each, a conference room, a very adequate bar, and a working room equipped with some excellent little Olivetti typewriters.

'But despite the fact that the press was making a tremendous effort to cover every detail the authorities were utterly unhelpful.

'The Prince set up his own censorship, while to cap it all, pictures which were intended to be sent by wire were printed the wrong size.

'No attempt was made to give everyone a chance and very few journalists felt inclined to attend "press conferences" kindly given by *France-Soir* or *Life*, for the benefit of colleagues.

'When Grace Kelly arrived, despite promises of fairness, many photographers had to pay as much as £100 for a place in a launch to meet the "Constitution" since they knew the facilities provided were inadequate.

'After dressing up his little State like a fairground, inviting all the crowned heads of the world and touching off the biggest publicity stunt ever, Prince Rainier suddenly realised that 1,350 journalists had not come to France to cheer him and his bride.

'By the time the galas started it was evident that relations between the press and Rainier had sunk pretty low. The first big gala at the Sporting Club produced an ugly scene. The press stand had been built so far away and placed in such an absurd position that it was impossible to get worthwhile pictures.

'On top of all this, sunny Monte Carlo wept like Manchester. For a whole week it rained cats and dogs, so reporters and photographers were not only frustrated but dripping.

'When members of the British press complained about facilities, they were curtly told that invitations had to go to those papers which had devoted most space to Monte Carlo over the past few months. This, evidently, was not the case of the British press.'

As the honeymoon yacht sped out to sea with the Prince and the new Princess aboard, Father Tucker – his great mission complete – stood watching from the palace ramparts, a slightly worried frown chasing the smile from his broad features. Had he perhaps heard the whisper that the Holy Father was not altogether pleased with the way in which the Wedding had been promoted and publicised?

For the last rumour in an innumerable string of rumours had already reached Monaco. It was that the Pope was refusing to receive the Prince and Princess in royal state at the Vatican in order to register his disapproval of the matrimonial missionary methods as practised by his underlings from the New World.

An entertaining aftermath of the wedding as viewed by the newspapermen and radio correspondents who covered the event was the Monte Carlo Memorial Game, 'created and executed in tribute to the men and women of the great wedding' by Jean Sakol.

It took the form of a game of snakes and ladders, with the casino at one end and the palace at the other. There were various pitfalls along the route, such as the Hotel de Paris, the Hermitage, Lady Docker's yacht, Onassis' yacht, Prince Rainier's yacht, and the Maison de Presse. The object of the game, as in snakes and ladders, was to get to the palace.

Small black cards, to be used by the participants in the game, had various instructions printed on them in red, thus: 'Trade picture of Grace Kelly for paw-print of Oliver'; 'Advance to Palace, wait three hours'; 'Make phone call to Hotel de Paris, wait twelve hours'; 'Disguise self as Prince Rainier go to Maison de Presse'; 'Advance to Cathedral: Warning: Cold seats, wear woollies'; 'Go to Lady Docker's yacht – drink champagne for three rounds'; 'Stowaway in *Deo Juvante*. Cable office for bail, walk backwards to Palace so you will look like you are just leaving'; 'Go back to Casino and start again'; 'Start rumour'; 'Go to London Airport and start again'; 'Advance one pace'; 'Change another 100,000 francs'; 'Somehow get around the royal hedge; if impossible, go back to Paris and start again.'

Barely two months elapsed after the wedding, before rumours started that Princess Grace was going to have a baby. These soon proved true, when she and Prince Rainier returned to the United States for a few weeks.

The hullabaloo, which followed as January 1957 approached, was intensified by expert publicity men. It was first announced that the baby would be born in Switzerland; next, that it would be born in the local Monégasque maternity hospital. Finally, of course, it was announced that the heir (or heiress, as it turned out to be) must, by Serene protocol, be born in the Palace on the Rock.

Reporters and photographers poured back into the Principality, sent by editors, who realised that their readers wanted some entertaining relief after the tragedy of Hungary and the infuriating position in which Great Britain found herself, as a result of being bullied into leaving the Suez Canal too early. The inimitable Father Tucker was, on this occasion, kept in the background. In his place, the Hollywood publicity man, Rupert Allen, took charge of the newspaper men, whom he called to his office for a press conference.

Said he: 'From tomorrow, you will have to be on the alert all the time, just as we were during the war. After all, in the war you never knew when the enemy was going to attack, did you?'

Arrangements were made to open the town information office when the baby was born, even if in the middle of the night. Information officers would then announce the baby's weight, the time it was born, and Princess Grace's condition.

A dark room was provided for Howell Conant, the American fashion photographer, who had been given exclusive rights to take pictures of the baby. Germ-conscious Palace officials informed him that he must wear a gown and mask, when taking his pictures, and that he was also to sterilise his camera. How do you sterilise a camera? One of the Press Attachés said, 'I suppose it will have to be immersed in boiling water.'

Other official promulgations included the announcement that, if the baby was a boy, there would be a salute of 101 shots fired from the medieval guns on the parapet of the Palace. If it were a girl, there would be a mere twenty-one shots. No provision, apparently, was made for twins. Another statement was that if it turned out to be a boy, the child would be called 'Gregoire'; if a girl, it would be called 'Caroline Louise Marguerite'.

A girl baby appeared on the scene on the morning of the 23rd January 1957, during a heavy storm with sleet and rain. At once the publicity machine got to work, announcing that by Serene tradition, it was lucky for Monaco if the heir, or heiress, to the throne was born in bad weather. The first man to be interviewed, the French gynaecologist, announced that the baby princess was (a) very pretty, and (b) took after the Grimaldis (her father's side) rather than the Kellys. Mrs. Kelly had been with her daughter for the two previous months.

Sitting in his suite at Claridge's in London, Aristotle Onassis was alerted by his secretary in Monte Carlo when the first boom of cannon began on the telephone line, which had been kept open for some time. He was able to tick off the shots until they ceased at twenty-one. He was, thus, the first person in London to know the sex of the child.

Princess Grace, unlike most film stars, had no anaesthetic, and so was able to drink a glass of champagne within a few hours of the birth of her daughter, which, it was officially divulged, she followed next day with a more prosaic bottle of local Monaco beer.

Once again, there were scenes when it became known that, apart from two photographs of Caroline issued to all the newspapers and magazines, the remaining sets would be put up to public auction.

What was of primary importance to Monaco was that His Holiness the Pope sent a message of congratulation, thus healing the breach which had occurred between the Vatican and the Principality caused by the unseemly prelude to the Roman Catholic wedding in the Cathedral, almost exactly nine months to the day previously.

BIBLIOGRAPHY

XAVIER PAOLI: *Leur Majestés*

JULES BERTAUT: *Côte d'Azur*

TOBIAS SMOLLETT: *Travels Through France and Italy*

A. M. STERLING: *The Ways of Yesterday*

AUGUSTUS HARE: *A Winter at Mentone*

CHARLES GRAVES: *The Big Gamble*

ELSA MAXWELL: *I Married the World*

MADAME BALSAN: *The Glitter and the Gold*

The Private Archives of Prince Rainier III

GENERAL PIERRE POLOVTSOFF: *Monte Carlo Casino*

THE AGA KHAN: *Memoirs*

THOMAS ROBINSON WOOLFIELD: *Life at Cannes*

INDEX